Re-Visioning Comparative Literature

Re-Visioning Comparative Literature

Anand B. Patil

AUTHORSPRESS

Worldwide Circulation through Authorspress Global Network

First Published 2012

by

Authorspress

Editorial

Q-2A Hauz Khas Enclave
New Delhi-110 016

e-mail: authorspress@rediffmail.com
authorspress@hotmail.com

Marketing

E-35/103, Jawahar Park
Laxmi Nagar, Delhi-110 092
e-mail: authorspress@rediffmail.com
authorspress@hotmail.com

Re-Visioning Comparative Literature
ISBN 978-81-7273-627-9

Printed in India at Tarun Offset, Delhi.

For my loving maternal uncles

Namdeo, Shripati and Bapurao

Acknowledgements

Re-Visioning Comparative Literature includes thirteen research papers and plenary speeches. They were presented at national and international seminars and conferences. Almost all of them were published in reputed journals. Had the individuals and institutions not created these opportunities. I would not have emerged as an Indian comparatist whose essay is included in *Cambridge Companion to Comparative Literature* edited by Steven Tötosy de Zeptnek (2011). I owe a great debt to Goa University as well as to innumberable friends and institutions for this "academic tourism".

This book is dedicated to my maternal uncles whose pen-pictures appear in my Marathi novel *Icchamaran* (desired death). It is their "inheritance of gain" that it is going to be released in the inaugural function of the UGC sponsored National Seminar on "Comparative Literature and Culture Study with special reference to Dr. Anand Patil's Literature" organised by Smt. Parwatidevi Chowgule College, Madgaon-Goa on 17-18 Dec. 2011.

I thank Sudarshan Kcherry and his team of the Authorspress for producing this fine work of art in a very short time.

The following details of acknowledgements will exhibit the nature and scope of my rich indebtedness.

1. "The Whirligig of Literary Taste: Impact or Alienation?" *Indian Literature* 157 (Aug. 1992): 157-169. International Seminar 28-30 Dec.1991; Dhaka-Bangladesh: "Impact or Internationlization?"

2. "Perspectives on the Folkloric Intertextuality in Goan Novel", *Indian Scholar* 15-2 (July 1993):19-41. ICSSR sponsored Workshop on Goan Folklore, 16, 17 Apr. 1993. Dept. of History, Goa University.
3. "Colonial and Post/Neo-colonial Discourse in Two Goan Novels: A Fanonian Study," *Ariel* 20-4 (Oct. 1997) 87-112.
4. "A Comparative Study of Nativistic Intertextuality in Indian Fiction", in Makarand Paranjape ed. *Nativism: Essays in Criticism* New Delhi: Sahitya Akademi, 1997: 177-210), National Seminar on "Nativism in Indian Literature" 21-22 Jan. 1995 at Kanpur.
5. "The 'Post' in the Post-colonial Fictional Discourse: A Comparative Critique", in Department of English Chh. Shivaji College, Satara (MS) ed. *Commonwealth Literature Recent Perspectives* (New Delhi: Creative Books, 1999): 102-119. National Seminar 78, Feb. 1997; invited by my alma mater.
6. "Images of *King Lear* (on the Bombay Stage) in Marathi", *Indian Scholar* 1-2 (July 1986):11-32. The Third World Shakespeare Congress, 1-7 Apr. 1986, Berlin.
7. "Bardicide in the Post-colonial Theatre: A Comparative Case Study" *Critical Practice* 3-2 (June 1997): 34-50. The Sixth World Shakespeare Congress, 5-15 Apr. 1996, Los Angeles, U.S.A.
8. "Contemporary Marathi Literary and Cultural Criticism from Comparatist's Perspective" was presented at the National Seminar: 4-7 Nov. 1997, Indian Institute of Advanced Studies, Shimla.
9. "Can a Subaltern Writer Write or Rewrite?" was presented at the National Seminar: Dept. of History, Dr. Ambedkar Marathwada University, Aurangabad, 28-30 Nov. 1997.
10. "Beyond Modernism: The Aesthetics of Resistance," *New Quest* 120 (Dec. 1996) 338-348. National Seminar at Bangalore, 24-26 Feb. 1996; organised by Sahitya Akademi, New Delhi.

11. “Re-‘visioning’ intextualities in R.K. Narayan’s Novels”, The plenary speech at National Conference on “Revisiting the Fictional World of R.K. Narayan” at C.D.V. College, Dasuya-Punjab, on 26 Feb. 2011, published in *Labyrinth* 2:3 (July 2011), 9-21.
12. “Literary into Comparative Culture Study: Internationalisation of Translation”, the plenary speech at National Seminar, University of Pune 26th March 2011.
13. “Contesting ‘Newness’ in Commonwealth Literatures”, the plenary speech at the National Seminar, Mount Olive College, Kohima, Nagaland 27-29 July 2011.

Introduction—Rewriting Wrong and Ethics of New Comparativism

> Lyotard demonstrates that knowledge has become a commodity that is bought and sold on the market, and is also the basis of power in society... The global competition for power is now fought out as a battle for knowledge just as it is used to be for recourses like coal, gas and oil. Lyotard foresees a time when nations may literally go to war over knowledge, past as they have fought over land and raw materials such as oil in the past (1984:5).
>
> —Simon Malpas, *Jean Francois Lyotard.* London: Routledge, 2007:18

It is rather difficult to know what the "postmodern condition" is about Indian literary studies in India. The key term in the title of my book "re-visioning" is taken from my speech at the National Seminar on "Re-thinking R.K. Narayan's Novels" held in Punjab. But reading of a German scholar's doctoral thesis: "R. K. Narayan as a Brahman Novelist" made me more aware of the limitations of our caste-conditioned and ill-informed "double colonized" single author studies. Will the Indian researcher be allowed to tread where angels fear to peep in?

Thirteen comparative research papers presented at international and national conferences and published during last twenty years demonstrate different phases in my development as a comparatist coming up from peasantry to the university very late at the age of forty. Looking back at my struggle of studying "Western influence on Marathi drama: 1818-1947" for the doctoral degree in the 1980s and "contesting 'newness' in 'Commonwealth Literature' in the 2011s are two distinct stages which brought me good recognition and rewards. After forty years of teaching experience in Departments of English realization of ignorance about domination of Western aesthetics and Euro-America-centric knowledge equated by production of intra- and inter-colonial ignorance has become very painful. What exactly did I teach and what is the output? What knowledge is produced in our non-interdisciplinary research, how is it generated, organized and employed in contemporary society? What is the 'nature' and 'status' of knowledge in humanities? Is there any Indian report on knowledge produced by teachers of specific subject and marketed all over the world? Isn't there some connection between the mushroom growth of low standard research, compulsory publications and corruption in the cultural match-fixing industry and farmers' suicides?

A glance at the research for M.Phil and Ph.D in Indian languages, including English, reveals lack of inter-disciplinarity and comparativism. For example, in the first decade of the twenty-first century nearly hundred doctoral works in Marathi are accepted by the universities. Only two partly comparative dissertations include four novels in Marathi only. It is the mockery of comparative literature and culture studies unheard of in the caste-based hierarchical society. Monolingual author studies amount to the production of ignorance in the obsolete terminology. The caste-conditioned Indian mind originally lacks "comparative imagination," which is the key concept in the global cultural market today. When Steven Tötosy de Zeptnek wrote the "Foreword" to my *Literary into Comparative Culture Criticism* (2011), he traced the cultural semiotics of British impact on the title and asked me to develop the "home grown" theory. It led me to the rethinking of various concepts and issues such as Indianness, newness in Commonwealth Literature, colonial consciousness, castealization of literary text, impact of the colonial twin process: Anglicization-Westernization+Sanskritization-Brahmanization in cultural industry, caste-determined interpretations, literary fakedom, rewriting wrong and ethics, etc. Our structure of literary feelings is too Euro-America-centric to think independently and too caste-conditioned to be ethical in truth telling.

A Report on knowledge of college and university teachers in India is likely to list the recent developments in literary kinds, author's life and works (wife?) studies, generic experiments, literary movements etc. What is at stake is much more fundamental and important. The Report will never explain why our experienced teachers of English fall short in translating comparative essays of the reputed alien comparatists into Marathi. The famous terms such as aesthetics of resistance, Prospero-Caliban/Crusoe-Friday complexes, Manichean divisions, Anglo-American project of modernism, grand narrative of emancipation, postcolonial project, empire writes back, de-scribe empire; dependence complex, daffodilization of mind etc. have not yet entered into our critical thinking. It means the comprador class of intellectuals imagined in 1835 by Lord Macaulay in his vision of future Indians not of the white man's colour, but of their "culture and taste" has been dominating our literati. Almost all comparative essays in this anthology explore various aspects of Western impact, the nature of intertextualities, interliterariness, and internationalization of indigenous literary culture. They attempt to compare the "unspeakable" in "postcolonial" terminology.

Indian culture, which leaves little space for comparativism, is hierarchical from Vedic times. Although the Portuguese rulers established separate villages for different castes, they failed to uproot the caste system even among the Hindus converted to Christianity during four and a half centuries. Three essays provide a good ground for further comparisons of literary and cultural transformations in British Bombay and Portuguese Goa. Indian criticism is ignorant of cultural transformations in Portuguese Goa, why? This pertinent question can be answered with RIA which demands not only use of politics of poetics but also of comparative poetics. For example, Professor Shrikrishna Adsul's experience of organizing the UGC sponsored multilingual National Seminar on "Comparative Literature and Culture Studies: With Special

Reference to Anand Patil's Works" in Goa recently shows how monolingual simplified impressionistic literary thinking still prevails, albeit the UGC has given top priorities to the comparative literature and culture studies. Barring a few exceptions, the majority of scholars wished to comment on Patil's fiction sans comparison. As a result he had to design two Marathi books: (1) Traditional mono-literary study of Patil's oeuvre and (2) Proceedings: Comparative literary and cultural study of his works. Hence there is a need to wage a war on individualistic and romantic myths of totality such as originality, authenticity, greatness, genius, etc. This can be achieved through creating greater awareness of Janus face of neo-colonial Indian literature with two layers/tones: one indigenous another alien.

The comprador diaspora is being used to produce and market the knowledge by the "First World". This liberalization of knowledge and in Frantz Fanon's phrase, "attack of cheap entertainment" has been responsible for the death of languages, literatures and cultures in the "developing countries". Comparatists and culturalists in the formerly colonized countries plead for constructing the "postcolonial project" to resist appropriation by the Anglo-American project of aesthetics and modernity designed in the 1920s. This is the breathtaking task for us at present. A single example of Emily Apter's brief "preface" to her doctoral thesis "Translation Zone: New Comparative Literature" (2006) will throw a flood of light on the weaknesses of our linguistic and literary "cultural capital". The 9/11/, 26/7 and many other numbers have become symbols of destructive terrorisms. Apter was a research scholar when the World Trade Center was destroyed by the terrorists. This traumatic experience changed her perspectives on translation study and she revolutionized the traditional concepts of both disciplines by merging them into one. We have undergone several experiences of terrorist attacks all over India, including the Parliament. Has anybody produced new knowledge like Apter? To the utter dismay of a well informed comparatist most of the papers recently presented at the UGC sponsored national seminar on "Comparative Literature and Translation" organized in the reputed university were non-comparative!

I had published the pre-review (*Lalit Dipawali,* 2010) of Steven Tötosy's layout of the "Cambridge Companion to Comparative Literature and Culture" to demonstrate the scope of international collaboration in producing and marketing knowledge in global competition. I was invited to contribute an article on "Comparative Literature and Culture Studies in India." Recently he edited it and has sent his article "The Comparative and Contextual Study of Literature and Culture in the Age of Globalization" written in collaboration with Louise O. Vasvri for my comments. It opens as follows:

> The perspective and use of comparison in scholarship and among several compelling lines of argumentation of with regard to comparative and contextual study in the humanities and social sciences is put forward by Marcel Detienne in his *Comparing the Incomparable (36-39)* (see also George M. Fredrickson's The *Comparative Imagination*).... It the West, comparative literature as a discipline remains- while embattled with regard to its institutional presence- an established field particularly in Anglophone regions such as the U.S., and to a lesser extent in Canada and Australia. In England where the discipline has not had a strong presence, the discipline has gained in interest today.

It was still born as a discipline in India; let it take rebirth in new schools of language, literatures and culture. These essays will prove that comparative literature is not dead in India.

I am grateful to many individuals and institutions in India and abroad. Sudarshan Kcherry and his team at Authorspress made this fine production available for release in the above mentioned National Seminar. I thank them. I am grateful to all my well-wishers Chowgules, Principal Dr. R, V. Gaonkar, Prof. Shrikrishna Adsul, Ashwini Naik and others on this auspicious occasion. Members of my family always encouraged my "academic tourism". Thanking them would be a mere formality.

— ***Anand B. Patil***

Contents

1

Impact and Internationalisation?

The formulation of the title, which warrants the complexity of the mechanism of global influences and the subtle process of alienation from one's own literary culture, immediately reminds one of E. E. Kellett's long critical essay: *The Whirligig* of *Taste* (1929) on the British literary taste. After half a century of the period of Independence the shadow of literary colonialism lies heavily upon our literary taste. The problem of decolonization of Indian mind, or say Asian mind, has not yet occupied the central position in our critical thought. A small upper caste/class anglicized section of Indian society still dominates the literary culture and skilfully retains intra-culture domestic imperialism to exploit the illiterate majority. It is this caste-class-based compartmentalization which conditions the imagination of our creative writers and arrests the growth of literature which is cross-pollinated (polluted?) after the colonial contact. Namwar Singh[1] (1952, 151), in his thought provoking keynote address 'Decolonising the Indian Mind', has not given a detailed exposition of the method and manner of spreading 'the lie of the land' through 'brokering' English literature in India. However, he has rightly pointed out:

> It is this small colonized class that has claimed to be the cultural and literary *avant garde* of India after Independence, and it lays claim too to having modernized and developed Indian literature. This class also lays claim to having effected decolonization, and never mind the fact that a lot of it is in reality pseudo-decolonization.

Namwar talks in terms of class conflict and fails to enumerate the nature and scope of the mixed processes: Anglicization + Sanskritization + Brahminization and Modernization or Westernization = Acculturation. Meenakshi Mukherjee has placed the 'Twice Born' Indian Writing in English in her Caste's perspective and opportunist nativist Bhalchandra Nemade has exposed its pseudo-native rootlessness. We have seen the end of 'socialism' recently but imperialism has been writing back through the colonized immigrant intellectuals such as Nirad C. Chaudhuri, V.S. Naipaul, Salman Rushdie and many others who write from abroad in English. The environmentalists have not yet noticed this literary contamination which spreads the *plague* of the poetics of parrotry and the art of mimicry.

Thus, many sets of problems are involved in the 'oppressive present' and our colonial consciousness. Every one of them derives from the general issues addressed in my article: 'The Whirligig of Taste: Decolonization of Teaching and Research in India' (*New Quest,* Dec. 1992 No. 96). The most important of them are: domination of the dwarfing influences of the First World Literature, responsibilities of teachers, writers, publishers and other mediators of alien influences, colonialistic modernity-tradition polarity, search of self-reliant indigenous literary traditions, awareness of Indian identity, ambivalence in the use of language as well as attitude to alien aesthetics, reformation of the narrow Hindu caste-based fundamentalism, extension of monopolized canon and so on.

Some scholars believe that decolonization has been the greatest event of world history in the twentith century, but vague notions such as the 'Third World', 'Difference' and the 'Destiny of the East' are yet secret devices of colonization. They opine that the focus of literary creativity has shifted from Euramerican centres to Asia, Africa and Latin America (Namwar Singh, 152-53). But this can be accepted with some reservations because postcolonialism does not mean postmodernism in our hierarchial literary culture, and revival of some indigenous literary traditions by commercialized elites does not mean that nativism is at the centre of our structure of literary feelings and creative or critical thinking. Western centres of learning control the thinking process of our writers, and Indian intellectual 'journey' to the West is considered a must for attaining an Indian identity. Our writers 'exhibit' their 'Indianness', which is a misleading concept, for a Western 'ideal-implied' reader by returning to the indigenous tradition without having its deep knowledge and intimate contact. Perhaps this false familiarity breeds contempt among students so they are attracted to the 'foreign things' such as American, Canadian or British literature. Either a survey of the university teachers of English carried out from sociological viewpoint or the scrutiny of any literary journal in Indian English or of a title such as Rajeswari Sundar Rajan, ed. *The Lie of the Land* (1992) would reveal a number of whirligigs of taste arising out of clash of alien and indigenous loyalties. The new open market economic policy is likely to multiply the number of èlite exiles in their own land, and give rise to pseudo-nativistic language revival movements led by the writers and publishers whose grandchildren are the citizens of the First World.

Our originally fragmented culture gives little scope to what Abdul JanMohamed[2] (1990, 1) describes as a 'theory of minority discourse'. Minority discourse is defined as 'a variety of minority voices engaged in retrieving texts repressed or marginalised by a society that espouses universalistic, univocal, and monological humanism.' We need to describe and define the common denominators that link various Asian minority cultures on the strength of the fact that they all share an 'antagonistic relationship to the dominant culture, which seeks to marginalize them all.' Madhav Prasad ,[3] (1992, 87), considering the Fanonian reading of the colonial context by Edward Said, Horni Bhabha, Gayatri Spivak etc., concludes that the critics of colonialism (1) share a belief in the continued existence of the primary antagonism at the heart of the colonial relation, between coloniser and colonised; (2) are committed to a 'repressive hypothesis' of culture; (3) their account of the colonial relation is only marginally receptive to the transformations in political economy and their relation to the psychodrama of the colonial encounter, (4) these discourses understand globality as a matter of 'international relations' resembling the notion of 'interpersonal relations' in their tendency to treat cultural entities as existing prior to their encounter in the imperialist era.... Prasad's analysis of Max Muller's essay on 'Caste' shows how culture was 'invented and deployed as a means of indirect rule' first by the Brahmins and then by the British colonisers. These masks of conquest, as exposed by Gauri Viswanathan in her *Masks of Conquest: Literary Study and British Rule in India* (1988), are still used for the universalization of its own ideology which seems to dissolve these identities into a 'new' and 'higher' unity. This background of the poetics of failure explains as to why we do not have among Asians a Chinua Achebe, a Gabriel Garcia Marquez or a Ngugi wa Thiong'o. It is better to limit this discussion to the Indian context only; especially to the mechanism of literary influences and the effects of alienation on the creative works.

A writer who has published some fiction in the regional language and an influence study in English entitled *Western Influence on Marathi Drama: 1818-1947: A Case Study* (1993), fails to identity his literary taste. My study of the English influence on Marathi drama of the British period in India revealed the following main findings: (1) The colonized literary culture has accepted the English dramatic genres as their own without keeping at the centre their own indigenous dramatic traditions. The desire of the colonized writer, to assimilate alien forms of drama with the indigenous gave rise to innumerable creative tensions. The tug of war between alien and indigenous tendencies disintegrated the work of art. The period of the British contact of one and a half centuries and consequent linguistic as well as literary acculturation shows four distinct periods of cumulative influences of English drama spreading like an epidemic. The process of institutionalization of English literature in India, based on imperialistic ideology, has been controlling those Indians who became 'experts', rewriters or translators of 'their-colonisers' literature mostly from priestly class. Literary works of such experts trained by the white Sahibs are 'mirrors' of culture as culture was interpreted by those who controlled the literary establishment. As the whole society was controlled on the basis of ideology by alien 'patrons', the literary system inside the society was governed on the principles of the master's poetics. So we had, to use Andre Lefever's[4] (1987, 60) words, 'rewriters', translators, mimics, adaptors, imitators, plagiarists and so on; but hardly any original creative writer of high stature.

The self-imposed mission of the colonisers to modernize (or anglicize) Indian vernacular literatures was guided by the models of literary renaissance in Europe. Their Shakespeare and English national drama were the products of the cross-culture encounter on equal grounds and produced in the mono-religious, mono-cultural situation. In India it was a meeting of two unequal literary traditions: one dominant; the other weak and enslaved. Shakespeare was a folk dramatist first and then a poet dramatist. On the contrary, our Brahman-Shastri playwrights looked down upon the folk drama which was preserved by the lower caste artists. Shastris were totally ignorant of the indigenous tradition of classical drama so they received English drama uncritically and the ambivalence in reception further complicated the generic confusion which reigned supreme in the British dramaturgy of the eighteenth and nineteenth centuries. The short-lived superficial 'honey moon' of two traditions begot half-baked, abortive or stillborn products of false influence. European writers enjoyed and enjoy great literary fortune so much that we should not use the concepts such as 'influence' or 'impact' to describe this literary hybridization during the colonial period. Moreover, Western theories of influence aesthetics, reception, response etc. fall short in the analysis of the literary cross-pollination in the colonial situation. Today it is internationalization It would be interesting to study the literary fortune of Shakespeare in a French colony and Moliere's fate in the British colony. This mixture and network of alien as well as native influences demands multidimensional approaches and varied methods. To cut the long story short, we have today the anglicized and Brahmanical caste/class-bound drama in Marathi but not the native 'Marathi' drama in the Marathi language. This leads us to the discussion of the paradoxical tautology, namely, the 'castealized' Indianness of Indian literature both in English and in any Indian language.

II

It is really difficult to define specific Indianness because our regional sensibilities and base lines for demarcation of alienation are not yet marked distinctly. On the contrary, in the First World literary critical thinking,[5] the problem of influences has been placed at the centre since long (1983, Intro). We have neither defined clearly what is meant by "Characteristically Indian" not given a serious thought to the missing links and inherent weaknesses in our indigenous literary traditions. The lack of identity and self-reliance, linguistic and literary competence complicate the problem still further. Acquisition of the strength to free oneself from all kinds of alien as well as indigenous dwarfing influences is a true test of the creative writer. But we have not yet understood "the other question: difference, discrimination and discourse of colonialism" as Homi K. Bhabha[6] (1986, 1487) stated. "It is the force of ambivalence that gives the colonial stereotype its currency: ensures its repeatability in changing historical and discursive conjunctures; informs its strategies of individuation and marginalization; produces that effect of probabilistic truth and predictability which, for the stereotype, must always be in excess of what can be empirically proved or logically ensured".

This is why our comparative approach to the study of English must begin with the assessment of the balance-sheet of alien borrowings during the colonial period first and then the microscopic stock checking of the indigenous survivals, Cyrena Pondrom[7] (1974, 22) aptly emphasised the significance of such a period study which enables us "to assess the full range of influence to identify the ideas or techniques most important" to the period as a whole, and "to examine the course of transmission rather than, the effects of influence alone. Observing the course of transmission lays the foundation for the revaluation of some literary reputation (25)." Among our caste/class-divided literati such indepth influence-studies seem to be discouraged in order to protect the vested interests and 'literary image' of the writer. It is cultural imperialism which does not favour influence-studies which tend to expose literary mimicry and parrotry bred by inter-caste colonialism. Extra-textual approaches to literature are deemed irrelevant and the alienated teachers' Utopian activities result in the sterile intellectual intercourse which yields no fruits. The Big Brother attitude of the First World Literature not only contaminates our teaching in the classroom by creating inferiority complex but it affects the creative process of the writer alienated from his soil.

In such circumstances it is a futile exercise to search for the features of so called Indianness, which we find in the literature of the less caste-compartmentalized medieval saint poets, or in the sophisticated yet nativistic films of Satyajit Ray and novels of Shivaram Karanth or in the modern writings of our anglicized Brahmin writers in majority both in English and in other Indian languages. The Indo-anglian literature of the Westernized minority has been enjoying a false prestige as representative Indian literature since the British contact. The dual standards of judging Indian writing in English and in the regional-languages by the borrowed paradigms of alien aesthetics has done much damage to our literary taste. For example, compare the disparity in interpretation and evaluation of Nirad C. Chaudhuri's writings in English. D. Anjaneyulu's recent article 'Nirad C. Chaudhuri: the Writer Extraordinary' *(Journal of Indian Writing in English,* Jan.-July 1992, 20, 1-2, pp. 243-36) is full of eulogies. To the other extreme, the spokesman of nativism, Bhalchandra Nemade[8] (1991, 22) finds Chaudhuri a very incompetent as well as hypocritical writer. He observes, "he (Chaudhuri) avoids in his *Autobiography,* how many 'children he bred' because breeding about a dozen children, the real cause of Indian poverty, would not create a good impression on the B.B.C. or the *New Statesman* reviewer". In a similar vein he further exposes the pseudo-Indianness in the English fiction of R.K. Narayan, Mulk Raj Anand, Raja Rao and others. He bluntly states, "Raja Rao, who opens his masterpiece *The Serpent and the Rope* with a statement 'I was born a Brahmin' hopelessly alienates himself from the general humanity all through his novel" (pp. 22-28). This onslaught seems to have provoked reaction from Raja Rao.[9] (1992, 1-4). Taking a defensive position, he asserts: "*So I assert that there is an echo of the mother-tongue behind all India English creative writings* (1-4)." But alas! these echoes are very feeble and marginalised by the mode of operation of English as a supra language. Nemade has rightly pointed out that such a written variety of English, which has not emerged from the native soil, is highly detrimental to creative use, and the sphere of its communication is limited to elitist upper castes, mostly uprooted. Further he questions the credibility and status of Indian Writing in English which he reduces to the level of "the fine art of parrotry." Finally he arrives at the conclusion:

> It is doubtful whether this writing will add any "Indianness" to world writing in English. A well planned programme of translations from the regional languages into English will at once make this writing obsolete. Until then let it survive as a clear case of mimicry. (p. 31)

One can understand Nemade's opportunistic; nativism but a study of the Marathi drama of the British period, as mentioned before, shows that the writings in Indian languages are also very much derivative, imitative and artificial offshoots of Western generic hierarchy. This is the imperial literary labyrinth which should be described as an Indian whirligig of literary taste in the static culture. It not only does affect the writer's identity but also the integrity of his literary work. Thrusting Indian reality into borrowed generic forms does harm either to the former or to the latter.

We always think in terms of our sub-culture or caste groups. In-group and out-group thinking give rise to the exo-culture concepts which condition the imagination and vision of our writers. Moreover, our pre-British literary tradition had established the poetics of plagiarism which encourages imitation. Individuality of the writer was totally absent in it. Stark reality, horror or tragedy in the Western metaphysical sense can never be found in Indian literature which favours romanticism, sentimentalism and idealistic representation of reality. The caste-based politics of representation in art is one more baffling problem for which we can never find solution in western theories. Under such circumstances how should we trace the Indianness in Indian literature? C. Paul Verghese (1975) and other scholars argue that true Indianness is to be found only in the speech of an Adivasi common man or an illiterate savage, a few folk forms, and to some extent in the writings of very few modern rural and dalit writers. But owing to the dominance of the anglicized Brahmanical literary taste, which canonizes literary works, the writers coming from the lower castes can hardly resist the compelling process of westernization in the disguise of modernization and are soon alienated from their artistic roots which are least recognized by the dominant taste. These intra-cultural and intra-literary conflicts dwarf our writers more than alien influence does. All such complexities and conflicts, which interlock around the 'power of translation', may be examined with special reference to our 'National language, Education, Literature' etc. Recent reports[10] on the distinctions between colinguism and bilinguism, plurilinguism and other kinds seem to be relevant in the Indian context. The creative work of a writer moves in the field where institutions and linguistic apparatuses interplay, and in the present day Indian democracy a change in the structure of the literary culture-bearing stratum is likely to change the sad conclusion drawn by Vilas Sarang[11] (1992, 167) and other critics regarding the development of contemporary Indian writing. Like Namwar Singh, Sarang finds Indian literature, at the end of the twentieth century, 'in grave peril'. He reminds us of the great achievements of the Latin American writers, and further adds,"... there is no reason why this vast sub-continent with numerous languages and subcultures cannot produce writers who will advance towards new territory. Let us hope that, in the 21st century, Indian literature will break out the barriers and forge anew 'the conscience of the race.'"

Sarang has not explained the "barriers" or a new 'territory'. In fact, our writers, who make "only a feeble effort towards expanding its scope and horizons", lack the poetics of resistance, the theories of the oppressed and the aesthetics of influence which the Latin American writers have developed through storm and strife. For example, a comparative study of Gloria Anzaldua's *Borderlands/La Frontera the New Mesiza* (1987) and any so-called experimental writing by the Indian elite woman writer would throw a flood of light on what is rotten in our literary culture. Gloria's multilingual book defies all norms of the generic classification. Her acute sense of identity is revealed in the following paragraph:

> Chicanos and other people of our colour suffer economically for not acculturating. This voluntary (yet forced) alienation makes for psychological conflict, a kind of dual identity. We don't identify with the Anglo-American cultural values and we don't totally identify with the Mexican cultural values. *We* are a synergy of two cultures with various degrees of Mexicanness or Angloness. I have so internalized the borderland conflict that sometimes I feel like one cancels out the other and we are zero, nothing, no one (p. 63).

This search of the internalized cultural conflict is a first step towards the decolonization of our deeply colonialized literary canon. A case study shows that in the majority of cases literary infection flows from the West. Except a few enlightened Indian intellectuals our writers and theorists are not convinced by the Fanonian attitude that 'it would be better for you to be a native at the uttermost depths of his misery than to be a former settler'. On the contrary, they take false pride in introducing the innovations and modernity copied through English. The Indian philosophy of tolerance, the temptation to harmonize homogeneity and heterogeneity and the elitist desire to maintain a dialogue with the Western world to retain literary monopoly and intra-culture imperialism are the chief obstacles in the process of distinguishing Indianness as cultural otherness, and also in the attempts at putting an end to colonialism, political and mental. So, to borrow from Georg M. Gugelberger,[12] (1991, 520) the 'tasks for us' are to undertake research in the area of "geo-thematics". It shows that the West has always understood how and why to marginalize the cultures and implicitly the literary works of 'the rest of us'. Indian writers have not yet learnt, unlike the African or Latin American ones, how plagiarism of the Western literature can be used as an effective weapon of decolonization[13] (See Randall, Marilyn 1991, 525). They have not paid much attention to the issues connected with the effects of' the borrowings from international cultural forms which are insensitive to the issues of 'cultural imperialism'. One would like to pose a question, in words of Kwame Anthony Appiah[14] (1991, 236), is the 'Post' in Post-modernism the Post in Post-colonial in India? To find answers to such pertinent questions we have to revolutionise not only linguistic code, which shows the widest gulf between the language of literature and the speech of the common man, but also the literary taste which has blocked the healthy development of the 'national literature'.

III

The sociology of literary taste is a totally unexplored area in Indian literature. During the colonial period the Brahman class and very few upper caste factions, which monopolized learning, dominated the process of the institutionalization of the English and the marginalized vernacular literatures under the guidance of the British rulers. There was little scope to question the relevance of literary texts to the Indian life. Hence the mastery of English language and literary forms made all the difference. English was the only factor which distinguished the modern from the traditional literary taste. In the post-colonial period the elitist taste has still retained its strongholds through the predominance of the medium of English; but the masses in the democratic country have begun to exercise their power. The lower castes, which have succeeded in asserting their rights with the spread of education, demand more space for incorporation of their taste which generally comes in conflict with the Brahmanical literary canon that is known for not admitting members from outside. Those who are not admitted into the inside circles of the literary culture adopt negative attitude to the native traditions and are soon attracted to the foreign theories of the oppressed. The dalit and rural writers' repeated attacks on the elitist anglicised literary taste demonstrated—they had found their predecessors in the saint poets like Dnyaneswar and Tukaram — that literary taste is not a constant quality or a universal organ. It is something that alters over time, between cultures and even societies. What matters most is to share the power that controls the literary canon. It is closely connected not only with the changes in social structure but also with the *zeitgeist.* The key to understanding literary history lies in an investigation of taste. Ultimately, the literature of protest produced by the writers of Little Magazines, mass movements and other oppressed groups stormed the strongholds of taste such as schools, publishing houses, universities and age old literary organisations. On the other side, the literary culture-bearing dominant elite group, which was basically alienated from the masses by the colonial force of Westernization, met with frustration and got disillusioned in the post-colonial situation. As it has failed to maintain the status quo, it has conquered other media such as TV, radio, immigrant literature etc., to retain its cultural imperialism spread indirectly through them by the West.

Levin Schucking[15] (1978, 81) has offered a theory to determine the dominant literary taste of a given period. He introduces the notion of a culture bearing stratum, which can be easily identified with the Brahman-Baman-Shastri class in India, in a society made up of those who propagate taste. According to him, art is dependent on those propagators of taste, and "the ability of such groups to assert themselves is again dependent on the degree of power they can exercise within the social structure." Their power is determined primarily by the extent to which they dominate "the mechanism of artistic life." This point has been already illustrated with a reference to the mixed processes viz. Anglicization + Sanskritization + Brahmanization = Modernization or Westernization. This dreadful process was controlled by the colonizers during the British period; but even now the formula works indirectly. It means that the 'classic' taste, which the post-independence generations of writers inherit, is only the choice of a very small caste/class culture group. It is not representative of the vast subcontinent which is full of variety of sub-culture groups, languages, dialects, thousands of castes and creeds and what not, In fact it offers a fertile field for presentation in a literary work. But why do our writers fall short? What has been canonized as great works of art by the dominant culture-bearing small class-caste are thus works selected by individuals in power. It is not necessarily the good that asserts itself through tradition; but rather "that which wins through will be regarded as good." So perhaps we have a number of mass canonized good books which are very often ignored by the 'classic' taste.

References and Notes

1. Namwar Singh, 'Decolonizing the Indian Mind', *Indian Literature* (Sep. '92) 152, pp. 151, 155.
2. Abdul JanMohamed and Devid Llyod, Introd. *The Nature and Context of Minority Discourse (N.Y. : OUP* 1990) p.1.
3. Madhav Prasad, 'The "Other" worldliness of Post-colonial Discourse: a Critique' *Critical Quarterly,* 34 (3) (Autumn, 1992), pp. 87-88.
4. Andre Lefever, 'Systems thinking and Cultural Relations' *Jadhavpur Journal of Comparative Literature,* 26-27 (1987), p. 60.
5. Stephen Berg, ed. *In Praise of What Persists* (1983), intro.
6. Homi Bhabha, 'The Other Question: difference, discrimination and the Discourse of colonialism', *Literature Politics and Theory,* eds. Francis Barker et al. (London: Methuen, 1986), p.148
7. Cyrena Pondrom, *The Roads from Paris: French Influences on English Poetry* (Cambridge Univ. Press, 1974) pp. 22-28.
8. Bhalchandra Nemade, *Indo-Anglian Writings* (Dharwad: Karnatak Univ., 1991), pp. 22.
9. Raja Rao, 'Pigeon-Indian: A note on the emergence of Indian English Literature', *The Journal of Indian Writing,* 20-2 (Jan. 1992) pp. 1-4.
10. Renee Balibar, 'National Language, Education, Literature', Francis Barker et al. eds. op. cit, pp. 126-47.
11. Vilas Sarang, 'Tradition and Conflict in the context of Marathi Literature', *Indian Literatrure,* 151 (Sept. 192) p. 167.
12. Georg Gugelberger, 'Decolonizating the Canon: Considerations of Third World Literature', *New Literary History,* 3-22 (Aug. 1991) p. 520.

13. See Marilyn Randall, 'Approriate(d) Discourse: Plagiarism and Decolonization', *New Literary History,* 2-22 (1991), pp. 525-39.

14. See Kwame Anthony Appiah, 'Is the Post-in Post-modernism the Post-in Post colonial?' *Critical Inquiry* 17-2 (Winter 1991) pp. 336-57.

15. Levin Schucking, as summarised in Robert Holub, *Reception Theory* (London: Methuen, 1978), p. 81.

2

Perspectives on the Folkloristic Intertextuality in Goan Fiction

A comparative study of intertwining of indigenous folklore in Indian fiction in English and in any regional language offers a model for measuring Indianness of one kind or other. It designates the borders between high art and mass culture. It brings out the limitations of the imported modernism's strategy of exclusion or 'anxiety of contamination' of folklore. The colonial contact perpetuated the separation of high art from mass culture. In this regard Western 'high art' dominated the native folk arts in the colonized countries. The postmodernist interest in the indigenous lore provides challenges to the institutions and conventions of both art and history. The function of the folklore in fiction is to make the reader aware of the distinction between alienated native elements in art. It also helps to distinguish between the events of the past real and the facts by which we give meaning to that past. Moreover, it determines the degree of alienation of a writer from his own culture. It explains the contradiction in the terms such as 'Indianness in Indian literature', 'Western drama in Indian dress' and so on. Is "Indianness" fact or fiction?

This paper is divided into three sections. At the outset, its objective, scope and limitations are defined. As a case study, it needs a theoretical frame of reference. A diagrammatic analysis of the problem of representation of folklore in literary works would provide further grounds for comparison. The second section is devoted to the scrutiny of the use of the Goan folklore in two sample texts. The folklores are classified and shown in a table format. The contradictions and paradoxes in the use of folkloristic literary devices are examined with suitable illustrations from the sample texts. The final section focuses on the aspects the folkloristic relativism in fiction. It suggests some means to reserve adequate space for indigenous lore and expansion of the boundaries of 'knowable community' in fiction. These means and ends of modernization of myth and lore are offered from the postcoionial as well as postmodern viewpoints. The concept of intertextuality is used to explain the interrelation of various texts in a literary work.

I

As a case study the scope of this paper is limited to the scrutiny of only two novels chosen at random. The following sample texts are prescribed for the postgraduate studies in the university curriculum:

1. Lambert Mascarenhas, *Sorrowing Lies My Land* (1955).
2. Subhash Bhende, *Jogin* (1974) in Marathi.

The choice of these texts, in English and in Marathi, shows what kind of fiction has been institutionalized in the neocolonial context. An inclusion of the Konkani novel in this study might have added the third dimension to it. Owing to the lack of adequate knowledge of the Konkani language and literature such sample has not been taken into consideration. A comparatist is likely to be tempted to select such samples which suit or support his preconceived conclusions. In order to guard against such pitfalls, already institutionalized texts, which are produced by two writers belonging to different culture groups of the same region, give greater scope for exploration of the folkloristic intertextuality. The first one is produced by the convert Christian writer in an alien language. He is expected to represent the insider's view of the cross section of the mixed ethnic group. The 'knowable community' and its lore depicted in his novel would differ from: that of the latter's. Subhash Bhende, a Hindu Saraswat Brahman, is a migrant but also the insider. Both of them have delineated the tales of the Christian families. Their texts would display varied features of the folkloristic intertextuality. Their works reveal different creative tensions. How far do they show interest in the folk culture, in collective discourse, and in semiotic codes?

Instead of a folk 'poetics', then, perhaps what we have here is a 'problematics'. It is a set of problems and basic issues that have been created by the various discourses of postcolonialism and borrowed postmodernism. These were not so problematic before but certainly are now. For example, we now query these boundaries between alien and native genres. We can interrogate these borders, and folklore serves to call to our attention both our continuing postulation of that difference. The discussion of the effects of commercialisation of the folklore at the popular tourists' resorts on literary works is beyond the scope of this paper. The culture industry in 'Golden Goa' is so complex that it certainly affects the literary culture. Under such circumstances, we need new tools for investigation of the role of lores in a very complex multilingual, multi-cultural and colourful society. The modest objective of this primary inquiry is to take stock of the indigenous folklore as represented in the sample text.

No text is without its pretexts. As cultural products literary works can't survive without folkloristic intertextuality. It is indispensable to the literary discourse. Whether the folklore tradition is more indebted to the standardised printed texts or vice versa is a bone of contention in modern criticism. But it is a universal trend that modern writers had to 'return to lores' whenever literature badly needed revitalisation and innovation. It is true that conscious experimental use of folklore to enrich layers of intertextuality in fiction saves it from becoming a stereotype composition. It provides local colour and vigour to it. It shows resistance to the overpowering alien borrowings which are hostile to its culture. The problem of contextual revival of fossilised folk forms is very complex. The works of T. S. Eliot, James Joyce, Rabindranath Tagore, Kafka. Albert Camus etc. were once considered experimental for their innovative myth making. But now they are revalued as products of the process of modernization of myth which had capitalistic exploitation at its core. The limitations of their modernism are brought out by the writers of self reflexive fiction. History and lore are subverted in their historiographic modification. Indian postcolonial fiction is not postmodern in this sense. I choose the term 'postmodern' as Emma Kafalenos (1992, 381) uses it to emphasise the gap. Here it is intended to focus on the gap that separates the folklore from the western modernism. It is distinct from the modern.

The sample texts selected for the scrutiny fall into the category of the 'well made' novel. They do not show the awareness of the impossibility of establishing a chronological fiction and indeterminacy in postmodern narrative. At the other extreme Gunther Grass, Gabriel Garcia Marquez, Salman Rushdie, John Fowles and other novelists have demonstrated, in Linda Hutcheon's words (1988, 118):

> Postmodern intertextuality is a formal manifestation of both a desire to close the gap between past and present of the reader and a desire to rewrite the past in a new context. It is not a modernist desire to order the present through the past or to take the present look spare in contrast to the richness of the past (see Antin 1972, 108-14). It is not an attempt to void or avoid history. Instead it directly confronts the past of literature and of historiography, for it derives from other texts (documents).

This extensive quotation opens the possibility of studying the so-called modernization or Westernization of Indian arts and literatures by the European colonizers. The folkloristic intertextuality is one of the effective literary devices to close the gap between 'past and present' of the reader. It helps to rewrite the past in a new context. Of course, we find a rich variety of the folkloristic intertextuality in Fanishwarnath Renu's *Maila Anchal* or, to some extent, in Premchand's *Godan*. But they do not contest art's right to claim to inscribe timeless universal values. This makes it clear that we need to return to the question of the relationship between the indigenous lore and modern literary kinds with fresh perspectives. Such an inquiry inevitably engages us with wider cultural and narrative issues in particular the dichotomy between, as Graham Law (1988, 335) has demonstrated, the relationship between the detective story and postmodern fiction, popular folklore and modes of elite fiction. According to Graham Law, these issues are connected with the dichotomy between 'popular' and 'serious' cultural modes and products. The role of popular folk forms have never remained dominant in questioning the assumptions which characterize the process of modernization introduced by the European rulers. The distinct folkloristic textual voices were never well organised into a hierarchy of literary discourse after the medieval Bhakti Movement lost its vigour and the colonizers' culture dominated the scene. A brief resume of this change will provide a base for the textual analysis. In fact, this configuration is complexly related to a specific bourgeois ideological formation during the colonial period. It is also instrumental in generating the cultural discrimination between the folklore and the modern literary kinds. A comparative perspective on the changing attitude to folklore would explain the factors involved in the lore.

The familiarity of folklore seems to breed contempt' everywhere. J.D.A. Widdoson (1990, 216) laments the loss of Briton's interest in their English folklore. He complains that foreigners are attracted to it but the British ignore their heritage. The indigenous folklore tradition had been always at the centre of the British literary thought. According to Richard Axton (1977, 1), they never lost sight of that stronghold even when the dominant Greek and Roman influences were received during the Renaissance. This is why they had their 'Willy' Shakespeare, the folk artist first and then a dramatist. On the contrary, the American immigrants suffered from the, 'anxiety of non-influence'. They had to create popular myths of the 'American dream' (see N. S. Pradhan, 1988, 87). We Indians, with fragmented sensibilities entrapped in the neocolonial situation, have not recovered from the culture shock. Paul Ricoeur observes:

> Every culture cannot sustain and absorb the shock of modern civilization. There is the paradox: how to become a modern and to return to source, (as quoted by Linda Hutcheon, 1988, 87)

The Third World writers face this problem more acutely. They live with the 'oppressive present' and 'archaeologized' past which are full of paradoxes and contradictions. How can we utilize the unacknowledged reservoir of available folklore in the modern context? Scholars agree that the meeting between East and West was one 'quite extraordinarily destructive' for Asia. Globalisation has threatened this cultural heritage.

Our postcolonial return to history and lore, both the Sanskrit and folk, must not be recuperation or nostalgia or revivalism. The tender yet unsparing anatomization of the postcolonial sample texts as well as those of the colonial period shows how native folklore traditions have been neglected in the process of pseudo-modernization. Elsewhere, the present writer (1993, 34) has discussed at length how and why the Marathi playwrights failed, on caste-basis, in making creative use of indigenous lore in their works. Their ambivalent attitude to native folklore has not yet changed in a meaningful way. They have not revived this centre as some writers in the postcolonial countries-Africa, America etc.— have done it with certain commitment. For imaginative reconstruction of our lore, the focus of our rethinking must be the mass culture. The past really did exist. The question is: how to revive it and with what or which thrust? The problematic nature of the relation of writing history, to narrativization and to fictionalization of folklore, demands new approaches. But the alien centres with hidden remote controls govern the creative process of our writers. Their thinking is controlled by the alien counters as follows.

It may be conceded that there is some change at the primary level. The varieties of documentations, festivals, workshops etc. are being organized. Yet folk arts remain, to a large extent, caste-confined. They are more prone to the cheap commercialization by the popular media, apart from the politics of popularizing folklore. Are there any purely nativistic, conscious or systematizing attempts to reveal unity in diversity of the Indian lore on the pan-Inian level? Conscious and organised efforts to perpetuate a folk culture can arise only when a society becomes conscious of the complexities of acculturation. The colonial background has complicated the problem still further. When the existence of our own culture is thus threatened the nativistic movements can take momentum. Ralph Linton (1943, 233) has distinguished the fourfold typology of nativistic movements as follows:

1. Revivalistic-magical
2. Perpetuative-magical
3. Revivalistic-rational
4. Perpetuative-rational

There is a further need to distinguish such types in terms of the situation of inequality between societies in contact. The factors involved in dominance of castes or creeds also obstruct the mastery of folk arts. The Europeans exploited this situation. So rational nativism of any sort did not develop in the colonial period. What we had were revivalistic-magical type movements of small groups. They sprang from hardships and suffering during the tyrannical rule of the alien rulers. The God-fearing Indian society and its writers fed on the mythopoetic imagination have always turned to revivalistic-magical types of nativism. They were guided by the Brahmins. But the hardships arising from subjection were not extreme for them as they were for the African Blacks and American Red Indians. So perhaps Indians showed/have been showing greater eagerness to assimilate Western culture. This eagerness is accompanied by a devaluation of its own culture. Some nativistic movements do develop as a response to frustration. But it does not mean that they are favourable to folklore and the Dalit literature is a glaring example. The direct effects of English education and cultural subjection are noticed in the sample texts. What we need today, to use Bhalchandra Nemade's obsolete concepts, is a team of 'savage writers'. Our new literary movements should originate with native source and not with alien roots. They must be rational with a combination of revivalist and perpetuative elements. They may not degenerate into the mechanism for aggression of only one caste or culture group. Now there are dozen kinds of nativisms.

Very few writers in the postcolonial countries have shown sharp awareness of the 'double exilement', and cultural alienation. For example, Latin American Gloria Anzaldua, in her *Bordelands* (1987, 61), strongly argues against importing too many foreign myths. The heart-searching account of her struggle for cultural identity reveals her yearning for the lost lore. In fact, it is the politics and sociology of representation of structures of feeling in literature that makes all the differences in the use of folklore. We need to examine the writer's sincerity and honesty in its use. His creative process may be complex. But we can analyse his method of seeing what is silenced by the dominant cultural discourse, and why'? In conclusion of *Culture and Society* (1961, 319) Raymond Williams observes:

> No community, no culture, can ever be fully conscious of its ever know itself.

Under such circumstances many difficulties are involved in the analysis of the folkloristic intertextuality in Indian fiction. The textual incorporation of native folkloristic past as a constructive element in it would function as a formal making of history both literary and 'worldly'. It would help to make our postcolonial fiction really postmodern, independent and distinctive. On this background, let us examine how far native lores are incorporated in two samples, and if not, why?

II

According to Somnath Komarpant (1993, 67-85), there are very rich Goan traditions of folklore tales, songs, music, dance drama, rituals, proverb, abusive terms and so on. Are all of them adequately represented by the Goan writers? One significant feature of the effect of alienation of the writer from a native folklore is revealed in both the sample texts. No consciousness or systematic consistency is noticed in the use of lore. Consequently, conventional attitude to it does not contribute much to the innovation in these novels. For example, a classroom scene depicted it Lambert Mascarenhas's *Sorrowing Lies My Land* (pp. 28, 29) reminds us of the similar satirical scene at the opening of Charles Dickens's *Hard Times*. However, it gives a deep insight into the process of linguistic and literary acculturation in the Portuguese colony in India. It not only does explain the process of alienation, but also throws a flood of light on the secret weapons of cultural aggression. It tells as to why nativistic movements did not take roots into the Goan soil. Portuguese colonisers like the British and the French, effectively used textbooks of conquest. A comparative study of the textbooks introduced by the colonizers in their colonies will further explain how native folk culture was skilfully suppressed and the alien one considered superior. Mascarenhas narrates:

> We learnt geography at school and how wonderful and beautiful Portugal was.... Great pride we children took in being Portuguese and every time we read about the exploits of heroes such as Vasco de Gama.... (p. 28).

This is why Garter G. Woodson aptly entitled his book as *The Mis-education of the Negroes* (1933). Such miseducation makes us look down upon the indigenous lores and mass culture.

Many scenes in this novel depict characters caught on the horns of dilemmas created by the colonial contact. A beautiful 'Brahmane' lady teacher has to become the 'machine of otherness'. A Christian pupil asks her if the Portuguese Afonso Albuquerque spoke Konkani. If the converted pupil and Afonso were both Portuguese, why were their languages so different? The puzzled teacher cannot support the native tongue. She helplessly tries to silence the innocent pupil by stating that their language 'was not Konkani but Portuguese'. The pupil practices in his home what his 'professor' has taught in the classroom. But his patriotic father punishes him for using the foreign tongue in his house (p. 29). Afterwards we read the accounts of the immigrant sons of Goa. They are trapped in 'lark mirrors' set by Europeans.

One more ironic situation shows how children were slowly alienated from their own culture. Mascarenhas has made an effective use of native history and folktales. One day Tobias proudly narrates the heroic tales of Indian and especially Goan kings and heroes. He compares their 'Ram rajya' (Utopia) with the tyrannical rule of the 'Portuguese traitors'. Children are shocked by such 'old women's tale'. Their teachers have never told them such heroic sagas of the Indian warriors. Their textbooks did never mention them. They ask Tobias not to 'tell yarns'. How can we expect that the traditional storehouse of indigenous folklore can be well preserved in such situation? The posterity was destined to grow under the dwarfing influences of the dominant alien culture.

The dramatic plot of the disintegration of a Goan Christian family unfolds on this background. Tobias's experience of the colonial life and the narrator's interpretations of this tragedy form the thematic structure of the novel. Like many other protagonists of the modern novels, the narrator is not an abnormal character. He suffers from the severe attack of paralysis. It is a symbol of the colonized human being. The tale is told in the first person singular. The narrator reproduces the extracts from his father's conversations with Dr. Aquino, the only enlightened social worker who sympathises with Tobias. Tobias argues:

> 'These damn Portuguese have so denationalized us that we may so well have no soul, of our own?' commented my father, bitterly and helplessly, 'We, the Christians in particular, are really a sorry sight. *More than four centuries of colonial oppression have made us foreign in our own country*' (p. 67, italics added).

This corresponds well with the poetics of resistance as demonstrated by many African and Latin American writers. Their slogan is 'BLACK IS BEAUTIFUL.' Neither Mascarenhas nor Bhende shows this kind of strong resistance.

The colonial consciousness is totally absent in Bhende's Marathi novel: *Jogin* (nun), why? Is it so because there is much transformation of the Goan Christian community after independence? Or is it so because Bhende is an upper caste Hindu writer who narrates the sufferings of a Christian nun? He is an outsider in this sense. Some biographical details of both writers such as the birthplace, education, caste, religion, etc., provide clues to their use of the folklore. Both the novels were published in Bombay. The first writer is a journalist, the second a professor. Both novels have the implied anglicized reader present in their formation. The novel in reader and reader in the novel make great difference in the use of folklore. It can be easily noticed that both the novels are written for the elite reader's consumption. This affective poetics governs their creative process. It has concern for power. It is related to knowledge. Neither the folklore nor the native dialect can easily penetrate into the steel frame of the Europeanized concepts of these novels. Here we need not evaluate them from the literary viewpoint. Our modest purpose is to trace the presence of the past in the form of folklore as it is present in them. It is neither experimental nor innovative. This leads us to the problem of the relationship between the popular fiction and the experimental one. 'Affective stylistics' and 'interpretative communities' are two important concepts in reader-response theories. We have to situate our reading of these samples in their historical setting.

The following Table shows the types of intertextuality of the Goan folklore in the sample texts:

Type of Lore	*Sorrowing Lies My Land*	*Jogin*
History	Used as intertext, not subverted patriotic, simple	Only anecdotes, no external field of reference.
Folk-tales	Three heroic tales, no folk tales	Poor intertextuality
Dance	A dozen references, no details, less variety, unconscious	greater in number, variety: waltz, fox trot, wedding, picnic, club, less symbolic, no subversion
Drama	No direct descriptions, terminology used figuratively, no conscious use	Ridicules Tiatr (p.100) no more references, no conscious use.
Song	Two stanzas, one nursery rhyme and folk ballad trans. in English, half a dozen references, not	Two stanzas of love song in Konkani, Mando, other varieties only mentioned, not a

	a single in Konkani, unconscious	single in English, short prayer texts in profusion, conscious but contrived
Music	Mainly Christian, limited, No reference to Hindu/ Indian music, unconscious	Jingle bells, orchestra violin, choir mentioned, absence of folk music, less conscious, artificial
Ritual	Mainly Christian fests, prayers, wedding, death etc., some subverted, only two Hindu festivals mentioned, very few references to crossbreeding in cultural affairs	Excessive references to prayers, but less artistic, few fests, wedding, no Hindu fest, no subvertion, absence of cross-pollination
Folk faiths super-stition	Absence of folk rituals born of blind faiths, black-magic, witchery, no subversion. No reference to Hindu faiths, ironic attitude, Sanskrit lore absent	Christian superstition used consciously, dream offering daughter as nun, no reference to Hindu blind faiths, Sanskrit lore absent.
Biblical, religion oath & perjury	Few biblical, some ironic, compares castes, Christian myths a few in English only, no Konkani or Portuguese, political perjury satirized	No scriptural intertexts, no comparison, nil conscious, half a dozen, simple, false swearing but no satire
Content	Christian (converts), insider	Christian but not clearly specified, limited knowable community. poor understanding, outsider
Commu-nity	Knowable community limited yet inclusive, selective	Writer outsider to the community in novel.
Form	Purely anglicized, no experimentation, bare tale, Victorian	Purely anglicized, no innovation, bare tale modern
Narrative Style	First person only Conventional, figurative	Third person only conventional, romantic

	lyrical, no deeper layers of folkloristic intertextuality, sentimental	artificial, decorative, no deeper layers of any sort of intertextuality, melodramatic.
Proverb	Half a dozen, simple, only in English, absence of Konkani	Only three, Marathi, simple, not in Konkani
Abusive words, idioms	Approx. 24 in English and Portuguese only, no Konkani	Total absence
Colonial consciousness acculturation, immigration	Progressive attitude, fine colonial consciousness anti-mmigration, sentimental, exhibits effects of acculturation, conscious	Conservative, elite, no colonial consciousness, least awareness of acculturation and immigration syndrome
Setting	Pre-independence village, good historicity	Town, no sense of historicity, weakness

The table shows that both the writers have not used the folk as well as classical lore consciously and effectively. In fact, the thematic structure of these novels demands harmonious cross-pollination of alien as well as native lore to portray acculturation at various levels. Regarding the problem of mastery of folk and classical lore, as both are excluded from our education, we can't expect that sort of mastery unless special efforts are made to reserve adequate space for the folk lore. On the contrary, contradictions in the use of lore as merely decorative features reveal writer's alienation from cultural roots. For example, the setting of Mascarenhas's novel and ethnology of a Goan village suggests acculturation of a very complex type. The absence of fisherfolk, other ethnic groups, their language and culture weakens its thematic structure. In Bhende's novel only two songs (pp. 36, 71) and half a dozen sentences in Konkani (p. 47, 62) are studded into the anglicized, in fact, over-anglicized, standard Marathi patterns like artificial jewels. A direct speech of the mother (p. 62) is a fine example of the incongruity. The mother speaks one sentence in pure

Konkani and immediately switches over to the elitist Marathi in the next one. He has not used any abusive word of expression with the realistic touch. To the other extreme, Mascarenhas has used a number of abusive phrases in English: rascals, pest, ass, a bitch, swine, dog, bloody bastard etc., and minimum Portuguese abusive words, but not a single abusive address word in Konkani. It is a paradox of colonialism that the writer who incorporates a number of Portuguese words and sentences: *regedor, schor, mestre, filbo de puto, patria* etc. and Konkani words: *gulmohr, battcars choli, hartal,* etc., in English novel fails to use native abusive tenors. Similarly Bhende overuses words and sentences in English: prayer, picnic, dance, examination of conscience, voice of god, secluded congregation etc. in the Marathi novel. He forgets totally that the ecclesiastical profession in Goa was governed by the Portuguese hierarchy and not by the British from Bombay. The absence of Portuguese in his novel does not seem justifiable.

As we live with several such paradoxes and contradictions which blur cultural identity, so do our literary works. This is why our literary texts exhibit maximum gap between the alienated elite culture and the mass culture. The mass culture is not adequately represented in these samples. So the folkloristic intertextuality is bound to remain very weak. Mascarenhas laments the lack of nativistic movements in Goa, but he falls short of expanding the boundaries of the knowable community in his novel for the other ethnic groups. The lack of resistance on the part of colonised means their desire to imitate and assume the white man's culture. Even Bhende's portrayal of nun's vocation and of Sister Agatha's family is so shallow that that it is not wonder that we cannot have *The Power and Glory* in our static literary culture. Our taste is rotten by borrowings and plagiarism. Isolationism and liberal humanism as well as simplistic mimesis have created both novels. Bhende includes one Hindu family – Shirodkar, in the plot without having to do anything with the problem of the cross-culture encounter. Mascarenhas also mentions some Hindu *mondakars* and labourers without the realistic touches. All this makes their novels readable but devoid of the rich intertextuality of native lore. The readers are not forced to acknowledge the inevitable textuality of their knowledge of the past. As the classical myths and folklores are excluded, there is the lack of intertextual intertwining of discourse ideologically and aesthetically. What Raymond Williams writes of the *English Novel* (1974, 78) holds more true of Indian novels. He observes:

> There are very few examples of written knowable communities in which the necessary connections with historical patterns of economy and culture are convincingly made. Yet to have understood the problem of the novel, ethnography and many other kinds of writing in this way is both a theoretical and a practical advance, in understanding.

But such advance in understanding of exo-cultural characters is also conditioned by many determinants in Indian contexts. All major characters in both novels are Portuguese-English educated. They live in the borrowed culture. They are alienated from the rhythm, rhyme and memories of the native lore. They do not exhibit how sociolects and idiolects, as parts of folklore, contribute much to the technique of characterization in the novel. Then 'discourse' in these novels ignores social practices, the historical conditions of meaning and the positions from which texts are both produced and received. In this sense these elitist productions do not allow much space to the mass culture which is the real guardian of folk arts. As these texts do not derive much meaning and significance from the indigenous lore, they fall short in fulfilling the condition of textuality. They show how art is separated from the world and our literature from our own cultural history. To bridge this wide gap we have to return to folklore to revitalize as well as 'resocialise' our literature. What Linda Hutcheon observes, by quoting Ronald Barthes approvingly, is a befitting conclusion for this section. She argues:

> A literary work can actually no longer be considered original: if it were, it could have not meaning for its reader. It is only a part of prior discourses that any text derives

> meaning and significance. Roland Barthes once defined the intertext as the impossibility of living outside the infinite text' (1975, 36), thereby making intertextuality the very condition of textuality (Hutcheon 128).

Making folklore the very condition of textuality in fiction in postcolonial context is the basic need of self-reliance. It is diagnosed on the basis of the samples examined in this case study. But what are the remedies and how can folklore enrich intertextuality ideologically and aesthetically?

III

If we accept these sample texts as representative modern Indian fiction in general, we arrive at some valid conclusions based on this case study. The microscopic scrutiny of the folkloristic intertextuality might further confirm and modify them. But glance at our theoretical as well as applied criticism of Indian 'fiction' reveals that neither a theorist nor a critic has ever examined the significance of folklore in fiction systematically. It means that they are also more alienated than the writers. However, very few folklorists, for instance except D. G. Godase (1989), have gone beyond the stages of collection, audiovisual documentation and methodical printing of folklore. They have failed in interpreting them in the modern context.

But none seems to have taken the postmodernist stance towards creative use of folklore in literary works. Various reasons of this discripancy and dilemma can be put forth. Godase has successfully brought out the differences and lacunae in our aesthetics. According to him (p. 84, summarised), the poetics of oral folk tradition has its primitive natural modes of expression. It exhibits collective consciousness, flexibility, speed, curves, and continuity of a stream. They may appear crude, disordered or craftless to the elitist aestheticians. The modern literary education overvalues techniques, artistic devices, traditional codes, sophistication individualism and so on. The modes of expression in folk arts have inherent power. They are total, symbolic, archetypal, universal and not linear material or bound by space and time. Further Godase explains why the European painters returned to the primitive culture of savages in the nineteenth century. He believes in the culture of the caveman. The urban education and conventions have alienated the pandits from the common people. It is impossible for the urban sensibility to create folk forms in their hothouses By citing passages from S.K. Kolhatkar and N.C. Kelkar on their response to the *pauranik natak,* Godase argues that these are the effects of anglicization. But he does not explain what was silenced by the alien as well as Indian upper class/caste elites in the discourse.

We need not go deep into the history of the monopolization of Sanskrit lore, condemnation of lower caste folk arts and contamination caused by the presence of English lore (Mande, 1975, 1-10, Moraje, 1985, 1-23). One thing is certain, the caste compartmentalized implied reader governs the creative process of the writer. That makes much difference in the reception of the folklore. Of course, there are many contradictions between the emergent and the dominative culture in India. From the nationalist viewpoint, we should accept the argument about culture and totality, but should also insist on a contradictory totality in the end. This is why we need to fix the space to be occupied by the indigenous lore in the creative works. In doing this we will face the tensions which are unsparingly pointed out by Ngugi wa Thiong'o (1984 3-5). According to him, the struggle between 'national democratic cultures' and 'imperialist cultures' or the national cultures of Third World and the imperialist cultures of First World give's rise to the real tensions. He believes that 'language is at the heart of this tension'. We have discussed the effects of these tensions on the sample texts. Our basic hypothesis is that the artistic intertextuality of folklore is a mark of true Indianness in Indian fiction. It is one of the remedies to get rid of this colonial dichotomy in our literary culture. This distinctiveness of our writing should primarily stem from its Indianness. Our findings based on the case study are confirmed by C. Paul Verghese's similar observations. He states:

> What I mean by Indianness in Indian Writing in English is the sum total of the cultural patterns of India and the deep seated ideals political, economic secular and spiritual

> that constitute the mind of India and are reflected in her writing. We have this kind of Indianness, in our regional literatures, but we do not make much of it. This is because the Indianness here is taken for granted (1952, 2).

Thus, the invitation of folk forms directs the attention of the writer to new themes and new techniques, and to the necessity of defining his position as a writer in quest of new frontiers. This quest should be necessarily guided by the postmodernism which subverts neocolonialism in literature. Then only the inherent potentialities of intertextuality of folklore in fiction will be tested. Let us conclude this paper with Linda Hutcheon's (139, 140) defence of the poetics of postmodernism which might vitalize our poetics of folklore. She argues:

> Postmodernism clearly attempts to combat what has come to be seen as modernism's potential for hermetic, elitist, isolationism that separated art from the world: literature from history. But it often does so by using the very techniques of modernist aestheticism against themselves The autonomy of art is carefully maintained: metafictional selfreflexivity even underlines it (p. 140).

This attitude to folk culture would enrich intertextuality in literature. There is no question of hierarchy. Breaking the native barriers of caste and creed is the chief task. The mastery of folk poetics is another challenge. The ambivalence in reception and study of folklore will persist as long as the English education dominates the cultural life. This is why there is a greater need to understand that folklores are parts of the signifying system. Culture is a system of meanings. In order to make our literature meaningful we have to dig our own soil deeper and deeper.

3

Colonial and Post/Neocolonial Discourse in Two Goan Novels: A Fanonian Study

Francisco Louis Gomes's *Os Brahamanes* (1866) was published in Portuguese in Lisbon. Lambert Mascarenhas's *Sorrowing Lies My Land* (1955) was published in English in Bombay.[1] I have chosen at random these two Goan novels written in two European languages during the period of Portuguese rule in Goa (1510-1961) for comparative study. The main objective of this analysis is to examine how fictional discourse changes in the different phases of colonialism and especially to test whether the two texts fit into or deviate from the Fanonian paradigm (Fanon 190-96). In the multilingual and multicultural situation in the Indian subcontinent, the problematics of race and imperialism become complicated. The resulting paradoxes and contradictions can be adequately explained only by comparative studies. For instance, Meenakshi Mukherjee treats novels written by Christian—whether originally so or converts—as a recognizable product of mid-nineteenth-century India. She goes on to argue: "The whole body of such works constitutes Christianity's contribution to the development of the novel in India. A comparative discussion of the themes and their presentation in some of these novels will enable us to assess the nature of this contribution" (21).

My comparative study of nineteenth-century literature in British and Portuguese Goa supports Mukherjee's presumptions.[2] It also unveils how the European cultural conquest of India gave rise to cross-pollinated literary genres. It demonstrates how elite Brahmanical literature was transformed in the contact situation in order to retain the cultural hegemony of the small Brahman minority. The Brahmans imitated the colonizers' generic repertory to preserve that hegemony. However, because of the different policies adopted by the Portuguese in Goa and the British in the rest of India, the Indian literatures put on different garbs and forms. On the whole, these literary types were, in Paulo Freire's words, the products of "antidialogic" education and "oppressive reality" (123).

The oppressive present creates various creative tensions in the colony. It is not an accident that Hannah Catherine Mullen's *Phulmoni-O-Karunar Bibaran* in Bengali (1852), Baba Padmanji's *Yamuna Paryatan* in Marathi (1857), Gomes's *Os Brahamanes* in Portuguese (1866), Mrs. Collins's *The Slayer Slain* in English (1864-66; translated into Malayalam, 1877), Samuel Vedanayakam Pillars *Prathapa Mudaliar Charitram* in Tamil (1879), and several other early novels in India, seek to "demonstrate the benefits available to Indians by converting to Christianity" (Mukherjee 21). Post-colonial critics and theorists will find in this cross-culture encounter fresh frameworks for their theories. All the problems interlock with imperialism of one sort or another, indigenous or alien.

Edward Said's and Homi K. Bhabha's concepts such as "culture," "imperialism," "ambivalence," and "stereotype," are especially useful in this discourse analysis. According to Bhabha, "there is a theoretical space and political space for such an articulation—in a sense in that world itself denies an 'original' identity or a 'singularity' to objects of difference" (149). This "difference" makes the difference between Gomes's *Os Brahamanes* (1866) in Portuguese and Lambert Mascarenhas's *Sorrowing Lies My Land* (1855) in English. The "difference" between the fiction.. discourses of these two Goan writers reveals two distinct phases of Portuguese colonialism. The first shows how the master's discourse confined the colonised and destined them to a half-life of misrepresentation. The second one exemplifies Fanon's phase of violence and resistance. Both reveal the different creative tensions caused by various pulls in the process of literary acculturation in the colonial situation.

I

It is interesting to note here that until the mid-nineteenth century, all Goan writing, both in Portuguese and in the vernaculars, remained mainly the literature of Christian porselytization. The Christian religion and the Portuguese language were predominant (see Xavier 184-92). Consequently, secular literature could hardly develop in Goa. In British India, however, English was made compulsory in 1835, and the first English-educated writers were encouraged to write in their native languages. Gomes's Chaddo-Kshatriya forefathers were converted to Christianity by force in the sixteenth century. His is a typical case of what Bhabha calls "the co-option of traditional elites into the colonial administration" (166). Inquisitions and language policies adopted for domination created, in Fanon's phrase, "the living haunts of contradictions" (175). These are the Goan exceptions to what Meenakshi Mukherjee writes of the converted Christians in nineteenth-century India (32).

Baba Mule, who came from the Kasar minority, embraced the Protestant Church in Bombay willingly. His *Yamuna Paryatan* (Yamuna's journey) was inspired not only by the Widow Remarriage Act (1856) but also by his conversion to Christianity. It mainly portrays the sad plight of the uppercaste, especially Brahman, widows. Both *Yamuna* and *The Brahman* end with the conversion of the Brahman protagonists to Christianity. The only difference is that Yamuna favours the Protestant and Gomes's Magnod the Catholic Church. A comparative study of these novels is a subject for further investigation. Non-literary determinants of a literary form like fiction can be easily traced in its paratexts. Moreover, the European rulers dreamed of converting all India to Christianity.[3]

Gomes was an experienced journalist, biographer, and politician who joined the opposition party in the Portuguese parliament. He is representative of "native intellectuals" in the colonies all over the world. His romance, written in Europe, reveals "the pitfalls of national consciousness" in the colonial situation which were systematically analysed by Fanon (148). Cultural estrangement, which is most characteristic of the colonial epoch, is more wide ranging in *The Brahman* than in *Yamuna*. Gomes speaks as a Goan and as a Portuguese. He boasts of his "universal standpoint" and pleads for humanism in his novel. This dilemma is caused by his two nationalities. Fanon points out how intellectuals avoid painful choices. Further he observes: "But most often, since they cannot or will not make a choice, such intellectuals gather together all the historical determining factors which have conditioned them and take up a fundamentally 'universal standpoint" (176). Gomes's novel reveals how he had thrown himself upon Western culture. Like an adopted child he tried to make European culture his own. The dedicatory letter, a pretext of *Os Brahamanes* (English trans, 1-4), revealingly invokes Shakespeare, Castilho, A. Herculano and other European stalwarts (Gomes was also influenced by Alexander Dumas.) His inferiority complex, born of his choice of the Portuguese language, is also mirrored in the dedicatory letter (3). We are told that he could write in Portuguese at the age of nine, and got his doctrate before he came of age. He stayed in Lisbon for eight years.

The Golden Age of the European novel reached its peak in the mid-nineteenth century. Historical romances in the tradition of Sir Walter Scott's Waverley novels were especially popular. According to Ernest Baker, a number of European writers, such as Bulwer-Lytton in England, Balzac, Victor Hugo and Dumas in France, wrote historical novels, plays and romances modelled on the Waverley novels (7, 63). Of course, the rise of the European novel is, as Edward Said has argued, closely connected with that of European imperialism (*Culture* ii-xv). Gomes's dedication to Clio the Muse was shared by historians like David Hume, Gibbon, and Carlyle in Britain, Grant Duff in India, Hegel in Germany, and Washington Irving in America. Under such circumstances it is rather strange to say that Gomes was "influenced" by "Lamartine and Victor Hugo" only (Menezes 6). The year and place of publication of

Os Brahamanes (1866) and the dedicatory letter are the paratexts which reveal how "the native bourgeois" created by colonizers was placed on the horns of a dilemma by setting his novel in British India. Postcolonial commentators such as Armando Menezes, Laxmanrao Sardesai, and Deepa Kolwalkar have not grasped the complexities involved in a colonial discourse connected with the circulation of power as knowledge.

Before analysing this discourse, I should offer a few comments on the role of the colonized writer and reader. The situation of the colonial Indian reader, deprived of writing for thousands of years, presents us with several problems. In such a society, every printed book was considered as holy as the scriptures. Very few could detect the weapons of conquest behind the masks. Nancy Vogeley writes:

> ... The colonial reader, whether a historical entity belonging to the days of the world's great empires or a present-day consciousness trapped in the prevailing linguistic systems and dominant artistic styles, finds it difficult to reach beyond these boundaries of control to embrace the texts. Critics using reader-response theories can only help in this task if they examine more closely the politics of a book's reception, if they acknowledge the varying degrees of text acceptance that the notion of the "colonial reader" represents. (796)

It can be easily judged that Gomes's implied or ideal reader was first the alien master and then the colonized èlite. Gomes was constructing a myth of Indian life in fiction as the European Orientatalists did. His choice of the Irish planter Robert Davis and the background of British Bengal is not intended to be a satire on the Hindu "brown" Brahmans and European "white" Brahmans as some commentators believe (e.g., Menezes 9). It is a colonial paradox that a colonized and yet romanticized Irish peasant is juxtaposed against the Indian Brahman. A Brahman can hardly be a thug or disguised as a Jew. Magnod does not disguise himself as a moneylending Pathan. Gomes's antisemitism and his portrayal of the Catholic Irish planter were meant to please the colonizers. Even in his handling of the 1857 Revolt there was nothing that could hurt the sentiments of the white masters. Edward Hirsch examined the romantic myth of the peasant in Irish literature (1116). In the nineteenth century, the British looked down upon the Irish peasant as a "white negro". Both the Jew and Irish peasant were stereotyped characters used to get laughter. Gomes did not challenge these myths because he had internalized the model of the white master's literature which spread myths to maintain white superiority.[4] His vehement demystification of the Brahmans can be well understood, of course, against the sociopolitical background of the struggle between two upper castes Kshatriya and Brahman, for supremacy (Olivinu Gomes 212-14). Ever though many of them had been converted to Christianity, they never forgot their original caste identities.

The setting of his novel also reveals the politics of representing reality. Goan natural scenes, sounds and colours can be traced in its pages; but it is not set in Goa. Goan critics have put forth contradictory views regarding this issue. According to Deepa Kolwalkar (61), Gomes was a Chaddo, so he wanted to portray the marshal race of Kshatriya in Oudh. But there was the history of the great Shivaji and the Marathas or Rajput warriors. Gomes did not want to voice the newly rising nationalist spirit, as did M.M. Kunte in his epic *Raja Shivaji* (1871). Gomes's choice of subject, setting, and even narrative mode was determined by colonialism. The colonized writer was left little space for free experimentation in fictional discourse. Goa had to wait for another hundred years till the arrival of Mascarenhas, who challenged the series of myths manipulated by the Portuguese rulers in his counter discourse. The present writer has commented on the myths of learned European administrators in Bombay (*Western Influence* 31, 80). The majority of them were non-English. The Irish or Welsh poor were sent to the colonies. So the presence of the Irish Robert Davis in Gomes's romantic fabula is not accidental. A brief summary of this picaresque novel might help in the analysis of its content, structure, and style.

It is a simple, third-person narrative, set in Oudh (West Bengal). The omniscient narrator tells the tale of the clash between a poor Brahman, Magnod, and the Irish tobacco planter, Robert Davis. Magnod is insulted by Robert at the dinner table. Suddenly, and rather unconvincingly, the orthodox Brahman decides to become a thug-highwayman to take revenge upon the white man. He abandons his wife and two children on the same night and secretly runs away to the jungle. Magnod's wife, Bima, reads the letter he leaves behind and immediately, and also rather unconvincingly, commits suicide. The Brahmans do not accept her anglicized orphans, but Frei Francisco, the Catholic Portuguese missionary, appears on the scene like an angel to save them. The conservative Brahmans are thus pitted against the "civilized" Christians. Gomes writes: "That same day Bima's body was buried. The Brahmanic faith refused her its prayers, and the Christian could not offer her its own..." (31). Such apparently humanitarian touches are numerous in Gomes's discourse. A number of sermons on topics such as spinsters, revenge, tolerance, dandism, gambling, love, jealousy interrupt the action of his pseudo-historical-cum-detective fiction.

Robert repents for insulting Magnod, and under the guidance of Frei Francisco, Magnod's children are converted to Christianity. They are sent to London for further education. There the Catholic Hartman family is expected to "civilize" the Indians in the company of Robert's daughter Helen. (Robert's wife had expired soon after giving birth to Helen.) Robert gambles, and is left penniless. At this point, Gomes employs the conventional device of the will. Robert's uncle has made one, according to which Helen must marry the dandy Richard; but she loves Thomas, Magnod's son. Richard seduces Emily, Magnod's daughter, who thereupon gives birth to a son, and breaths her last. Meanwhile, Magnod, who has disguised himself as Sobal the Jew, detects all these crimes. Instead of taking revenge on Robert, he murders Richard. Finally he confesses his crime; but he is not punished. On the contrary, the romance ends on a optimistic note: "A month after the capture of Delhi, the French priest Lebrun blessed the union of Thomas and Helen in the Church of Saint Francis Xavier and administered baptism to Magnod with the name of Robert Davis. (181). Thus the long-awaited assimilation of white and black is achieved, at least in fiction. The great freedom struggle of 1857 is used as merely a backdrop. It has nothing to do with the main plot of the picaresque novel which is full of disguises, weird caves and valleys, romantic love scenes, beautiful scenery and adventures patterned on the Waverley novels.

Gomes's inspiration is wholly European. We can link his romance with definite trends in the European novel. He himself chose the label "romance," which appeared on the title page of the original novel. Thus his only novel belongs to what Fanon describes as "the period of unqualified assimilation" whereas Mascarenhas's fiction belongs to the third phase "which is called the fighting phase" (178). The desire of the natives to assimilate with the culture of the alien masters was stronger in Goa than in British India because nativistic movements were ruthlessly uprooted by the Portuguese.[5] In Goa, the forces of resistance gathered rather late. (In British India, neo-Hinduism counter-checked the onslaught of Christianity.) Gomes's attitude to religious and other reforms was determined by his understanding of the history of the European Reformation and Renaissance.

There is a peculiar ambivalence in Gomes's delineation of themes, in his portrayal of characters, and even in his attitude towards Indian history. Although he pleads for the liberty of the enslaved Africans and Asians, he fails to voice an indictment of the white imperial rulers in India. One can understand his harsh satire on Brahmans and condemnation of Maharajas (22, 23); but the tone of this discourse changes suddenly when he consciously juxtaposes the European masters with them. The following excerpts demonstrate his tug of war between loyalties:

> Cholera and the Thug were born in the same country and in the same year. India is their native land; the year 1818, the date of their birth... (36)
>
> Frei Francisco did not approve of the English rule in India, but he preferred it to the despotism of the Nawabs and Rajas.
>
> With Magnod, whom he treated as his friend, Frei Francisco used to discuss at length the system of castes

> and slavery. The Sheridans and the Wilberforces might speak more eloquently; *but* never with greater indignation or more sincerity than the humble priest of Fyzabad; for conviction *is* worth more than the showy fineries of eloquence. (63)

Gomes seems to interpret Indian history and politics through Portuguese eyes (174-77). The myth of the "White man's burden" makes him somewhat inconsistent. For instance, he offers a sincere plea in his novel as well as in his essays for the enslaved Africans (131) but entitles Chapter XVI of the second part of *The Brahman* (which fails to interpret the 1857 Uprising in the nationalist spirit): "1857—The Sepoy Mutiny." The title echoes British policy. To show his humanism he criticises the policies of the white "Brahmans of Europe and America." But the alien pull is stronger than the native one in his analysis of historical events. Consequently he concludes the chapter on the epoch-making event of 1857 revolt with the pro-colonialist sentiment: "The Society of Jesus was all this" (177).

As a novel of the first phase of colonial "unsuccessful assimilation," *The Brahman* gives proof that Gomes has assimilated the culture of the occupying power. Gomes refers to his native Goa only twice in it. These passing references are necessarily meant to project the superior image of the Catholic Church possibly as a reaction against the native imperialism of the Brahmans. In order to expose native Brahmanism, Gomes has juxtaposed to it a larger-than-life portrait of Frei Francisco. His praise for the priest is unbounded: "At a very tender age he had gone to Goa, where the Order of the Hermits of Saint Augustine possessed a stately convent and the college de Populo" (60).

At least 50 per cent of Goans, mostly Christians, continue to maintain the image of the Portuguese Goans. The Christian press helped to manipulate the myth of the Vatican Goa in India. However, Mascarenhas's fictional discourse of the fighting phase exposed many such myths. These differences are born of colonial history. Gomes's discourse exhibits a number of the tactics of colonialism. Although his vision was historically conditioned, his views were progressive for his own time. But he could not escape the dichotomy of rejection or assimilation of alien culture. The dual heritage disintegrates his creative process. The resulting inconsistencies and dislocation of sensibilities can be discerned from the following mode of narration:

> To men of liberal principles and to mankind it is perfectly indifferent whether India is called English or Brahminical; what they cannot consent to is, that the domination be exploitation instead of paternal tutelage .... Europe ought to sympathise with the land that formulated democracy in the game of chess, the land that sang with the voice of angels all the sublimities of Heaven, and with the voice of the nightingale ail the beauties of earth; in its poem, the *Mahabharata* — the true Himalaya of literature. England fortunately comprehends what is her mission in India. (175)

The narrator hardly comments on the "double game" played by the colonizers to exploit India; but he takes every care to appreciate England's divine "mission in India." He repeatedly professes that "The most powerful instruments of civilisation are two: the Christian religion and education" (176). Deepa Kolwalkar has rightly observed Gomes's neglect of the other downtrodden Hindu castes. She argues: "However, Gomes himself was guilty of believing in this Brahmanism. He advocated that the lower castes should be converted to Christianity in order to liberate them from the ancient prejudices of their religion. Why could Gomes not advocate for them education as a means of liberating them as he did for the upper castes? Perhaps he felt that they could not be educated as he might have thought that their intellect was weak" (51-52). She does not explain the causes of this cultural dilemma in the mind of the creative writer. We get the answer to her question in Paulo Freire's theory of oppression: "Cultural invasion, which serves the ends of conquest and the preservation of oppression, always involves a parochial view of reality, a static perception of the world, and the imposition of one world view upon another. It implies the 'superiority' of the invader and the 'inferiority' of those who are invaded, as well as the imposition of values by the former, who possess the latter and are afraid of losing them" (129). In fact, the Portuguese "lost" Goa too late to the Indians.

Gomes shows some awareness of the art of characterization (3). He tells us how he would "create one or two characters and breathe life into them, clothe them as best" as he could (3). But his novel is populated by European administrators, women, dandies, missionaries, and soldiers. On the native side, only one Brahman and a few Thugs are depicted, and with less ingenuity and skill. Gomes delightfully portrays "the festivities at Cawnpore"; but he never questions their economic and social implications. He simply states. "The Englishman in India travels like a Nawab" (111), bypassing all other, more complex sociopolitical realities. The handling of character, incident and setting is in the Romantic mode. The characters tend to be types which symbolize some abstract principles. Very few of them grow into round characters.

Even the artificial or contrived scenes show how characters are made to play as puppets in the author's hand. Magnod's test of killing his pet dog and Frei Francisco's decision to sell canaries to Sobal make the melodramatic stuff much needed for a popular romance. The world in this romance is divided into two compartments. The colonial world is divided in turn by barracks and police stations. All the aesthetic expressions in Gomes's fictional discourse show respect for the alien established order. They serve to create around the exploited characters an atmosphere of submission and of inhibition. This point can be further explained by weighing the elements of native and alien intertextuality in Gomes's colonial discourse.

A close scrutiny of intertextuality at various levels reveals the nature of the writer's colonial consciousness, which depends on his level of linguistic and literary acculturation. In *The Brahman,* allusions to European scriptures and literature include: the biblical image of Christ (173), the gospel (106, 132), Job, Paul, Noah, St. Xavier (23), Eden (123), Eve (144), Paradise (105); Alcibiades and Byron (79), Machiavelli (80), Dante (122), Mozart, Cameons (145), Virgil (137), and so on. There are a few figurative expressions such as a "bastard son of Hyppocrates" (152), and the fire of Helea, David, and Goliath. Among the

Indian allusions include: the *Vedas* (21), the *Shakuntala* (122) the *Hitopadesha* (138, 190), the *Mahabharata* (39, 175). Very few native words and expressions such as "a sacred noose," "nachny," "apas," "cruel Vishnu," "the mild Shiva" (175), find place in this discourse dominated by the European texts. Gomes's use of Sanskritic literary devices (for example, the characters scream and swoon) shows that he was not completely alienated from the tradition of Indian classical literature. Although he is called a Konkaniphile, his novel exhibits very little use of Konkani words, idioms and proverbs. Naturally in this elitist discourse we find hardly any folkloristic intertextuality. The novel is set in Fyzabad but it was not possible for Gomes to use Hindi or Bengali heteroglossia. Ironically, we do not find a rich variety of Sanskritic or Brahmanical literary intertextuality in a novel named after the Brahmans. Both Gomes's urge to demystify the dominant Brahmanism and his alienation from native culture must have contributed to these incongruities in his prose style. (This judgement is based on his novel's English translation.)

As pointed out before, Gomes's centre of inspiration is European. We can link his novel not only with definite trends in Europe, but also with Indian romantic novels like Bhikaji Gunjikar's *Mochangad* (1871), and Romesh Chandra's *Jiban Prabhat* (1873). Gomes's novel may seem far superior to a number of contemporary Indian novels. Many of them do not fulfil the primary conditions of a good novel. Even Gomes's romance, however, tends to be a religious tract. Its proselytizing purpose is clearly stated by Gomes (176, 177) and is further confirmed by his letter to Lamartine, written on *15* January 1861 (1853-85). Many of its chapters are independent journalistic essays. It abuses history. Meenaksh Mukherjee observes that underlying "the use and abuse of history in Indian fiction of this period there must be intimations of the cultural crisis that was overtaking Indian society as a result of the impact of Europe" (39). Gomes imitates the Waverley model to achieve an authority in that craft of fiction. That makes his work ironic today. It does not show any use of indigenous modes of narration.

Gomes was aware of the limitations of his novel. We are told that there was not any "outstanding Portuguese novel with a clearly articulated liberal message" before *Os Brahamanes* (5). Owing to my lack of an adequate knowledge of Portuguese language and literature I cannot comment confidently on its reception. The secondary sources reveal that it was patronised by the white masters. It was "interesting" to different culture groups for different reasons (11). A comparative study of its reception in Lisbon and Panaji might throw more light on the colonial consciousness of both the dominators and the dominated. Sudhir Chandra's recent comparative study of nineteenth-century prose in Indian languages examines the dichotomy of West and East in that oppressive present. The West assumed a civilizing mission and the East was perceived as in need of civilization. The spectre of the polarity between tradition and modernity still haunts our literary culture today. Very few men of letters have consciously attempted the task of decolonization.[6] In this context, Mascarenhas's *Sorrowing Lies My Land* is a striking example of the novel of the "fighting phase."

II

After *The Brahman*, for the next hundred years we do not find any remarkable novel in a Goan language. The Portuguese tyrants suppressed native voices and encouraged only Christian religious literature. T.B. Cunha has examined 'the denationalization of Goans' in detail (59-109). It was Lambert Mascarenhas who fictionalized this reality in his Dickensian novel *Sorrowing Lies My Land* (1955). This Chaddo-Kshatriya, whose ancestors were converted to Christianity long ago, is a living Goan journalist and a prolific writer. He was exiled from Goa by the Portuguese rulers in the 1950s, when the freedom-for-Goa movement had gathered full momentum all over India. He sought refuge in Bombay and published *Sorrowing Lies My Land* in English. It shows how the colonial counter-discourse could change and challenge what Gomes believed a century ago. In fact, *Sorrowing Lies My Land* is not really postcolonial, although it was published in independent India. Goa was still not free. The place of publication of this novel and its alien medium seem to have influenced its partially postcolonial discourse. It stands in contrast to *The Brahman* in many ways. However, both Goan fabulists share a condition which Gareth Griffiths describes as "a double exile" (9-19). It is a paradox of the colonial history of Goan literature that the first novel was published in Lisbon and the second one in free Bombay. The first was set in British Bengal, the latter in Portuguese Goa. Both were written in alien tongues. This bilingualism is a special problem.[7] It is not, however, possible to isolate it from its political contexts.

Sorrowing Lies My Land is more realistic than *The Brahman*. It is the tragic saga of a Christian peasant family. Its contemporary reviews (ix), reprinted with the text, enthusiastically allude to modern novels by Pearl S. Buck, Charles Morgans, Tolstoy and others, and place Mascarenhas in their rank. We should not be misled by such enthusiastic reviews in free India. They show how anti-Portuguese militant movements were making progress there. This acute consciousness of the resistance to colonial forces is absent from Gomes's romance.

The third edition of *Sorrowing Lies My Land* (1970) does not contain any pretext except a subtitle: "a novel of Goa." As noted before, it does provide an epitext, consisting of ten pages of extracts from newspapers and periodicals. Its division into two parts and the numbers given to the chapters are pretexts in it. But it does not have chapter headings or subtitles like *The Brahman*. On the whole, its paratext does not provide any information about the "historical author" or about his creative process. We have to construct the image of the "implied author" from the text. Since the novel is in the first person singular, the narrator is likely to be identified with the writer himself. It depicts the narrator's and his father's experience of the last phase of Portuguese colonial rule in Goa. The narrator reminiscences, "May 28, 1926, what a gay and carefree day it was; yet what misery, ignominy and terror did it usher in for us, in years to come ..." (59). Thus he slowly develops an anticolonial discourse by constructing effective dramatic scenes. The novel has an episodic structure. Its discourse design is determined by the paradigms of anglicization rather than those of nativization. The Portuguese cultural conquest overshadows it; but it is intended to shake the people. The narrator seems to adopt the role of awakener of the people. Fanon aptly analyses the salient features of the rise of the "fighting literature." What he says in general is applicable to Mascarenhas in particular. Fanon states, "During this phase a great many men and women who up till then would never have thought of producing a literary work, now that they find themselves in exceptional circumstances—in prison, with the Maquis or on the eve of their execution—feel the need to speak to their nation, to compose the sentence which expresses the heart of the people and to become the mouthpiece of anew reality of action" (178). Gomes stood poles apart from this stage of the colonial consciousness.

If Mascarenhas's realistic, traditional *Sorrowing Lies My Land* met with such critical acclaim, it was because of the subject rather than the treatment. Mascarenhas did not write an imaginary romance to entertain the European masters and to spread their message, as Gomes had. Neither he did write "tourist fiction" to introduce Goa to foreign visitors. In recounting the travails of Tobias Costa, the peasant protagonist who wants nothing more than to escape from Portuguese domination, Mascarenhas created a novel which is not only predominantly realistic but also nationalistic. It is a plain narrative which unfolds the tale of the sorrowing Goan land, as represented by the family of an ordinary Catholic farmer. Tobias is an educated, but hardly Westernised, peasant. He is patriot of the village called Copena. He heads a family of nine members. His first daughter dies on the eve of her marriage, and the second one's engagement is cancelled because of difficulties created by the colonized elites, who dislike nationalists. She joins a convent. The eldest son marries a Hindu convert of a low caste and migrates to Bombay. The narrator himself is the second son. The vagabond third son is lured by the masks of conquest put on by the colonizers and migrates to Africa, never to return. The fourth son swallows the bait of the colonizers' agents. He is used by them against his own nationalist father in a court case filed by the Portuguese soldiers against the freedom fighters. The narrator himself somehow survives an attack of paralysis; but he is crippled forever. Emma, Tobias's humble, God-fearing wife, cannot stand such upheavals. She dies, leaves Tobias alone with a crippled son, Babush. Finally Tobias concludes his nativism and patriotism have driven all the members of his family to despair. Yet he never betrays the native freedom fighters to the alien rulers. It is the basic feature of colonization that those who resist it are slowly alienated and ruined. Tobias courageously faces these ordeals when he is arrested and tried. He dies cherishing his dream of a Golden Goa freed from Portuguese chains.

The socio-political, economic, and religious tensions under alien rule are well brought out in this partially post-colonial discourse. Gomes's colonial discourse is quite different from it. Gomes voiced the principles of liberty, equality and fraternity which were never practised by the colonizers. Otherwise, after the fall of the Portuguese monarchy, Salazar would not have reduced Goa to misery. The narrator's paralysis in *Sorrowing Lies My Land* symbolically presents the sufferings of generations of Goans crippled by colonization. The narrator's awareness of the cultural invasion by the Portuguese, of the effects of acculturation, and of imperialism, is disclosed in the course of the narrative. Compared to Gomes's borrowed European humanism and liberalism, Mascarenhas's transparent counter discourse adopts a strong, ironic, anti-colonial tone. This is why his treatment of characters is more complex than Gomes's. Whereas Gomes's characters remain abstract types. Mascarenhas's become more "round". They grow with every new experience.

Mascarenhas's indictment of Portuguese colonialism becomes apparent at various levels. The narrator hardly needs to comment directly on the conflicts caused by the cross-cultural encounter, because the tensions are revealed through situations in which the characters are made to act. The words and actions of the colonizers never match, and this tension varies from character to character. The attitudes of the colonized towards their rulers assume diverse and complex forms, ranging from total acceptance of Western culture—like that of Emma, to the staunch refusal to submit to it—like that of the nationalist Tobias. As the text is populated by Catholics, the voices of the Goan Hindus are rarely heard in it. It is one more colonial paradox that whereas Gomes's fictional discourse concentrated on the demystification of Brahmanism, Mascarenhas emphasises the ideology of nativism by exposing the myths manipulated by the alien dominators. Gomes's evaluation of European imperialism remains at the verbal level and is restricted to his parliamentary scenes, but Mascarenhas portrays fiery fights against imperialisms of all kinds.

Gomes did not show a consciousness of the crisis of identity faced by a conquered people. He did not expose the myth of the lazy native implied by the Portuguese in their use of the degrading word "sossegad" for the Goans. He glorified the victory of the British in the 1857 war. On the contrary, Mascarenhas's protagonist wants to drive the Portuguese "pests" out of Goa. His narrator's double name—Babush and Felipe—points to his dual identity. When is a boy of seven he asks Anastasio:

> "What was it like during the Monarchy, Ansu? What's the difference between then and now?"
>
> "...To me it's all the same ...We drank a lot during the Monarchy and we are drinking the same quantity now during the Republic. That's a liberty, isn't it?" (5-6)

Such dialogue, which comments ironically on European imperialism and Christianity, is not be found a hundred years earlier in *The Brahman.* Gomes greedily fell upon Western values and recommended the Christian religion and Western education as remedies for India. Mascarenhas finds them futile and at many places parodies them. For example, he ridicules the shallow effects of the Europeanization of the Goans. Emma discovers her son Antonio kissing Dona Propercia's daughter, Clara. Although caught red-handed, Antonio pretends that he was "learning English with her" (8). The narrator comments: "But worried my mother really was. For nothing worse could have happened to her, religious and God fearing as she was, than to see her children drift from the straight and narrow path of recitude" (9).

Gomes's idealised images of the Catholic Church and the European conquerors come under vigorous attack in *Sorrowing Lies My Land* (22, 30, 33, 36). The Europeans ruthlessly divided the natives and ruled them. Their school system encouraged distinctions among the sons of peasants, labourers, and elite landowners. The poor learned to read and write in the vernaculars while the elite were taught Portuguese. The condition of the native teachers was, as usual, bad: "Old Jairam was a good soul. Teaching was not his sole means of livelihood which he actually eked out by selling provisions and groceries to the village folk" (13). Among the socio-cultural problems featured in Mascarenhas's anticolonial discourse are the poverty of the peasants and labourers, their exploitation by the rulers, and their dislike of learning the alien language (14-15). Gomes dispatched Magnod's children to London for their education, which he glorified; but Mascarenhas boldly condemns the "mis-education" of the Goans: "English education was not much encouraged in those days in Goa, and in our village every son of landlord and the well to do had pursued higher studies in Portuguese. A few who had gone to English schools and studied up to the fourth or fifth standard, and then gone to Africa or Bombay to take up a job..." (24). In short, this education has no relevance to Goan life and culture. Gomes pleaded at length for Western education, but did not clarify his idea of such an education. Mascarenhas exposes the myth of educating the "savage" natives. Moreover he touches upon the problems of unemployment and migration, which Gomes never dreamed of.

A fine satirical scene in *Sorrowing Lies My Land,* which reminds us of the opening of Dickens's *Hard Times,* brings out several contradictions in the colonial approach to education. An alienated young Brahman teacher faces the problematics of linguistic identity when Babush asks her whether their language is Konkani or Portuguese (28-30). Her true answer is suppressed by the fear of losing her job. She hesitantly tells the inquisitive student that their language is Portuguese, and that he should always speak in it at home. Babush faithfully follows the teacher's advice; but his patriot father beats him for using the tyrants' language in his house. Such confrontations and contradictions are many (18-19). The novelist seizes every opportunity to ridicule superstitions and blind Christian faith. Emma likes Christian rituals. But Tobias asks a pointed question about why the Christian converts have never shed their original Hindu or Muslim caste distinctions.

In *The Brahman* the conversion and baptism of the Brahman orphans are glorified. Mascarenhas depicts a similar scene with greater depth and insight, and brings out the complexities involved in poor Laxmi's forced conversion to Christianity (30-36). There is a great difference between Thomas's marriage with the white (Irish) Helen and the black Laxmi's marriage with Tobias's son. The former symbolizes the colonized's desire for total assimilation with the superior European culture; and the latter, the impossibility of such assimilation. It is Emma who arranges for Laxmi's conversion. She never does willingly accept her as her daughter-in-law. Tobias wants to leave "Laxmi alone as far as religion was concerned, and let her decide for herself when she (grows) older..." (34). His criticism of Christianity in Goa stands in contrast to Gomes's divine mission to spread it all over India. Tobias calls it a farce and prefers a peasant's primitive paganism to corrupt Christianity. On the auspicious occasion of Laxmi's conversion he frankly tells the vicar and the congregation: "Who are the Christians? Are we? No! We are only supposed to be Christians. Let me tell that I would rather be a pagan than a Christian of this type—for that would amount to one and the same thing..." (36). This type of religious counter-discourse was imaginable neither in Gomes's era nor in the Portuguese Goa of Mascarenhas's period of exile. The empire was writing back from Bombay. How strange are the ways of colonial history!

According to Mascarenhas's vision of reality, problems like migration and the absence of an authentic culture or identity are consequences of exploitation by the Portuguese. Gomes did not interpret colonial reality in these terms. Adriano, a boy of nineteen in *Sorrowing Lies My Land, is* "promised a clerkship in the Anglo-Iranian Oil Company in Abadan, and he [leaves] for this Persian town..." (40). Aunt Aspulquel is the native spokesperson for the Portuguese rulers. She prefers to be associated with them in order to prosper in her business. She looks down upon Tobias's peasant status, and advises him to abandon it to start a new business under the grace of the white masters. She goes on gossiping and influencing the non-Europeanised Goans. The Carbral girl elopes with the soldier. Carlos becomes a priest. According to the decree issued by the Vatican in 1684, it was compulsory for at least one son from every family to become a priest.

The Konkani language was banned and Portuguese was imposed. Aping Europeans became the convention (46-51). Ligorio's match-making business unravels the mystery of colonial acculturation. He is a tailor but succeeds as a match-maker. Caesar joins the seminary. Francisco goes to Africa with Leandro. Donato goes to Burma. Only the crippled Babush resolves to stay with old Tobias to continue the tradition of cultivating the :and of their forefathers. For all the others, foreign things are more attractive. Babush observes, "Young and impressionable as he was, Francisco was dazzled with Leandro's talk, mannerisms and possessions" (53). Tobias's ardent love of the land fails to prevent his sons from being entrapped by colonialism. His family slowly falls apart. Colonized people are people without a centre. Antonio's decision to marry Laxmi is convincing, but it is a last stroke that kills the sentimental Enuna. Tobias's fight for the freedom of Goa ends with his own death. Babush is left alone; yet he concludes the tale on an optimistic note: "When that happens, I shall perhaps not be here, but I shall be happy in the knowledge that those will tread on my grave, will be free men—free as my father always wanted them to be" (179). A century ago Gomes might have dreamt of an independent India but did not mention it in his novel.

The difference between the political consciousness of these Goan writers becomes clearer in their attitude to Europeans and their institutions. Gomes's discourse frequently echoes Orientalists and humanists from the West. His device of the disguised Jew Sobal is not incidental. Like that of the Irish (represented in the novel by the planter Robert), the image of the Jew has a long cultural history. Edward Said writes:

> Whereas in the past it was European Christian Orientalists who supplied European culture with arguments for colonizing and suppressing Islam, as well as for despising Jews, it is now the Jewish national movement that produces a cadre of colonial officials. (*Orientalism* 221)

It is interesting to compare Gomes's Robert with Rudyard Kipling's *Kim*, who was an Irish outcast boy and later an essential player in the British secret service. Both Kipling and Gomes present a false picture of the "mutiny of 1857." What Said writes of *Kim* is equally applicable to *The Brahman*: "*Kim* is a major contribution to his Orientalized India of the imagination, as it is also to what historians have come to call 'the invention of tradition'" (*Culture* 181). Under such circumstances. Mascarenhas's challenge to that Orientalism and colonialism is a challenge, in Said's words: "to the muteness imposed upon the Orient as object." Where his predecessor feared to tread, he dares to develop a counter-discourse albeit at the periphery of Portuguese Goa.

The Prospero-Caliban and Crusoe-Friday complexes were not developed during Gomes's times. But Mascarenhas's *Sorrowing Lies My Land* needs to be interpreted in terms of these complexes (see 59-60). Tobias, the author's mouthpiece, bluntly tells his wife: "Well I want this land of my fathers to be free of this Portuguese pest, so that Goans may rule it the way we choose" (60). He has suffered the ravages of an alien imperialism. He is aware of the lack of strong nativistic movements in Goa, He is "sick to see our people so emasculated, so complacent, so devoid of self respect and political consciousness." According to him, "these damned Portuguese" have done nothing for the Goans during their four-hundred-year regime. A hundred years ago Gomes had good words about British rule in India, and was very silent, or let us say "muteness was imposed," regarding Portuguese rule in Goa. In Mascarenhas's view, the Revolution in Portugal (1926) brought for Goans "a life of repression and humiliation." The narrator's mature analysis of the political fate of Goa (65-66) is the exact opposite of what Gomes wrote of the role of the British in Indian politics. Tobias rightly diagnoses the ills of imperialism:

> "These damn Portuguese have so denationalised us that we may as well have no soul of our own!" commented my father bitterly and helplessly. "We, the Christians in particular, are really a sorry sight! More than four centuries of colonial oppression have made us foreign in our own country! Pffah!" (67)

We have already commented on the limitations of Gomes's attitude to Indian history. Mascarenhas has outgrown some of the limitations imposed on it by Oriental myths. Tobias always speaks proudly of native history. In particular, he glorifies the pre-Portuguese native rulers. He tells his children: "Do you know, children, that Goa was fabulously prosperous before the Portuguese arrived here? Our forefathers were already reading and writing and painting when the Europeans were still eating raw fish and meat and wearing skins" (29). Further he narrates tales of the brave Kadamba kings before Albuquerque invaded Goa in 1510. Children ask him not to "tell yarns" because their teachers never tell them such heroic tales of the Indian heroes. Instead, they always speak highly of the Portuguese warrior-heroes. Their textbooks are designed to impress the superiority of the white race and inculcate inferiority among the black. Compare Gomes's devaluing remarks on Indian nawabs and rajahs with Tobias's views. His romance reflects the hope of the regeneration of India under alien domination, while Mascarenhas throws light on the sinister side of it.

The second part of *Sorrowing Lies My Land* shows how an ideological system can operate beneath the surface of an imaginative fiction. It depicts the last phase of the freedom movement in Goa. Its leader was Dr. Ram Manohar Lohia. "'Jai Hind" became anathema to the colonialist and Gandhi cap like the red flag to a bull" (152). The chapters on the mock elections, *Satyagraha* and the court trial are charged with intense conflict, suspense and high drama. Once again the absolute demarcation between East and West is reinforced. The saga of the Catholic family might have ended with the protagonist's defeat and sad demise. But the invalid narrator's epilogue sounds a new optimistic note. He declares, "India is free. Asia is asserting itself. Britain, wise and perspicacious, has bowed to the will of the people. So has France. Yet the Portuguese still holding down with a brutality that is inconceivable" (179). Finally he expresses his belief that the land of his forefathers, which now lies sorrowing, will soon be free and smile again. He has traversed a long path from where Gomes stood.

From the sociological viewpoint, *The Brahman* did not incorporate all the varied cultural and socioeconomic groups in Indian society. Gomes intended the idealised characters in his romance to be taken as real human beings. They were larger than life, as almost all characters in nineteenth-century European novels were. They were elite types rather than individuals. Individualism was unheard of in Indian feudal society. Gomes's characters were not the natural products of the socio-cultural conditions of the time. They cannot be related to the history or geography of that period. *Sorrowing Lies My Land* presents a richer variety of characters. Many voices are heard in it. The hierarchy of characters in both novels is dependent not only on the caste system, but also on the author's degree of loyalty to the alien rulers. Very often the interests of castes and classes clashed. The present revolts were suppressed due to such fractions among Indians *(Sorrowing Lies My Land* 68-70). Mascarenhas's narrator elucidates:

> Economic conditions had deteriorated in Goa a great deal during the last two years, and the price of coconuts having reached a new low, the landlords of our village whose income dependend mainly on the sale of it, called a meeting to decide upon the reduction *in* the wages of the labourers (68).
>
> Portugal, which was systematically suppressing us, introduced *in* the Parliament a bill which meant to put last nail *in* the coffin of our slavery. (85)

These novels echo contemporary politics in different ways. Yet mass culture is not represented in them at all.

Mascarenhas's style is neither rhetorical nor bombastic like Gomes's It is plain and simple. Occasionally it takes lyrical flight, especially when he describes the beauty of Goan nature (30, 57, 121). The twin processes at work in the nineteenth-century Goan prose style were Westernization and Sanskritization. The impact of these processes is deeper on Gomes than on his successor. By the mid-twentieth century the indigenous elements of style were weakend by strong alien forces. Since Mascarenhas has chosen English as his medium, a strong process of Anglicization is inevitable. Yet his use of several Konkani and Portuguese words and expressions in his English fiction marks a new phase in the process of stylistic acculturation. In a separate research paper (1993) I have examined folkloric intertextuality in *Sorrowing Lies My Land* and a Marathi novel, *Jogin.* This comparative study revealed that both these Goan writers were equally alienated from native folk literature and culture. Gomes's novel retained some allusions to the Indian classical heritage. Folkloric intertextuality, however, was absent from it. The intertextuality of Goan song, music, dance, drama, tales, and rituals is greater and richer in *Sorrowing Lies My Land.* Perhaps this is the outcome of the nationalist movements. In this sense *Sorrowing Lies My Land* displays more features of realism and Indianness than Gomes's romance. Briefly put, the prose styles of both writers are representative of the different phases literary acculturation in the colonial situation.

From the point of view of narratology, these novels stand apart from each other. Gomes is a detached and distant observer. His omniscient narrative and authorial intrusions, contrived plot and digressions, typed characters and dramatized dialogue, make his discourse artificial. To the postcolonial reader it seems to be a historical document, an imitation of European forms, devoid of Indian reality. Mascarenhas's realistic fiction is more authentic. Babush is the eyewitness of this colonial drama.

Sorrowing Lies My Land is postcolonial literally. It was produced in the independent part of India. It depicts the colonial reality of Portuguese Goa. *The Brahman is* fully colonial. What is distinctive about the languages and genres to which they both belong is that they are produced for the West. Their readers are educated in the Western style. Their critical revaluations—even of *Sorrowing Lies My Land*—are not really fully postcolonial, in Kwame Anthony Appiah's terms (336). Although Mascarenhas tries to escape from Portuguese domination and construct an anticolonial discourse, his theories of fiction are irreducibly informed by his interpellation in a British-American literary tradition. All aspects of Goan cultural life have been influenced by the passage of Goan society through Portuguese colonialism. Now a writer can not easily escape the traps of neocolonialism. Not all Indian societies today are in the fullest sense postcolonial. The same is true of Indian literatures. So more space-clearing gestures are needed to decolonize the canon. The revaluation of the Indian literatures of the colonial period from a comparative perspective would be a first step in this direction.

Notes

1. Owing to a lack of knowledge of the language I have not consulted Francisco Louis Gomes's *Os Brahamanes* (Lisbon, 1866) in Portuguese. All references to the text are taken from the English translation, entitled The *Brahman.* The name of the translator is not mentioned; but the introduction is written by Armando Menezes, who must have done the translation for the Dr. F.L. Gomes's Centenary Committee. Gomes (1829-1869) was a medical practitioner, administrator, journalist and politician. Before 1866, he had published three biographies and some essays in Portuguese. In 1861 he became a member of parliament. In 1865 he suffered from tuberculosis and went to the Portuguese island of Madeira for a rest cure. He must have written Os *Brahamanes* during this period.
2. Lambert Mascarenhas is the leading contemporary Goan writer in English. All references to *Sorrowing Lies My Land,* first published by Hind *Kitab,* Bombay, 1955, are taken from its third edition, published by Goa Publications, Panaji-Goa, in 1970. Both novels have been translated into Indian languages and have been placed on postgraduate curricula in some universities.
2. My research project on "The 19th Century Literature in British Bombay and Portuguese Goa: a Comparative Study" was sponsored by the Dr. S. G. Malshe Research Centre of S.N.D.T. Women University, Bombay, through a Dr. Malshe Research Fellowship

(1993-94). See Anand Patil, *British Bombay ani Portuguese Govyateel Wangmay,* Mumbai: Granthali, 1999. The paper was presented and discussed on 24 September 1994 in a Seminar organised by the Centre.

3. Books by British writers like Mary Carpenter, Dennis Kincaid, and others of the colonial period present similar views. I happened to read many references of the same kind in the unpublished letters, and other manuscripts housed in the Indian Office Library, London. It is apparent that after the 1857 Revolt the British rulers adopted more neutral policies in native religious matters than their Portuguese counterparts in Goa. The differences between their policies have left long-lasting marks on the literatures produced in these neighbouring regions.

4. It is interesting to note that the romantic myth of the Irish peasant prevailed because of the Celtic Movement. Similarly, the Indian peasantry and village life were glorified after the nativistic movements gathered momentum in the early twentieth century. Only recently have the Dalit and rural writers begun to interrogate this elitist myth-making.

5. My study of Western influence on Marathi drama 1818-1947 confirmed that the native generic elements do assimilate with or resist the alien literary kinds according to the phases of acculturation. The colonial textual politics of representation is another interesting topic for study. In "Appropriate(d) Discourse: Plagiarism and Decolonization," Marilyn Randall argues: "In the pre-revolutionary phase, colonial theory posits an inevitable double bind situation in which the colonized culture, desiring assimilation, is condemned either to a steric and disempowering repetition of the discourse of the colonizer or a cultural self-devalorization: the notion of Culture cannot exist outside of the validating influence of the institutional centre which is its source and guarantee."

6. In two research papers, "The Whirligig of Taste: Decolonization of Teaching and Research in India" and "The Whirligig of Literary Taste: Impact or Alienation?" I have explained various aspects of literary, inter- and intra-cultural imperialism in the neocolonial situation and emphasised the need to decolonize literature. See *New Quest* (Nov. 1992): 341-352; and *Indian* Literature 157 (August 1992): 157-169 respectively.

7. In Goa, multilingualism is common, but it has not been studied from the sociological viewpoint. Jane Miller's *Many Voices: Bilingualism, Culture and Education* provides a model for such a study (110-42). Goons have been facing the crisis of their linguistic identity since 1510. It has affected their literature and culture deeply; and their fiction is no exception.

4

A Comparative Study of Nativistic Intertextuality in Indian Fiction

At the outset, it should be pointed out that the meaning and scope of the term 'intertextuality' has not yet been defined clearly in the context of 'Indian Literature' in more than two dozen languages. There is the mushroom growth of so-called 'influence' studies mainly dealing with the Euro-american influences on Indian literatures, But the network of indigenous and alien 'texts' in a work of art remains still unexplored. Much fuss is made about alien allusions and quotations. In fact, over weighing alien allusions and quotations in our text should be considered a symptom of the alien oppressive forces in our literary culture. Basically there persists an age old tension between the Sanskrit and Prakrit forces. This division between indigenous *margi* (metropolitan, elite, mainstream, Sanskrit) and *deshi* (regional, subcultural Prakrit- *bhasha,* languages) traditions[1] has always given rise to a different kind of the problemetics of intertextuality in the Indian multilingual and multicultural situation.

A post-structuralist would claim that a text cannot exist without a pretext. True, every text is an intertext, but how to establish their interrelationship is the major problem in the neocolonial context. Let us accept a working definition of intertextuality as a base for further comparison. Terry Eagleton (1993, 138) states:

> ... All literary texts are woven out of other literary texts, not in the conventional sense that they bear the traces of

> 'influence' but in the more radical sense that every word, phrase or segment is a reworking of other writings which precede or surround the individual work.

There is hardly any need to comment on the domination of an English 'word,' 'phrase', or 'text' over literary texts in Indian languages produced after the colonial contact with Europe. By 'Europe' it is intended to suggest the presence not only of the British but also of the Portuguese, French, German and so on. The presence of 'superior', novel and attractive 'foreign' textual elements always leads to metaplagiarism. Our critics have not yet willingly accepted the dictum: "all literature is intertextual". Once we accept it fully, Indian literature would no more seem to be Indian but would be exposed as white masters' European generic form in Indian dresses. However, a few Indian intellectuals are now struggling to decolonise or 'de-educate' it, and the aim of the present National Seminar seems to be the same.

It is no wonder that the sixth edition of M.H. Abram's *A Glossary of Literary Terms* (1993) fails to exhibit any reference to nativism. It is, therefore, of interest to examine if our 'regional'/rural/ 'country' *(pradeshik)* novels are really nativistic or not. It is often claimed that they are likely to reveal less distorted Indianness. In order to test this hypothesis Abram's following definition of "the regional novel" is of some help.

> The regional novel emphasises the setting, speech, and social structure, and custom of a particular locality, not merely as local colour, but as important conditions affecting the treatment of characters and their ways of thinking, feeling, and interacting ...(34).

All these features can be sorted out and displayed in a chart to show the nature and scope of the nativistic elements in Indian 'regional' fiction at a glance.

Only four Indian novels[2] written in different 'regions' and languages by the writers belonging to different religions/sects/ and castes are selected at random for the comparative analysis. The objectives of this scrutiny are twofold:

i) to examine the scope and nature of the network of the nativistic intertextuality in modern Indian novel.

ii) to trace the possibilities of counter-discourses in Indian fiction and to review the implications of the term *desivad-nativism in* the post-colonial contexts. It *is a* simple but comparative case study. It has its own limitations as a general case study. Owing to the lack of special training, an in depth analysis of all sociolinguistic features is not undertaken. The samples of fiction selected for scrutiny may not be the masterpieces in respective languages; but they are considered 'mile stones' in the development of Indian 'regional novel'. The majority of these writers have won the Sahitya Akademi awards for literary works. The focus lies on their treatment of the nativistic techniques and not on the revaluation of their novels in totality. It is not a microscopic scrutiny of all elements of fiction, but it suggests new directions in developing the poetics of resistance to unhealthy alien generic element. The short stories are not taken into consideration.

From the point of view of methodology, the major problem in this comparative study is concerned with a choice of the base line for comparison and the salient features of nativism. On the whole, all the pie-British oral and written forms of Indian narrative can be considered "native", Some of them may be decadent and would need modification in the present contents. Bhalchandra Nemade (1990, 12-13) has demonstrated how a base line of the pre-British Marathi prose styles can be reconstructed for examining the effects of English prose styles on Marathi. It is a good model for expounding the sociolinguistic and stylistic aspects of the influence of English on Marathi. The influence of English drama on the Marathi drama of the colonial period also revealed a very weak nativistic intertextuality in the corpus of modern Marathi drama. Ganesh Devi (1992, 119-2) briefly assessed Nemade's contribution to nativism in literature. Yet the task of the evaluation of the role the nativistic literary elements in the fictional construct waits further explorations. So the intertextuality of native and alien components of novel is examined mainly at three levels: content or themes, form and structure, and language and style.

Meenakshi Mukherjee (1985), who described Indo-anglian fiction through Brahminical eye as "twice born" has further explored the rise of Indian novel from 'Purana to Nutana'. In her partly comparative study she has taken into account the indigenous forms of narratives which contributed to the development of modern novel, and concluded that it is not 'purely a legacy of British rule.' However, she has neither demonstrated how far the structural and stylistic norms of *purana* or medieval prose tales- *Harikatha* or chronicle persist in the modern Indian novel, nor explained how far it is different from its European counter-parts. It is clear that Indian literary criticism has not yet become really "post-colonial" as it is in Africa and Latin America. Likewise no Indian novelist has really attempted to cast the work into a nativised mould in order to make up a testament of dissidence with respect to the West. Jawarharlal Handoo (1994, 89) has rightly pointed out as to how and why we have failed to reclaim the soul and authentic voice of the folklore. He observes that "folklore-oral literature and related genres—the semantics of folklore and the cultural categories it represented, have remained much neglected areas in Indian academics". Perhaps, this is one of the reasons for the over determination of Indian novel by alien paradigms. So we do not have a novel like Toni Morrison's *Jazz* which canonizes the indigenous dance and music. My research findings (1993, 19-14) regarding the folkloric intertextuality support Handoo's views. It was confirmed that our fabulators, especially the English educated and the upper caste ones, exhibit a very weak competence in enriching the texture of novel by employing native lore effectively and creatively.

Despite various kinds of nativistic movements in the colonial past our modern novel shows the peak of its Westernization. It mens it does not have its own native centre. We have not succeeded in formulating true centre of the native oral literature. Yet Makarand Paranjape (1991, 27) believes novel to be "the battleground for an ideological struggle" on "cultural" ground. Let us see how four novelists have fought it on their own "cultural" grounds, and whether they have won or lost it.

Instead of discussing each novel in isolation, they are juxtaposed and compared at various levels. *Garambicha Bapu* and *Adha Gaon* are translated into English, but these versions are not used. These translations delete many native words and expressions which are vessels that carry discordant ideologies, social values and religious beliefs. True dialogic and dialectic language of specific regions resists translation. Yet at present a pan-Indian comparative study of literature has to depend on English translations. A comparative study of the colonial and post-colonial discourse in fiction is one more aspect which demands indepth studies for the assessment of nativity in fiction. So Raja Rao's so called "national epic in prose": *Kanthapura* (1938) is juxtaposed with three postcolonal novels. They are expected to exhibit different degrees and types of nativism. It is a colonial paradox that a fully anglicized romance like *Bapu* (1952) reveals less awareness of *deshiyata-nativity* than the colonial *Kanthapura;* and yet it is institutionalised as a best 'regional novel' by anglicised elite literary taste.

The following table shows not only nativistic intertextuality but also displays various shades of the British empire which writes back through fiction. It fails to indicate the powerful possibility of these erstwhile peripheral fictional discourses setting up rival centres of nativity and creatively capable of challenging the hegemony of European novel. The ethnic affiliations of its authors seem to be a proof of their recognition. In the main, the relevance of adopting the nativistic position depends on a challenge given to the traditional centrality of the Anglo-American literary axis. Can we trace in these samples an example of syncretic creativity shorn of mimetic dependence on Western models?

The Chart Showing the Nativistic Intertextuality in Indian Novels

Sr. No.	*1*	*2*	*3*	*4*	*5*
1.	Novel, language and author identity	Raja Rao, *Kanthapura* (1938) English Hindu, Brahman	S. N. Pendase, *Garambicha Bapu* (1952) Marathi Brahman	Rahi Masoom Raza *Adha Gaon* (1960) Hindi, Muslim	Pundalik Nayak *Acchev* (1977) Konkani Hindu (Kharavi-Kunabi)
2.	Title	Named after a village.	After a village and protagonist Bapu.	After half village; ironic.	After theme of upheaval.
3.	Subject, content and themes	The story of how the freedom struggle becomes reality in a tiny village in Karnataka, South India. Socio-politico-religious themes of colonial period. Brahmanical vision, elitist. classicist, humanistic. Minority discourse heard but Brahmanical tradition dominant.	The melodramatic plot depicts Bapu's rise and revolt; intercaste, remarriage. Themes: love, marriage, lust caste conflicts. It indirectly glorifies the Brahmans in Garambi on the West Coast of Maharashtra. The herione Radha belongs to Gurav	Represents faithfully the cross-section of the Muslim community in Gangauli, a village in Uttar Pradesh, deals with the transformation of Muslim families during the partition of India and after independence. Themes, love, sex marriage: migration,	Depites the disintegration and destruction of the peasant family in Kolamba, a village in Goa, after the development of mining industry. The themes of love, sex, intercaste manage and poverty. The drama of human relations in the Kunabi-

(Contd...)

(Contd...)

			minority group. No other culture group adequately represented. Artificial, individualistic elitist portrayal of rural life.	violence, death, politics, religion etc. Profound awareness of history, very rich and complex picture.	farmer's family effectively portrayed with fine native touches.
4.	Paratexts: Preface	'Foreword' with self-defence mechanism, contradictions, defines *sthala-purana* without using those conventions, ignores folk-oral tradition, yearning for assimilating the West.	'Preface', short, making loud claims with autobiographical notes, spent early eleven years of childhood in Konkan, then shifted to Bombay.	'Preface' added after last but two chapters to clarify his unbiased non-communal position. Raza's plea adds new dimensions to nativism.	'Foreword' anonymous, perhaps by the publisher or friend as a note of appraisal, shows, how lately standardized Indian literatures are patronised.

(Contd...)

(Contd...)

	Chapters	No headings or numbers, shown by blank space.	All numbered but without headings.	Have significant subtitles.	Divided by blank space and some coloured pictures.
	Footnotes	Only three, meant to explain Hindu and religion specific concepts.	No footnotes but its English translation contains many.	Hundreds of footnotes are added to facilitate reading	Nil.
	Dedication	Nil	To late Nana with devotion	To a Hindu, Kuwarpal Singh with fine compliments	To the contemporary poet Nageshab Karmal
	Reader	Can't be defined in the colonial situation; footnotes indicate non Hindu, especially Western implied reader.	Elite middle-class implied reader, especially of the Brahmanical literary taste.	Besides speakers of Urdu and Hindi wide non-Muslim readership is also expected; mixed-readership; 'ideal reader' impossible.	Necessarily Konkani and then Marathi; class taste distinction not clear.
5.	Setting and	A tiny village of 24 quarters houses in	Garambi on the West Coast of	Gangauli, a small village in Uttar	A Goan village called symbolically

(Contd...)

(Contd...)

	Characters	Karnataka, South India, structure less complex, majority Brahmins, except potter Muslim and Red-Sahib. Characters are types, attitude to nature romantic, Westernized but nativized repre-sentation of some facts and objects.	Maharashtra, only Brahman and Gurav. Cultural caste groups depicted; simplified attitude to nature; anglicized, artificial non-Hindu characters, stereotypes.	Pradesh. Its half part of Muslim community represented with all subdivisions; characters are gifted with complex individual traits, less stereotypical. Attitude to nature realistic.	Kolamb with interesting myths and legends and folk-tales, characters are drawn from various strata of Goan society. Attitude to nature nativistic.
6.	Colonial Conscious-ness	Determined by British imperialism yet expressed satirically through disguises of myths, legends and stories (pp. 80, 98, 102, 107, 116, 118, 122). Gandhism authentic but no	More influenced by formalism-*riti*-type theories of autonomy of literature, no awareness of after effects of any kind of colonialism. Attitude more	Acute sense of British imperialism and divide between Hindus and Muslims, satire unbiased, problem of regional identity of Muslims well represented.	There are hints to the Portuguese legacy, no satire intended; weak consciousness of national, socio-political reality, but realistic picture of the

(Contd...)

(Contd...)

		reference to other kinds of movements.	coloured by intra-colonialism.		tragedy of mine workers.
7.	History	Profound awareness of Gandhian. movements but weaker sense of Netaji's freedom struggle and other international affairs; does not aubvert history.	Total lack of contemporary history, politics and other upheavals.	Fine interpretation of historical events in the present context, subverts history.	Lack of historical awareness and class-caste distinctions
8.	Form and structure	Determined by the old women's tale, loud claim of the *sthal-purana* structure; simple, episodic, no romances nati-vistic formulae of *puran-katha*.	Completely *riti*-type, formalistic; deter-mined by English romances and pic-aresque novels, episodic but full of lengthy, artificial Sanskritized dislogues, loud authorical voice; a non-nativistic.	More complex, loose structure, self-reflexive not fully imitative of any Western model non-episodic, some mixed elements of oriental story telling; tending to be post-modern	Well-made novel of Western type, *ritiwadi*, formalistic, like *Bapu*, fully epidodic, mixed with several folk-oral elements, tends to be filmy at the end.

(Contd...)

(*Contd...*)

9.	Narrative technique	First person singular; a Brahman elite woman narrator-character, less experimental but authorial voice and narrative mode apparent, no digression; good mastery and conscious of technique but no resistance to Western mode of first person narrative, no presence of *puran-katha* fully felt, *kriti*-action oriented.	Third person, omniscient, less narration, more dialogues, lack of experimentation and innovation; purely imitative of Western prose; picaresque and romantic novels, nativistic elements, narrative totally absent; mimetic.	Mixed, first person singular also third person, omniscient alternate, slightly shadowed by the Western post-modern; historiographic metafiction; oriental modes of *Arabian Nights* often become apparent, mixed native elements.	Third person, omniscient, more descriptive, narrative; dialogues short crisp and in local dialects; *ritivadi* like *Bapu*, perhaps influenced by the romantic trends in Marathi; mimetic & diagetic.
10.	Language and style	Indianisation of English to some extent, naming characters, waterfall Venkamma,	Highly Sanskritized and anglicised, local dialects totally ignored, style romantic, artificial	Influenced by Urdu, but regional dialects effectively blended. 65% of proverbs, idoms, expressions,	Purely Konkani, fine mastery of local dialects, less Sanskritized, but adopts standardised

(*Contd...*)

(Contd...)

	nose-scratching Nanjamma, purely native months. seasons used after Sanskritic vocabulary like *karma, dharma, mlencha* used freely but no more *chutnifcation* like Rushdie; style metaphoric but not of the *bhasa* tradition.	not native Weaker literary competence.	address words are similar to Marathi and Konkani. Mastery of local dialects superb, the narrative is full of ironies, metaphors and poetic touches; greater literary competence.	conventions of Marathi, English and Portuguese words used freely, less conscious of individual style, indicates speedy process of acculturation.
a) Folklore	No presence of the rustic oral folklore, a few legends, mainly of gods and goddesses are heard; poor folkloric intertextuality reveals author's alienation from rural fold;	Local myths and legends used as a decorative part, rustic lore totally absent, elitist, Westernized sensibility seems to look down on mass	Unrivalled mastery of folk literature, introduces a number of anecdotes; a very rich folkloric intertextuality, especially tales about the village,	A very rich folkloric intertextuality, especially, tales about the village, but Sanskrit lore absent.

(Contd...)

(*Contd...*)

	domination of Sanskrit lore.	culture.	tales—both Muslim and Hindu.	
b) Allusion	Repeated references to the *Mahabharta* and *Ramayana*, *Veda* and *Hari-katha*, ample classical allusions, absence of alien texts suits the character of the narrator.	Blurred intertext-uality of *Hamlet* as a backdrop; native textual allusions absent; a few dialogues in Hindi (*Dakhani*).	Allusion to Muslim scriptures and Hindu holy book; Shairs, poets and other literary works are many; surpasses the other three.	Only to *Harivijay Ramvijay* and *Puranas*, alien texts not mentioned, it suits the cultural background.
c) Pro-verbs,	Mostly translated from Kannada into English, but they example: squeeze water out of stone, misses flavour of the endless proverbial rhythm of rural language, original Kannada proverbs not used at all.	Only half a dozen; rural alliterative idiomatic expressions totally absent, poor competence of mass culture and its expressions.	Fine mastery of proverbial rural dialects, characters' proverbial wisdom truly nativistic; local slangs and idioms many, the rhythm of local language adequately represented.	Ample use of proverbs and idioms is the true mark of Goanness in the novel, it is the part and parcel of sweet Konkani dialects, author deeply rooted in it.

(*Contd...*)

(Contd...)

d) Abusive terms, address words, swearing and perjury	Mostly translated into English: ass, pig, a bitch but elitist; rural rough expressions avoided, good awareness of swearing, oaths and perjury.	Very limited use of simple abusive wods, so called obscene address words and expressions are indicated by asterisks or avoided; incongruity in this regional novel.	A number of abusive words: *madarchod*, *behanchod*, etc, freely used by Raza. They help the techniques of characterization, realistic, nativistic swearing, oath and perjury is natural here.	Hundreds of abusive word and expressions and fine native touch to the styles, even loving expressions and phrases are likely to be misinterpreted by the sophisticated as pornographic.
e) Dance	Only passing references, not described in detail, restricted to the sacred.	Only *Kirtan* mentioned, absence of secular forms.	Fine carnivalization, Hindu and Muslim culture specific; good awareness of festivities and secular forms of dance.	Dance drama, music and song—main components of Goan Culture—adequately represented, picture-squely described, passing references to *bhajan*, *kirtan* and other dance-dramas are many.
f) Drama and other media	Only *Harikatha* mentioned.	Only *Kirtan*	Actual performance of *nautanki* described, a few	*Dashavatar* and *tiatr* performances are mentioned

(Contd...)

(Contd...)

			references to folk dramas.	repeatedly.
g) Music	*Bhajan* music and music associated with rituals and festivals of only Hindus, a few musical instruments—pipe, drum, symbols.	Nil	Varieties of musical notes adequately incorporated in the text, folk as well as classical.	References to folk music are ample.
h) Songs	Sixteen songs in English translations, including *bhajan,* prayer, elegy, patriotic songs, toddy songs, highly Sanskritized absence of folk songs, "Oh such were our men of 1857" reminds of a ballad.	Only two lines of refrains from musical drama, highly Sanskritized, absence of folk songs and music.	Muslim and Hindu prayers, songs, *sher dods, doha, kawwali* and other types are quoted freely, many *shahir* poets are mentioned, hundreds of extracts, rich intertextuality.	Three *abhanga*-songs eleven, *dhalo* and *phugadyo* songs are quoted partly. The Shigmo-songs introduce a new variety, hundreds of other references add to the local colour, purely native.

III

This table mirrors the Janus-face of fictional discourse in India. Such East-West dichotomy reveals creative tensions and disintegration in it. The samples do not show that the 'nation' has been narrating from its own cultural centre. The 'locality' of national culture as depicted in them is neither unified nor unitary in relation to itself. The process of hybridity in them exhibits the changes in them. They undermine "the myth of imagined communities" and also one united "nation". The problem of outside/inside, especially in the representation of Muslims in *Kanthapura*, and *Bapu*, is evident. Hindus in *Adha Gaon* and Christians in *Acchev*, generate other sites of meanings. It produces several sites of political antagonism and unpredictable forces of political representation. Rao and Pendase have selected protagonists Moorthy and Bapu respectively-from their own Brahman/culture group. By portraying them too subjectively and individualistically in the Western fashion, the writers hopelessly alienate themselves from the rest of the rustic people who are least conscious of their own individuality. On the contrary, Raza and Nayak, Muslim and Bhandari-Kunabi respectively, have not much concentrated on the individual protagonists as such. The contents of *Kanthapura* and *Adha Gaon* are determined by Gandhian movements and the partition of India respectively. But both the novels do not become truly *krati*-novels (to mean action on the part of the novelists) in the real *desi* (native) sense of the term. Perhaps Rao's vision was determined not only by his presence in Paris while writing the novel, but also by the British Press Acts. All these novelists have not resisted to the European trap of design conscious, formalistic *riti*-novel.

The diversity of cultural differences is exhibited in the stereotypical portrayals of the 'Other', both from inside one sect/caste/religion or from outside it. Bade Khan (Muslim), Seetharamu, Pariah and Lingyya (Hindu lower caste), Red-man and Anthony (Christian) in *Kanthapura*, Musasheth (Muslim) and Ravaji (Gurav lower caste) in *Bapu*, Parasuram and his wife (cobblers) and Swami (Brahmin) in *Adha Gaon*; and Manuel (Christian) in *Acchev* illustrate the effects of 'incomplete signification' and indicate the boundaries, limits and the in-between spaces through which the meanings of cultural and political authority are negotiated. In a way multiculturalism in India should give greater scope for more complex delineation of life in India, but it seems that our writers are either overdetermined by our own culture or they fail to perceive reality through their castealised and anglicized eyes. A typical Indian ambivalence of language is revealed in these samples. Here we have to link nation, narration and native-*desi*, and try to understand these forms of cultural elaborations in the light of Homi K. Bhabha's (1993, 1-7) project: *Nation and Narration*. It is the problem of investigation of the nation-space in the process of articulating nativistic elements in a novel which is already fully Westernized in many respects.

In fact, these four writers wrote in different parts of India and in different languages. How come that they all fall back on European modes of prose fiction and not on any native-*desi* element which gives their work a distinct Indianness that has no counterpart in the Western tradition? Perhaps, it could be argued that Rao had consciously adopted the *desi* mythic mode of Indian old woman tale and of *puran*. No, he does not display any convention of *purana*-style of narration except a few repetitive phrases and address words. His narratology and myth-making is Joycian and not of our *Harikathas*. Similar contradictions in the history of 'Modern" Marathi drama were revealed. For example, the most outstanding Marathi dramatist[3], the predecessor of Rao, used to proclaim that all his plays were nothing else but *Kirtan*-plays; but he never used any convention of the indigenous *Kirtan* in his totally anglicized drama. It is the common tendency of the majority of Indian writers to show superficial loyalty to the *desi* culture as well as 'bogus' internationalism. In order to seek answers to such dilemmas we will have to rewrite the history from the *desi* point of view. A comparison with the rise of novel in other "Third Word" countries might add a new dimension to the study. It is a paradox of our colonial history that the rise of our novel was partly connected with the rise of the modern nationstate in the Asian subcontinent when its people were being denationalized by the European rulers. The rise of Western novel is closely connected with the rise of the modern nationstate in Europe in the late eighteenth century. European nationalism directed the course of literature through the concept of indigenous folk character and national language. Of course, these were their romantic concepts; but the colonized were deprived of them because they would have led them to the nativistic movements. The effects of alienation from the folk and *bhasha-traditions*[4] are revealed in the samples. It is believed that novel was an incarnation of the epics but our epics and *puranas*, plays and verse rhythms suffered from serious cultural amnesia. The styles and forms of master narratives readily available in Europe were imitated uncritically by Indians. The elite upper-caste writers pioneered that literary 'renaissance'. They were least conscious that they were doing more harm than good to Indian reality by imposing 'ready made' alien forms. It has remained a very thin minority discourse in India till today.

Here the term 'minority discourse' is used in the specific Indian context to point out hundreds of caste divisions and their subcultures. In this sense Indian literature, which is often described as a Brahmanical creation, is a minority discourse. Such minority discourses have their own strong points and weaknesses. Pseudo-secularism had evaded these culture differences which are the bases of the regional identities of thousands of culture groups in India. They are rooted in the indigenous soil, and constitute the history of the place. It is a challenge for the nativist writer to do justice to the maximum culture groups by showing greater mastery of the culture competence. Nobody can claim full knowledge of one's own culture. The sample texts demonstrate how our novelists have depicted the theme of love through the 'romantic concepts' of love. Pendase and Nayak have excelled in this matter. It is the Westernised concept of love and sex that dominates their texts. One can understand that Pendase's Radha might have learnt the traits of individualism and acquired ideas of romantic love in the Westernized city like Bombay, but the anglicization of Bapu of Garambi is larger than his life. This makes *Bapu* the English romance in the Konkani (West coast region) dress. Similarly, many of Raza's characters also express their love through non-native words and gestures. It is likely that other westernized medias such as films, radio, plays etc., might have " civilized" them, but the authors have not shown awareness of that intertextuality. The nativistic intertextuality of indigenous architecture, painting, and photography is nearly non-existent in these texts.

All the samples delineate an unsettled mixture of ideas. Their themes are distinctly local and connected with specific ethnicity. But the composite quality of a 'regional novel' cannot be evaluated only ethnically or by regionality. What is important is the perception of reality through the *desi*-native sensibility. The samples demonstrate how the 'high' and the low cultures are represented in the framework of fiction. Yet it is the problemetics of the politics of representation of certain themes. Thematology would throw light on the degree of the *deshiyata*-nativity in their portrayal. Do these samples carry the weight of new perceptions made possible by the changes in society? Do they adequately express the collective consciousness of the rural illiterate society and the fullness of their life? Neither Rao nor Raza shows the nativistic or colonialist consciousness of the key events of the freedom struggle to expose the methods of colonizer's construction of history. Their relation to the imperial history is not fiercely political. Their treatment of themes and characters is meant to comply with the metropolitan literary taste. Pendase and Nayak are no exceptions to this, but Nayak is less succeptible to it directly.

From the foregoing discussion, it seems that the manner of presentation of Indian reality in fiction has not yet reached the distinct native consciousness which would differentiate our novel from Western models. Is it because the wave of anti-colonialism has not yet touched our literati? While expounding 'the national longing for form,' Timothy Brennan has commented on the relationship between nation and novel by comparing the development of different countries. According to Brennan (1994, 47), the rise of nations is accompanied in the novel "by mimicking the structure of the nation, a clearly bordered jumble of languages and styles." The first part of

Brennan's statement is more applicable to the Indian situation than the latter half. Brennan's observations on the neocolonial Third World novel, which seeks to project the neocolonial Third World novel, are more helpful in the analysis of the problems faced by the Indian writers in their creative process. It also explains the colonial paradox of the need to trace the imagined Indianness of Indian literatures in an independent India. Brennan writes:

> And yet it is here that the greatest paradox of the new novel can be seen. For under conditions of illiteracy and shortages, and given simply the leisure time necessary for reading one, the novel had been an elitist and minority form in developing countries when compared to poem, song, television, and film. Almost inevitably it has been the form through which *a* thin, foreign-educated stratum (however sensitive or committed to domestic politics) has communicated to metropolitan reading publics, often in translations. It has been, in short, a naturally cosmopolitan form that empire has allowed to play *a* national role, as it were, only in an international arena. (57).

Under such dwarfing circumstances do our novelists struggle to free themselves from the imprisonment? All samples scrutinized in the chart reveal several structural family resemblances to the European, especially English, novels. 'The constraints imposed by an alien form are discerned in the "beginning, middle and end" components of these novels. They exhibit the straight line of traditional European narrative and not the *lambak* and *tarang* (modes of narrative which have several curves and discontinuities) which move in a zigzag manner in Gunadhya's tales or in the Arabic stories. All the samples generally fit into the pattern of British fiction. They do not formulate a cultural independence by Calibanizing the European traditions. Caliban has not yet possessed his own *desi* land even after the independence of India.

The plot structure and narrative technique of *Kanthapura,* a typical product of the colonial time, displays elitist paradigms. Rao's internationalist stand is revealed in his 'foreword'. He argues, "We cannot write only as Indians. We have grown to look at the large world as part of us. Our method of expression therefore has to be a dialect which will some day prove to be as distinctive and colourful as the Irish or the American..."(5). Yet neither had he succeeded in evolving the regional English dialect except Sanskritising it to the minimum degree, nor has he shown staunch resistance to what Homi K. Bhabha (1986, 152) describes as, "logocontric discourse" of European masters. Both Rao and Pendase continue the legacy of the master who "differentiates the gentleman from the native, culture from civilization." The result is that the Indian fiction becomes stereotypical. The chapter based on segregation is not broken by any one of these novelists. Except a few patches of *desi*-native songs and sayings they have not used any indigenous pre-British oral or written narrative technique consistently. The final victory of white discourse is disclosed in the immediate material conditions of these literary products. *Kanthapura* was designed and published in Europe. *Bapu* and *Adha* are translated into English. Thus, in James Snead's (1993) words, "fateful historical intervention of European" in Indian society, and the effects on the village life and culture here "find a striking and unsettling narrational and institutional resonance."

The range of writer's language determines the range of his world. Already it has been pointed out that the antidialogic colonial education led, to use Paulo Freire's (1977) phrase, to "the cultural conquest" of the Indians by the colonizers. The indigenous rhythm and voice was disturbed by the dominant Western prose styles. Our rich oral tradition of the *bhashas* was suppressed by the written ones. The notion of culture is always defined in relation to language, music, production of artifacts, rituals and customs of specific people. That is the ground of their cultural identity. Such a drum beat in the indigenous culture provides, in view of Kumau Brathwaite (1974, 727), an "alternative" folk or alternative tradition with which one can resist alien dominant influences. This leads us to the discussion of the use of language and style in these samples.

Language and style alone cannot make the nativistic hegemony but to some extent rural and dalit writings in

Marathi have demonstrated how they can revolutionize it. They are nonetheless particular patterns of thoughts conditioned by innumerable factors. In nativistic terms such patterns can be differentiated on various grounds such as Brahmanical *Kantha*pura and *Bapu*, non-Brahmanical *Acchev* and Muslim *Adha Gaon* and so on. The language of the first two is more Sanskritized and Anglicized than the latter two. The latter two are more heteroglotic and close to the *bhasa* traditions. They demonstrate, especially Nayak's *Acchev,* how the language and style are bearers of certain feelings and expressions of specific kinds in particular region. Those too are crucial to the experience of stormy rains in Garambi and greenery of Kolamb.

In fact, the difference of the spirit of the people is distinguished from all others of the same genius by their folk literature. Folk songs and folktales according to Mikhail Bakhtin (1981, 38), are the prototypes of the novel form: 'The novel's roots must ultimately be sought in folklore. But the roots of our modern novel are more alien than native. During the colonial period there was weak revival of the Sanskrit lore but the Shastri writers always looked down upon the indigenous folklore. Bhalchandra Nemade (1994, 79-78), while examining the semantics of orality, writes:

> For centuries we have been accustomed to literature primarily as an oral manifestation of languages and for our rural and tribal population literature has meant only the spoken word. Of 1,652 distinct languages spoken in our country not more than 24 can be associated with the written culture. Even in these so-called "recognized" literary language, a very marginal population has had a hand in their literatures. In fact until the Gutenberg phantom entered this country and T.B. Macaulay could measure the entire Indian literature by his notorious bookshelf, nearly all our literature was purely oral or in manuscripts that were interpreted by somebody to a gathering of expectant listeners (79).

The sample texts demonstrate how written language is mostly monologic and oral language is dialogic. Moreover, they reveal that the indigenous tradition of oral and manuscript literature in *bhashas is* relegated in the fiction. Rao's "intellectual make-up" allows him to use only two folk songs: "at least a toddy pot, sister..." (132). Ten extracts of other prayers and patriotic songs are highly Sanskritized. Similarly, Pendase makes Bapu hum only two refrains of the songs from Anglicized and Sanskritized Marathi drama (30-31). Very few words used by Rao to nativize English also show the elitist choice of the Sanskrit vocabulary and not of the *bhasha* or folk. His list includes: *prayaschitta, gayatri, arati,* a *kumkum* worship etc. Even the number of idioms and proverbs translated from Kannada into English does not go above score. This kind of folklore intertextuality is still more weak and thin in Pendase's *Bapu.* It contains less than half a dozen rural riddles and sayings. One of them is "Sushila's wed into Garambi, now she is rolling in sweaty money" (translated by Ian Raeside 1969, 1). Rao has used a number of sophisticated abusive words and expressions rather freely but Pendase has totally banned them. Perhaps both these elite writers do not know that all abusive or so-called obscene words and phrases in rural dialects are not always bawdy and "beat and bawdy", rhythm and gestures show the magnificent range of orality. The socio-linguistic and stylistic analysis of these sample texts discloses the class or caste, religion and education, rootedness or uprootedness in the soil and indigenous literary traditions, and different degrees of alienation of these writers.

It is interesting to compare dialogues in *Bapu* and *Acchev* from the nativistic point of view. Now "recognized" as an independent Konkani language, Konkani was considered by the elite Marathi literati as dialect of Marathi. Nayak used to write in Marathi at the beginning of his career, but his "regional fiction" in Marathi was neglected by the Anglicized culture bearing stratum in Pune and Bombay. The language dispute in Goa was not purely a nativistic literary movement. But it gave rise to the Goan writings, albeit overshadowed by English and Marathi models, which display the dialogic features of Konkani. Pendase's monologic language was standardized by the Sanskrit pandits long ago under the guidance of British masters. Nayak's dialogues in *Acchev* are crisp, short, less artificial, and very close to the speech of the common man. On the contrary, Pendase's use of dialogue is monologic, artificial, elitist, bombastic, anglicized and over Sanskritized. The conversations of the characters run into many pages in this contrived melodrama. A comparison of *Bapu* with its dramatised version is another topic of dispute. No doubt, *Bapu is* an expression of Mardhekarian modernity in Marathi, decultured by fake universalizing and colonial amnesia; and Nayak's *Acchev* is the product of true nativistic sensibility, but misled by misinterpreted Western aesthetics of fiction. Nayak did not have any predecessor in Konkani to wrestle with. Let us not delve deep into the caste-based family romance of Indian writers, but it should be noted that they have been used to employing European weapons for fighting with the writers in their own language. Pendase has his predecessors like Phadke and Khandekar who conditioned his fiction, but Nayak enjoyed more freedom in creating a medium for himself that had a tonal stretch and an intrinsic musicality although partly acculturated by the Portuguese legacy in Goa. The heteroglossia in *Acchev is* richer than that in *Bapu.* Words in Portuguese: *khamos, patranv,* or in English: best, driver etc., flow smoothly in *Acchev.* The language surface is not disturbed by heavy Sanskritized or Anglicized words in it like those in *Kanthapura* and *Bapu.* Pendase's voice has a loud and static register, while Nayak's has low but dynamic one. When Rukmin and Babusha, Nany and Devaki talk in *Acchev* (43-45, 87-91,134-136) the Konkani vernacular with its flicks of irony, its touches of humour, and its under statements comes alive and resonant, especially in its first part. Where Pendase failed, Nayak, perhaps unconsciously, removed the print-quality of language to put back the oral quality, where intonation, volume, gesture are all there. He makes his story appear more oral, meandering, effortless, and spoken story than Pendase's highly sophisticated life history of *Bapu*. Yet we have to wait for some time for a truly nativistic aural novel in India.

Often Nayak uses the rhetorical device of repetition to intensify the implications of festivities, rituals and seasons. Repetition, which is the native popular device, does not merely generate the rhythm of pause and emphasis and release, it calls attention to and dramatizes the psychic wounds that foster silently in the marginal peasant family. Pendase over-dramatizes every episode and often consciously uses typography to convey signals. Nayak is not so conscious of experimentation guided by the Western models. On the whole, he submissively abides by the conventions established by the linguistic acculturation during the colonial period. Whereas Pendase puts asterisks in place of so called pornographic words and phrases, Nayak unhesitingly uses such four lettered words as *ayavzavrya* (mother fucker), *hhanzavrya* (sister fucker), *rangya* (son of the 'keep' concubine) etc., smoothly.

The folkloric intertextuality in *Acchev* is richer than in both *Kanthapura* and *Bapu*. It is difficult to translate all of them into English. Mouthing chats leads to begging (14), read-*Gita* (scriptures) to a donkey (67) and many other expressions endlessly expound the rural wisdom. Kolamba has its own myths and legends (101). Allusions to the classics such as the *Mahabharata* (58-60) and *Ramayana*, folk tales (67-68), rituals: the *Satyanarayana*, (124), *Harivijay* and *Ramvijay* (29), invoke the world of rustic faiths and superstitions. In this respect Raza also has enriched his *Adha* Gaon by allusions to the *Koran* and other scriptures. Moreover, he has faithfully portrayed the cultural and sectarian differences between the Shiya and Sunni fractions. Like Nayak his language is more dialogic and he uses abusive address words and expressions such as *sale, madarjad chut, hahinchodan, haram-jadan* etc. appropriately. In fact, the presentation of sex, violence and communal conflicts is more complex in his novel. Consequently, the content itself demands richer heteroglossia, and he has surpassed all the three novelists in use of proverbs, literary allusions, rituals, oaths and perjuries.

A comparative study of sample use of the *dhalo* and *phugadyo*-songs (46-56) the *shigmo*-songs (70,71), *khelsongs (73)*, Goan music (70), dance (47, 52, 72) folk drama 9125) and painting in *Acchev* and folk songs (1, 160), love song (33), a marriage song (1.61) humourous rhymes (167) skiers (254), satirical folk songs (266), *gajjal* (264), *jalasa* songs (219), poems (full text quoted with a footnote, 291), and a number of references of *kawali*-songs, couplets, *kirtan* (281), variety of both Muslim and Hindu dances: Hussen (47), Chanda Bai's dance (280), and rituals and prayers in *Adha Gaon* bring out a number of differences and similarities in geographically isolated regions. It also shows that Raza's vision of village life is more complex and nativistic than any other novelist discussed above. His mastery of the folk culture surpasses all of them. Yet Raza's *Adha Gaon* cannot be described, like other three "regional/country/rural novels" a wholly Indian product because it is overshadowed by the Western post-modern technique of the historiographic metafication.

IV

This, in Edward Said's words, a "contrapuntal" but brief analysis four samples, shows that the novel in India, as a cultural form, is not and soon cannot be, purely nativistic. It confirms Edward Said's (1993, xii-xxvii) observations on the relationship between culture and imperialism. The focus of his study is on the modern Western empire and the role of the novel form in "the formation of imperial attitudes; references, and experiences (xii)." The fictional narrative is crucial to his argument. He approvingly modifies Homi Bhabha's statement that nations themselves are narratives by adding that:

> .... The power to narrate, or to block other narratives from forming and emerging, is very important to culture and imperialism, and constitutes one of the main connections between them (xiii).

Broadly speaking, the nativistic intertextuality in our sample texts seems to be blocked by both the Western first and secondly *desi*-native imperialism. Nativity has not yet fully emerged in them. We need the grand narratives of emancipation and enlightenment which would be known as distinctly Indian master narratives. One way out is to develop a new indigenous aesthetic of fiction.

Among younger generation a new awareness is emerging that the Euramencan theories of aesthetics do not cater to our need. Our indigenous aesthetics was lost in the colonial amnesia. We have not yet even begun an aesthetical experience after the imperial experiences. Let us adopt Kumau Brathwaite's working definition of aesthetics as quoted by

Synthia James (1994, 662). According to him, "the aesthetics is a critical communal sense of the essence of one's own culture." Our national longing for the native form of fiction should not only show a revolt against the dominance of Western models, but also against the quality of modern life made possible by the uprooting of communal, village life. In such a resistance we have to explore our traditional culture, and structure a new one.

But in the age of globalization and 'instant' cultures it is a very difficult ask to study the literatures of global dependency for the understanding of our own traditional cultures. Our affluent intellectuals, who have migrated to the first world, are/will mediate Western forms of narratives. S. Sankar 1994, 479-488) has aptly interpreted the famous story of "The Thumb of Eklavya" to explain the situation of the "Third World" scholar in a neocolonial world. In his view, it is a story about "subalternity and pedagogical institutions." Its major theme is "knowledge and power" politics. It suggests the possibility of a resistance. Finally Sankar urges:

> Hence, let me suggest that we all, as students and teachers, as scholars and intellectuals (all those subject position that readers of this essay may aspire to cover), consider the case of our thumbs... (486).

It would be befitting to conclude this paper on the same note with plea for fighting the fictional battle without losing our thumbs in cultural battle grounds.

Notes

1. Two essential components of tradition *parampara* in India are:
   a) *Marga* or *Margi*—the metropolitan or mainstream, especially of the elite, classical origins;

   b) *Desi*—regional and subcultural or later known as folk and Prakrit, See Ganesh Devi's *After Amnesisa* (1991, 18). After the colonial contact of the European rulers in India there developed the "tripatrite"relationship which made the alien forms of intertextuality superior to the native one. It is an universal tendency that an unidentified colonized reader diffuses writer's "horizons of expectancy" of the literary intertextuality. On the creative writer's side the presence of the foreign texts gives rise to the tug of war between the alien and the indigenous generic elements in his creative process. In the colonized writer's fiction little space is left for the native intertextuality. My survey (1993) of the influence of British drams on the Marathi drama of the whole colonial period proved it.

2. There are 24 Indian languages recognized by the constitution. Each one has its distinct, well-developed literature. But owing to the lack of knowledge of them a number of texts are not chosen for the analysis. Only four samples, chronologically selected from the corpus of fiction in English, Marathi, Hindi and Konkani, are studied. There are 1652 spoken languages in India, and a number of tribal writers are now using their dialects for literary works. Yet their literary sensibilities and the spirit of their writing is shaped by the Western aesthetics. If they become aware of 'de-education' of literary culture and consciously revive the nativistic textuality and succeed in assimilating it with healthy alien elements, authentic Indian voices array be heard in our fiction.
3. Krashnaji Prabhakar Khadilkar (1872-1948) consciously used the myth of the *Keechak wadh* killing of Keechak for his famous play of the same title. But its structure is completely Shakespearian. It is interesting to compare it with the *Kirtan* (folk dance-drama) performances of the same myth. The latter were more popular. See Anand Patil's *Western Influence on Marathi Drama (1993, 53.106).* As yet it has nor been explored how far the 'implied' reader either in the colonial or neo-colonial situation determines intertextuality.
4. The word *bhasa* (language) is used in the sense of modern Indian languages which have literary histories of many centuries. Ganesh Devi argues, "Thus, *hhasa* literature or *bhasa* criticism; but the label merely indicates a manageable group of many different literatures. It should be understood in the same manner as label like 'European literature', and 'Commonwealth literature...(3)

5

The "Post" in the Postcolonial Fictional Discourse: A Comparative Critique

The title of this paper is intended to echo the pertinent questions raised in Kwame Anthony Appiah's much anthologised article: "Is the 'Post' – in Postmodernism the Post in Postcolonial?" (1991). A number of theorists of anti-colonialism have defined two concepts[1] namely "postcolonial" and "decolonization." Almost all of them have tried to distinguish between "the postcolonial and the postmodern" from different points of view. True, all alien "posts and isms" come to us through our Post-offices' "Foreign mail" only. We are told by the "First Worldists" in Bombay and Pune that we live in a "Postmodern Age"; but we are hardly likely ever to find in Bharat that we live in a "Postcolonial Age". It is because the "post" in postcolonial is not the same as the "post" in postmodernism. Post-modernism does not appear to be the primary condition for the majority of people upon this earth. Western postmodernism has affected the rest of the world to some extent. It also means that the imperial Eurocentricism is still active. This activity itself becomes the subject of postcolonial fiction and novels of Salman Rushdie and Gabriel Garcia Marquez, for instance, have demonstrated how the" "empire writes back". There may be some similarities in theoretical positions, but the practice of poststructuralist and postcolonial readings are quite different. The very idea of postcolonial text refuses to return to a canon established by the 'master narrative'. In this context it is interesting to compare postcolonial novels produced in different countries and cultures.

So far, comparative studies of the Third World literatures have not been conducted on the larger scale owing to the neocolonial situation which makes claims upon our experience. Attempts at literary decolonization involve a radical dismantling of European codes and a post-colonial subversion and appropriation of the dominant European discourses. Of course, contradictions are inherent in this project, but the history of Indian criticism in English or in any Indian language does hardly display any work which carries a title with the word "decolonization". It is clear that precolonial purity of our culture can never be attained; and pre-British monolithic Indian culture may be one more Nomadian nativistic myth. Yet the colonial literary myths must be exposed and the comparative literature studies are very effective means to do it. So the following sample texts are juxtaposed comparatively:

1. Lambent Mascarenhas—*Sorrowing Lies My Land* (1955)
2. Chinua Achebe — *Things Fall Apart* (1958)
3. V.S. Naipaul's — A *House for Mr. Biswas* (1961)
4. Gabriel Garcia Marquez — *One Hundred Years of Solitude* (1967)
5. Salman Rushdie — *Midnight's Children* (1980).

These samples are selected at random, and are not necessarily 'fully' postcolonial. Their choice was (over) determined by the availability of the text in the neocolonial situation. Moreover, some of these samples defy binary opposition such as colonial and postcolonial or Indian and alien and so on. Some of them exhibit various kinds of mimicry of which Homi K. Bhabha speaks as "of mimicry and man" (1994, 85 - 92). They illustrate how fictional representation and resistance are very broad arena. Helen Tiffin (*PSR* 1995, 95) aptly commented on this drama of colonialist relations and post-colonial subversions of those relations as follows:

> Post colonial cultures are inevitably hybridized, involving a dialectical relationship between European ontology and epistemology and the impulse to create or recreate independent local identity. Decolonisation is process, not arrival; it invokes an ongoing dialectic between hegemonic

> centrist systems and peripheral subversion of them: between European or British discourses and their postcotonial dismantling. Since it is not possible to curate or recreate national or regional formations wholly independent of their historical implication in the European colonial enterprise... ("Post-colonial Literatures and Counter Discourse". *PSR* 1995).

Thus I want to mark out, what is the general focus for the following discourse on the postcolonial fiction written or translated into 'English'. A comparative study of these samples with their counterparts in the 'regional' or indigenous languages of the respective countries would throw more light on the complex process of the hybridization at different levels of literary productions. The issues I have emphasized have been those selected by critics but hardly with what Edward Said (1993, 36) cautiously describes as "contrapuntal" attitude to the relationship of European fiction and imperialism. He has interpreted the colonizers's fiction in the context of their imperialism. Our samples are the counterparts of those cultural products. Examining these samples with the paradigms of Western aesthetics is a mistake, because the values of that European-based culture with respect to fiction are not suited to the actual Indian or African readership. They are suited less to the novelists, who have their own mixed literary value systems. Achebe's novels demonstrate how the "black" aesthetics has brought about the tremendous change in their fictional discourse and the Caribbean or Latin American novelists of the postcolonial period also display the results of their struggle to have their own aesthetics of fiction. But more threatening to the critical process of appreciating postcolonial Indian novel, as John Oliver Perry (1992, 32) writes of the contemporary understanding of Indian English poetry, "are the expanding forces in middle-class English reading Indian society that, as elsewhere in the world, offer only a capitalistic aesthetic of consumption" (32). Perry's concept of "absent authority" which he calls the aesthetic of "indigenizing, strategies" may be of much help in this respect.

In using the term "post" in postcolonial it is to be argued that there are separate grounds for the claims of postcoloniality in fictional products of the decolonized countries. On the basis of sample texts it is to be tested how far our historical reading of the 'post' in 'postcolonial, like one in 'postmodern', is adequate, In Indian fiction the postcolonial does not necessarily follow the colonial in time. Coloniality had always contained its 'postcolonial' moments. Same is the case with postmodernism. For the sake of discussion we accept following meaning of the term 'post-colonial' as implied by theorists. It is the 'post' of:

1. The space clearing gesture, post-realist, post-nativist.
2. Post-colonising impetus or a process as much as an identity.
3. The overlap between the post-colonial and the postmodern.
4. Concept of contamination.
5. Hybridity as a source of creative strength.

Thus, by proposing, in Lisa Lowe's (1993, 47) words, postcoloniality as a heterogeneous, non-binary terrian we can compare the sample texts. In her analysis of the postcolonial literary nomadism she argues:

> Postcolonial Francophone literatures of North Africa and South Asia are not only symptomatic sites of the struggles and contradictions analysed by Fanon and others but in certain cases, the literatures also offer narrative allegories of these struggles and contradictions (44).

Postcolonial Anglophone fiction is not an exception to these observations. A comparative scrutiny of postcolonial Francophone and Anglophone literatures from this perspective would suggest another manner of reading and thinking of postcoloniality. Here we restrict our discussion to the concept of 'post' in the postcolonial as revealed in a few select samples of fictional discourse.

II

At the very outset, let us examine the colonial consciousness as it is revealed in these texts. For this, according to Perry, "very basic understanding of the place of writing seems required" (35). If we consider novel as a cultural battlefield where inter- and intra- imperialistic armies 'clash by night' for domination, we need as Perry rightly argues, "some vision of a fundamental cultural esthetic for its literature (35)". By using such indigenous perspective we can estimate various directions taken by the 'post' in postcolonial fiction. For instance, postcoionial or partly colonial novelist becomes riot only the 'double exile' but the triple one in the Indian elitist neocolonial contexts. Lambert Mascarenhas's *Sorrowing Lies My Land* (1955) was written and published in Bombay, the metropolis in free India when he was exiled by the Portuguese rulers in Goa, the inseparable part of India. It was written in English, and has some links with Raja Rao's much canonized bogus 'prose epic': *Kanthapura* (1938) which was drafted in Europe and published in England. Elsewhere, it has been demonstrated comparatively how it is less 'regional' and Indian. On the contrary, Mascarenhas's *Sorrowing Lies My Land is* the first Indian anticolonial peasant novel in English, but its 'place of writing' and publication made all the difference in its noncanonization in the 'great colonized tradition' of Brahmanical fiction in India. This statement is again proved by the representation of reality through the brahmanical perspective in V. S. Naipaul's *A House of Mr. Biswas* (1961) which was written during his self exilement in England. His novel can be easily transplanted to the Indian soil by transferring some of the Caribbean names of persons and places, but it is very difficult to do so in case of Mascarenhas's Goan regional novel of the last phase of the freedom struggle. It was just published six years before Goa was liberated in 1961. It cannot be easily shifted to any region of Portugal. Peter Nazareth (1978, 62-70) has rightly described it as " the Novel as Anti-Colonial Weapon".

It is interesting to compare the representation of cultural reality by four fictionists in the 1950s and 1960s. Emilio Francisco Lamberto Mascarenhas, who hails from the family of Chaddo-Kshatriyas converted to Christianity, was born in Goa in 1914, but was sent to Bombay to study English literature in the postgraduate class. Consequently, his novel opens with the similar pattern which we notice at the outset of Charles Dickens's *The Hard Times*. Is it the colonial coincidence that the jacket cover of Naipaul's A *House for Mr. Biswas* exhibits the following statement by the reviewer.

> ...It has the Dickensian largeness and luxuriance without any of the Dickensian sentimentality, apostrophising or preaching.

The patronizing tones of the British reviewers of Naipaul's novel and of the Indian commentators of Mascarenhas's fiction differ widely because of the socio-political contexts of these texts. In a way, both the novels fall into the pattern of the British well-made fiction of the realist school of modern times. To some extent both deal with the theme of growing up under the col^nial shadows. Yet their attitude to the colonial reality is totally different.

In a way Mascarenhas's counter-discourse of the colonial phase of violence is partly postcolonial. He constructs the tragic saga of the disintergration of the family of the Goan Christian peasant Tobias Costa. Tobias's crippled son Babush is the narrator of this episodic tale told on the background of the struggle for freedom of the inseparable part of India. In order to bring out the differences between the fictional discourse of the colonial phase of assimilation and that of the violence, in Fanonian theory, Patil (1995) had juxtaposed this novel with another Goan novel in Portuguese by the Goan Catholic parliamentarian Francisco Louis Comes: *Os Brahamanes* (*The Brahman* 1866). *The Sorrowing Lies My Land* is an unique example of the oppositional fictional aesthetics which exposes, in Nazareth's words, "Portuguese imperialist exploitation in Goa" and it was "intended to arouse the political consciousness of the people" (62).

In contrast to the anticolonialist fictional discourse of the Goan Christian author we have the example of an immigrant novelist belonging to the Hindu Brahman family in Trinidad namely V. S. Naipaul (b. 1932) whose *A House for Mr. Biswas* displays the following features of his writing in general:

> One local journalist wrote: "...we resent Naipaul's criticisms, but claim his achievements. Alienated by his bleak, unsentimental vision, we see him in isolation, overlooking the fact that his themes of meaninglessness and the threat of chaos are also the themes of much modern American and European literature. If Naipaul has portrayed life in the Third World as nasty, brutish and short, in these post-oil boom days (in Trinidad) it's harder to contradict him" (Williams, Raymond 16 as quoted by Kelvin Jarvis 1995, 72).

It is interesting to note how the majority of Brahman writers, to name only one Raja Rao whose narrator opens *The Serpent and the Rope* with white man's arrogant capital "I" and a reference to his being a "Brahman by birth," hopelessly alienate themselves from the rest of the humanity. It is this Brahmanical world-view which dominates the poetics of colonial reality in *A House for Mr. Biswas.* It is this tendency to look down upon the mass culture and also its: 'wounded civilization' that was ironically hinted at in a sharp taunting tone by Naipaul's competitor Derek Walcott in his 1992 Nobel lecture. Of course, Naipaul is highly critical of his own caste and its creeds as Mascarenhas is, but the latter is a nationalist. While the first ridicules ruthlessly the traditional Hindu rituals, myths and manners, the latter pines for the lost glory of the precolonial past. Tobias tells the heroic tales of the Kadamba kings and other heroes in Goa, but his Portuguese oriented children do not believe them. He condemns the Portuguese for denationalization of Goa. Finally he insists:

> "So you don't believe it, children? Well, I don't blame you! You are at least children, while even the adults and the so called educated people of this land don't like it." Then he began to tell us of the great Ashoka whose empire extended to the shores of Goa, and the Kadambas who ruled for nearly seven centuries and under whom Goa had been very prosperous ...(30)

Naipaul's displaced protagonist, who spends his whole life in search of an adequate 'house' for himself, is totally cut off from the Indian history. Only a few fragments of the Brahmanical culture, which he laughs at, follow him. His orthodox father Jairam Pundit teaches him Hindi, As Tobias beats Babush for speaking in the Portuguese language at home and not in Konkani as usual, Jairam also punishes Mr Mohun Biswas for not performing rituals in the disciplined manner. The narrator tells us:

> Jairam was no flogger. When he was in a rage he might box Mr. Biswas on the ear, but usually he was less intemperate. For a badly conducted *puja,* for instance, he might make Mr. Biswas learn a dozen couplets from the *Ramayana* by heart, confining him to the house until he had. All day that day Mr. Biswas wondered what punishment the eating of the bananas would bring, while he copied out Sanskrit verses, which he couldn't understand, on strips of cardboard, having revealed to Jairam his skill in lettering (52).

Soon Mr. Biswas relieves himself on the handkerchief instead of using the latrine. He throws it on Jairam's cherished oleander tree of which flowers were used for the *puja*. In the morning Jairam told Mr. Biswas, "you are no Brahmin (56)". Emma, Tobias' wife, cursed her elder son for marrying a Hindu convert of a lower caste and the son left for Bombay. On the contrary, Tobias approves of that wedding but disapproves Laxmi's conversion at an early age and criticizes Christianity in Goa that retains caste barriers even after conversion (34, 36). Such colonial contradictions and stereotypical situations are many in these novels. We can trace the process of Western education which represents the intervention of imperial values and the amnesia of the indigenous ones into the family. We will see how Marquez metaphorically depicts the effects of the colonial amnesia in his *One Hundred Years of Solitude*.

A number of parallel events and similar transformations can be sorted out from these novels. For example, Naipaul's Jagdat lives "with a woman of another race and had some children, no one knew how many, by her" (244). The Tulsi family in the Hanuman house celebrates Christmas (365), Shekhar's wife calls herself Dorothy "without shame or apology; and for her daughters chooses" the Hindi names – Mira, Lena which were "meant tc pass as Western" (356). This craze for the Western, especially Portuguese, foreign thing is symbolically represented by Tobias's own sister in *Sorrowing Lies My Land.* His son migrates to Africa. Migration is a common factor in both the novels. Mr Biswas's daughter and son go to England for further education, many others migrate for jobs. It is significant to note that Naipaul's novel is set in the Caribbean West Indian islands but nearly all characters proudly carry their Hindu names such as Tara, Shama, Anand, Pankaj and so on. Mascarenhas's 'regional' novel depicts the colonial reality in Portuguese Goa by giving all the characters strictly Portuguese names such as Maria, Antonio, Thomas and so on. Such cross-cultural pollination in both the fictional discourses differs only in degrees and not in kinds.

Thus 'the Oedipal structures of colonialism', to use Mary E. Donnely's terms (7), can be discerned in both the novels. The presence of 'mother country' and 'father country' in them matters most in the postcolonial criticism. Frantz Fanon's following observations are more applicable to these 'family romances'. He states in *Black Skin and White Masks:*

> There are close connections between the structure of the family and the structure of the nation. Militarization and the centralization of authority in a country automatically entail a resurgence of the authority of the father. In Europe and in every country characterized as civilized or civilizing, the family *is* a miniature of the nation (147-4).

In both the novels the presence of the European authority is constantly felt, especially it is more dominant in *Sorrowing Lies My Land:*

> "Yes the same fellow, Tob," replied my aunt in very low tone, "He seems to have a terrible influence on Robu, and Robu appears to have become more Portuguese than the Portuguese themselves. He even hit someone the other day for talking againsts the Portuguese" (120).

In the colonial situation in Goa obedience to king, who was far removed from the daily life of his subjects, was required. In

Naipaul's novel the situation is post-colonial; but the image of the cultural empire of the Queen of England appears in the form of journalism, which transforms less educated sign-painter Mr. Biswas's life; and of the British education, which liberates his son Anand from the drudgery of the plantation labour. The English literary texts also 'fix the paradigm of the cultural father', as Donnely writes of George Lamming's *In the Castle of My Skin,* 'far removed from the schoolboys' own daily lives' (7). Although Naipaul's characters parade their 'high caste' brown colour and Hindu upper *varna* names, their own culture is continually devalued and affected by the process of their education based on British patterns. Jairam compelled Mr. Biswas commit the *Ramayana* to memory, but the latter wants his son to win the scholarship which will lead him to 'father country', i.e., England:

> *Mr.* Biswas said, *'Boy,* get me the *Collins Clear-Type Shakespeare,* and my pen'. .....
>
> On the fly-leaf, below the four masculine names that had been chosen for Savi before she was born, Anand read: *'I, Mohun Biswas, do hereby promise my son Anand Biswas that in the event of his winning a college Exhibition I will buy him a bicycle'* signature and date followed (467-68).

The autobiographical elements in both the novels are disclosed in such dramatic situations, and such colonial processes continue even after the fictional discourses of two Third World writers appear in print. Mascarenhas won a prize for writing a novel in English in the competition for Indian Authors held by Grove Press in the United States; but it was banned by the Portuguese rulers in Goa. A number of British Awards for literary works are pocketed by Naipaul, and American reviewers of A *House for Mr Biswas* considered it to be a masterpiece and placed him in the hierarchy of living 'writers of whom the English language can be proud' (back leaf).

This leads us to the discussion of the role of the English elitist readership in shaping the spirit of the postcolonial fiction. Both samples exhibit the collaborationist inclinations of these novelists in constructing the fictional discourses in the standard British English. Naipaul's novel hardly displays any features of the creole language and culture. His culture conditioned anti-dialogic imagination vigilantly guards against heteroglossia which is of great importance in Mikhail Bakhitn's theory of novel. Almost all characters speak correct and 'chaste' English, and hybrid dialect is not used at all. For instance, Mrs. Tulsi speaks both English and Hindi but not a single phrase or sentence is produced in Hindi.

> 'All right, miss. All right.' Mrs. Tulsi pressed her thin lips together repeatedly. 'Tell me what happened.' She spoke English in a slow, precise way which surprised Mr Biswas... (84)
>
> Mrs. Tulsi spoke some abuse to Shame in Hindi, the obscenity of which startled Mr. Biswas (85).

We will see later how Rushdie and Marquez make a very creative use of mixed dialects; but here it should be noted that neither Naipaul nor Mascarenhas makes use of Indian languages or of the folk traditions except few words such as *puja, baba, mai, maharajin* etc., in *A House For Mr Biswas* and in *Sorrowing Lies My Land* the Konkani words are totally banned. Naipaul has made use of song and dance but in alien or European fashion. A comparatist has analysed the folkloristic intertextuality in *Sorrowing Lies My Land* and demonstrated how Indian writers are torn between the culture in which they live and the culture they are indoctrinated to believe to be superior (see Patil 1993). Both of them are aware of the tensions in living in the borrowed culture. They are caught, to use Donnely's metaphor again, "in a bind not unlike that of a child facing the Oedipal conflict, forced to choose between comfort and law, the mother land and the father culture." Here the originality of the writer is tested in facing this conflict, and his 'space making gestures' make his writing truely 'postcolonial'. In this respect both upper-caste English educated Indian (immigrant nonresident included) writers are totally alienated from the folk culture and crippled by the twin processes of Sanskritization and Westernization. That is why they have failed in an attempt at evolving an independent aesthetic model like Brathwaite's idea of 'the jazz novel'. Chapter One of *Biswas* is titled as 'Pastoral' which seems to be a misnomer, because it fails to contribute rustic touches to the texture of the novel. In the scene of the nomenclature of Mr. Biswas, we notice the continuation of the nineteenth century 'punditi tradition' of setting the pastoral scenes on the background of Lord Krishna's Mathura. Such stereotypes are innumerable in our regional language literatures produced by 'pundits'. One example form *Biswas* will show how Naipaul uses Indian lore:

> The pundit was surprised and genuinely pleased. 'But that is excellent. Excellent, Mohun. I couldn't have chosen better myself. For Mohun, as you know, means the beloved, and was the name given by the milkmaids to Lord Krishna'. His eyes softened at the thought of the legend and for a moment he appeared tc forget Bissoondaye and Mr Biswas (17, 18).

Similarly the Goan Christian writer is more alienated from the rich folk traditions which had survived for four centuries despite the Portuguese cultural conquest. Peter Nazareth has aptly pointed out the limitation of *Sorrowing Lies My Land* that it "is liable to be misunderstood once its time is past or when it is seen in a different context" (69). He has advised him to write a new novel modelled on Yamho Ouologuem's fiction in Africa. What is obviously distinct in the Black aesthetics of fiction is its resistance to European master narrative and struggle to achieve the text's postcoloniality in its apparent 'folking up of the novel form'. African and Afro-American texts exhibit a different approach to what Indian imitators of Euramerican new criticism describe as 'universality'. They are inclined to display a certain linguistic and cultural eclecticism. Their thinking and writing deeply rooted in oral culture stands in contrast to racially based pedigrees of Western European tradition of fiction in Indian English. Chinua Achebe's fiction provides fine models for comparison.

III

Achebe (b. 1930) had his primary education in Igbo and was one of the first graduates of the University College, Ibadan in Nigeria. His *Things Fall Apart* was written in response to Joyce Cary's *Mister Johnson* which depicted the Nigerian life through the eyes of a 'white' outsider. For a long time Joseph Conrad's portrayals of the Negroes in *The Heart of Darkness* and other novels intrigued him. Edward Said (1993, XXi) ironically points out how Conrad was on the pay roll of the Empire's queen and his ficition "confirms habitual Western suspicions about Latin America, Africa and Asia" (xxii). It is interesting to compare his critical assessment of the novels of Naipaul, Achebe and Marquez (xxii, 320-21, 372). He includes the names of Achebe, Marquez and Rushdie in the list of writers who have learned Conrad's ironies so well. They have done their work *after* decolonisation, after the massive intellectual, moral, and imaginative overhaul and deconstruction of Western representation of the non-Western world, after the works of Frantz Fanon, Albert Memmi, C.L.R. James... and many others (xxiii).

Achebe's *Things Fall Apart* depicts the history of the village Umuofia from 1850 to 1900, i.e., the period of colonization. 'Uma' means children and 'ofia' means 'bush'. The history and novel meet in it. It was influenced by Negritude' (1930s) which meant the awareness, defence and development of African cultural values. It delineates through a series of scenes the clash between traditional society and British Christian imperialism. Its title suggests the intertextuality of W.B. Yeats's 'Second Coming'. The protagonist Okonkwo falls a prey to the confusion created by the colonizers and hangs himself. The missionaries divided them and ruled:

> The three white men and a very large band of other men surrounded the market. They must have used a powerful medicine to make themselves invisible until the market was full and they began to shoot (126).

The supposedly savage Ibo believe in their dictum 'Never kill a man who never says anything'. Thus, an autocratic rule of the whiteman under the guise of democracy shocked the Ibo whose rule was based on open decisions taken collectively. Although Achebe focuses on Okonkwo much of the frustration at the end of the story is (that of) the entire community that underwent the colonial harrowing experiences after the contact with an 'intimate enemy'. Mascarenhas, like Achebe, had shown similar anticolonial consciousness; but Naipaul tends to be the collaborationist comprador novelist.

In a way their plots are episodic and conventional. Achebe also admits the literary influences of the British novelists such as Conrad, Graham Greene, Evelyn Waugh and others. Yet he more consciously resists these influences by using indigenous folklore. In this respect he stands in contrast to Mascarenhas and Naipaul. However, their texts are modernist in the European sense of the form of the novel. Achebe's incorporation of the anthropological details in the first chapter of *Things Fall Apart* offended the Eurocentric literary taste. Then followed the series of loosely linked events: throwing of the cat, killing of Ikemefuna, shot fired at Ekefi and the pilgrimage of Chielo. The second part depicts the punishment of Okonkwo; and finally the denouement contains his suicide. The tale is based on the document: 'The Pacification of the Primitive Tribes of Lower Niger.'

This subaltern writer adopts the nativistic tone of the fictional narrative:

> In this way the moons and the seasons passed. And then the locusts came. It has not happened for many a long year (49).

The nativistic intertextuality of folk songs serves the purpose of parodying the treacherous Kotmas:

> Kotmo of the ash buttocks, he is fit to be a slave. The white man has no sense, he is fit to be a slave (158)

Similarly the tale of the tortoise and the broken shell may seem an extrinsic element in the novel. The third-person omniscient narrative provides scope for introducing such 'archetypal' patterns, Achebe consciously reshapes the European prose genre into something distinctly African in form and pattern. This kind of resistance at the structural level is not seen in *The Sorrowing* as well as in *Biswas*; and hence there is more, effective postcoloniality in *Things Fall* than the other two fictional discourses. It is said that a subaltern writer hardly speaks with his own voice and technique. Achebe has challenged this muteness by juxtaposing the 'minority discourse' against the 'majority discourse'.

Achebe's creative use of the English language is very different from that of the fictionists discussed before. Achebe plays with the foreign tongue in order to expose anthropocentric values and to celebrate the native culture. Note the indigenous modes of narratives in the following sentences:

> As I began to fend for myself at an age when most people still stuck at their mother's breast (20).
>
> Eneke the bird says that since men have learnt to shoot without missing, he has learnt to fly without perching (20).

He treads freely where Mascarenhas and Naipaul fear to walk. He uses .indigenous ritualistic words and phrases in the original: *chukwu, chika ant,* etc. The slogans, proverbs and sayings are many. "When the moon is shining the crippled become hungry for a walk" (10). It was like pouring grains of corn into a bag full of holes (21). If one finger brought oil it soiled the other (114). *The Sorrowing* or *Biswas* can be read without the help of glossary; but *The Things* had to include it in the second edition. Achebe's similes are based on African and not on European realities: "Okonkwo's fame had grown like a bush-fire in the harmattan" (7). The alien reader is made to assume the vulnerable position.

Achebe's commitment as a postcolonial Third World writer is revealed in his article "Named for Victoria, Queen of England" (1973) which opens with a sentence:

> I was BAPTISED Albert Chinualumogu. I dropped the tribute to Victorian England when I went to the University

> although you might find some early acquaintances still calling me by it.

Thus, his comments on the hybridity of the literary culture and the creative writer's role in the postcolonial contexts are exemplary. He writes about the creative process of his fictional discourse:

> At the university I read some appalling novels about Africa (including Joyce Cary's *Mister Johnson)* and decided that the story we had to tell could not be told for us by any one else no matter how gifted or well-intended.

He continues by quoting the inscription on the coffee shop wall:

> Take care of your boss
> the next one may be worse.

The trouble with writers is that they will often refuse to live by such rationality (see *PSR* 190, 193).

Indeed the 'trouble' with Indian writers is that 'they' have rarely lived by what Achebe calls 'such rationality'. Neither Mascarenhas nor emigre Naipaul exhibits Achebe's awareness of postcoloniality. 'Writing postcoloniality' means, in Helen Tiffin's words, "the project of postcolonial writing to interrogate European discourses and discursive strategies from a privileged position within (and between) two worlds; to investigate the means by which Europe imposed and maintained its codes in the colonial domination of so much of the rest of the world" (93). Further, she evaluates Achebe's contribution to this 'textual revolution' in the postcolonial world:

> ...Achebe's essay, 'The Novelist As Teacher' (Achebe *1975: 167-74)* stresses the crucial function of texts in post-colonial social formations and their primacy in effecting revolution and restitution, priorities *which are* not surprising given the role of the text in the European capture and colonization of Africa. Post-colonial counter-discursive strategies involve a mapping of the dominant discourse, a reading and exposing of its underlying

> assumptions, and the dis/ mantling of these assumptions from the cross-cultural standpoint of the imperially subjectified 'local' *(PSR* 97, 98).

Although Achebe's resistance to colonialism is multifaceted, involving language, history, space and the Negritude, our focus lies primarily on postcoloniality in his fiction, because it informs his conception of individual and collective identity on the one hand; and concerns the relationship between the 'colonizer and the colonized', to repeat Albert Memmi's famous title, on the other. One instance will suffice. James Snead has explained how Achebe employes counter–discursive strategies in using W. B. Yeats's 'Second Coming' in *Things Fall Apart* and T.S. Eliot's 'Journey of the Magi' in *No Longer at Ease* to "rewrite the text both of European historicism and of the cyclical view that was its hopeful antidote". James Snead states:

> Achebe reverses this view to highlight the negative impact that his hypothetically 'positive' Christian phase has already had upon the 'falling apart' of African culture' *(242).*

In defining postcoloniality it is the 'new morality' in the use/ misuse of the European text that matters most. It depends on how the postcolonial writer does use European textual model for a specific purpose. A comparative study (1996) displayed some aspects of intra-colonial commercial (mis) use of Shakespeare plays in post-colonial India. It is clear as light that the majority of English educated writers instead of using the European texts against both infra as well as inter-colonial conquests, misuse them against subculture groups to retain the cultural hegemony of the comprador Westernized class. Fighting against both alien and indigenous forces of colonialism is the main feature of postcolonial textual revolution. Let us see how the postcolonial writers make the most of postmodern condition in constructing counter-discourse in their fiction.

IV

From the foregoing discussion it can be safely stated that it is not only 'writing back' to the European authors and their canonical texts but to the whole of the discursive field within which such a text operated and continues to operate in postcolonial countries. At least two models of future postcolonial studies are useful and we will have to blend them harmoniously (1). The postcoloniality would reside in the discursive features of fictional discourse (2). Its material situation will determine its nature. The combination of these two features certainly shapes the spirit of counter-discursive strategies. This is a broad field of fictional counter-discursive strategies and a number of subgroupings are possible. Unfortunately these subgroupings are not yet fully exploited in the doubly determined Indian literati. But the Latin American 'magic realism' and the 'boom' of typical fictional discourse provides glimpses of postcoloniality which are closely connected with postmodernity. Gabriel Garcia Marquez's *One Hundred Years of Solitude* demonstrates how the replacing of carnivalesque European genre like the picaresque novel can be achieved in postcolonial discourse. Reality and fantasy hobnob with each other, and the truth becomes as powerful as the truth of a fable. What Susnigdha Dey (1988:19) writes of Marquez's *The Autumn of the Patriarch* is equally true of his *One Hundred.* She writes:

> ... It is a novel of political and social protest. We are again at a loss to find out who among the many dictators of Latin America, could have provided him with the model. Violence and poetry, magic and realism, heighten the effect (19).

Marquez's deep commitment to anticolonialism as well as his friendship with the Chilean supremo Fidel Castro are known facts. The real and the mythical are interwoven in his novel in such a way that his novel does not appear to be the fiction of protest at the surface level. His "story-telling is not lineal" (5). He is a Marxist novelist but with a difference. He has carried the fictional discourse to a higher subversive power, and paved the path for Gunther Grass and Salman Rushdie. His fiction exhibits the potential of allegory as a privileged site of anti-colonial or post-colonial discourse. Helen Tiffin aptly calls it "canonical counter discourse" (97).

He is more known for political prose writings on Chilean reality. *One Hundred* made him known all over the world. It is a socialist novel. Its first sentence demands on part of the reader that one should know the history of foreign exploitation in Latin America:

> Many years later, as he faced the firing squad, Colonel Aureliano Buendia was to remember that distant afternoon when his father took him to discover ice (11).

In the next sentence we are introduced to the imaginary village Macondo in Latin America. After these two opening sentences we are told how Colonel Aureliano Buendia's father, Jose Arcadio Buendia, is fascinated by the latest discoveries from the outer world brought by gypsies led by Melquiades. He buys toys from them. He tries to extract gold from the soil with the help of magnet bought from them. Later he buys the telescope to invent weapons of war. Then he is obsessed by the idea to device a formula for doubling the quantity of gold. He wastes Ursula's inherited gold. He gets obsessed with several things in his laboratory till he goes mad. In the end he is tied to the tree and dies there. He is forgotten.

This is a family chronicle but very different from those discussed above. It is the complex history of a family which reflects innumerable transformations in Latin American history. Apparently it covers one hundred years but refers to hundreds of years. The family tree is given at the beginning of the text. Such paratexts help the reader to remember the 'family romance' of four Jose Arcadios. However, it is not the plain and simple family chronicle like John Galsworthy's *The Forsyte Saga.* Marquez, like Achebe, explores Latin American reality of underdevelopment during nearly 300 years of imperialist exploitation. He goes a step ahead of Achebe in depicting the harsh realities of the neo-colonial exploitation by the most powerful of developed countries over a hundred years.

This kind of postcolonial as well as postmodern sensibility was not revealed in the three samples discussed before. Marquez has turned upside down the European technique of so called stream of consciousness and other experimental novels. It is difficult to analyse the stylistic features of his Spanish prose fiction translated into English. The grotesque elements and black comedy are the most significant features of his narrative. The Latin American absurdity is linked with the outside world through fantastic events and strange characters. The episodes which delineate the adventures of the 'foreign banana company' symbolically illustrate this point. The exploiter contemptuously refers to the exploited Latin American countries as 'Banana Republics.' This is the symbolic name given to the monoculture introduced by the colonial contact.

There are other ways of creating that "marvellous reality" in this historiographic metafication. For example, the entire episode of the loss of memory caused by Rebeca's arrival in the village is a fine satire on the cultural amnesia caused by the colonizers' 'cultural conquest' (see pp. 44-55). The well-made lengthy dialogues are not to be found in decentered self-reflexive fiction. Here everything is straight forward:

> "I have come to sleep with you," 'he said.
>
> His clothes were smeared with mud and vomit. Pillar Ternera, who lived alone at that time with her two younger children, did not ask him any questions. She took him to the bed (62).

Similarly aphorisms and antithetical subversions take the reader by surprise:

> 'How strange men are,' she said, because she could not think of anything else to say. 'They spend their lives fighting against priests and then give prayer books as gifts' (137).

There are reincarnations, incests, premonitions, ghosts, voices from the grave, and what not. Different narrators narrate different stories. We have number of versions of the same event. For instance, see the reports of the police firing at the workers on strike. It is difficult to grasp reality under such circumstances. Similar scene is introduced by Rushdie by asking the readers to see if they can observe any image on the TV screen when they go too close to it.

In *One Hundred Years of Solitude* there is no tragedy as such. The farcical scenes are many. It is the rich intertextuality of different texts introduced by the cross-cultural encounters in the colonial situation that makes Marquez's cyclic narrative more innovative. There are repeated references to a Sanskrit Book (288-89). Even Milton's poems figure in the list. He demystifies the literary works. Literature is a bull's shit. At another place he tells through one of his characters:

> 'The world must be all fucked up,' he said then, 'when men travel first class and literature goes as freight.' (323).

The central theme is the problem of distortion caused by the colonial and neocolonial experience which is relevant to almost all colonized countries. Peter Nazareth observes:

> The gigantism, the dark humour the marvellous reality of Gabriel Garcia Marquez is meant to draw our attention to the absurdity of our underdevelopment as a result of continuous neocolonial exploitation ....Through marvellous reality, Gabriel Garcia Marquez is showing us that the people themselves are responsible for their reality as underdeveloped people, not being marvellous (111, 112).

Parody, subversion of history, hybridization, indeterminacy of meaning, decanonization, carnivalization, construction, irony, performance and several other aspects of postmodernity are well displayed in Marquez's novel. It shows how historical accuracy is not an idea one usually associates with fiction. However, he presents 'tyrannically documented life' effectively. Marquez insisted that he is 'a realist' and his sensibility is very close to that of the ancient Greeks. The postcolonial novelists such as Achebe, Marquez, Rushdie have been struggling to construct fictional counter-discourse by challenging orthodoxy and authority. The present movements and migrations have brought about several changes in the postcolonial literary scene. Edward Said has explained how new theories in the West have replaced the old ones, and one of them is 'post-modernism'. Post-Marxism and post-structuralism are also affiliated to it. Said establishes the links between these ideas in the West and changes caused by them in the postcolonial literary culture. Ire states:

> ....This is similarly the case in the Caribbean, East Europe, Latin America, Africa and the Indian subcontinent; these movements intersect culturally in a fascinating cosmopolitan space animated by internationally prominent writers like Salman Rushdie, Caros Fuentes, Gabriel Garcia Marquez, Milan Kundera, who intervene forcefully not only as novelists but also as commentators and essayists (399).

It is interesting to explore the intertextual relationship among three masterpieces of the self-reflexive historiographic metafications, viz, Marquez's *One Hundred Years of Solitude*, Gunther Grass's *The Tin Drum* and Rushdie's *Midnight's Children*. Jaidev has demonstrated how the intertextual play in the latter two is a wholly 'self-conscious and consciously managed activity'; but ignored the first one. According to him, *Midnight's Children* 'appears inconceivable' without and 'derivative' of *The Tin Drum*. What he writes about the parallels in form, theme, technique, approach to history etc. in it, to some extent, is equally true about *The Tin Drum* and *One Hundred Years of Solitude*. Jaidev observes:

> ...Its (*Midnight's Children*) multi-generation epic form, its going back in time to begin with the protagonist's grandparents, its miracle protagonist who is not subject to the human limitations of time, space and subjectivity, its juxtaposition of the protagonist's private crises and the nations tragedies: its employment of polarities, its mixed mode, fragmented chronology, invention of fairy tale motifs, games and self-reflexivity, its use of an insided reader figure or interlocutor, its intention to demythologize history ... all these and more come bearing a stamp of *The Tin Drum* (134).

It is not a coincidence that three novels written in three different languages of different countries exhibit such similarities. All these three novels are political writings. Like Marquez's, Salman's "Anglepoised" writing is a way of co-opting political and literary power. It should be noted that their brand of metafiction, especially of Marquez and Rushdie, is not "vainly narcissistic, nor does it fall into the nihilism of linguistic determinism that much 'postmodern' fiction does". Arena Srivastav has pointed out how Rushdie recognizes, as Saleem does at the end of *Midnight's Children*, that "life unlike syntax allows one more than three and at least somewhere the striking of the clock, twelve chimes, release" (463). Further she comments:

> Having been released from the syntax of the novel, the reader nevertheless is left with the unmistakable taste of pickles and the assurance that Rushdie's novels, for all their complexity and playfulness, are deeply committed "acts of love" (477).

It is interesting to compare the essays and interviews of Marquez and Rushdie. Marquez's essay on the Chilean coup, for instance, deals with Latin America. Rushdie's "The Empire Writes Back with a Vengeance" discloses his attempts at 'chutnification' of the English language and its 'great tradition' of novel. In his writings recurring acts of reader estrangement serve a political end. Marquez as well as Rushdie wants the reader question his/her own ideological assumptions about literature, language and culture.

As Saleem thinks of writing a novel, like Oskar Matzerath at the outset of *The Tin Drum*, he opens it as a family chronicle; but it becomes a historical history of the decolonized nations namely India and Pakistan. Saleem wrestles with a chronological view of the 'whitened' history from the European rule to the present one in the Indian subcontinent. He meddles with events and misremembers dates. Like Marquez, Salman Rushdie also believes that history is a method of fictionalizing experience as is biography or autobiography. For him reality and truth are not, as explained before, ascertainable. He explains it with the example of images on the TV screen (p. 211). Through Saleem's narrative, which seems to acquire autobiographical overtones, Rushdie wants to put the distorted imperialist view of Indian history straight.

One of the important features of Rushdie's cyclic narrative technique is its self-reflexivity and playfulness which is less Western but Oriental. This aspect of this fiction has not been adequately elucidated by the Western critics who give undue importance to Rushdie's religious and political satires and parodies. The cyclic and playful narrative tradition of the *Arabian Nights* and of Gunadhya's winding stories within fiction have attributed complexity and heterogeneity to his postcolonial novel. As colonized one Saleem tries to come to terms with his personal and national histories. Both the author and his protagonist explore notions of history, time, autobiography, writer and the act of creative writing itself. In *One Hundred Years of Solitude* the omniscient narrator changes roles and occasionally disguises. Rushdie's first person narrative or Saleem's 'self-writing' defines the protagonist's relation to Indian history to which he is mysteriously 'handcuffed' (3) and fathered by 'History as She is Writ'. By adopting the mode of auto writing Saleem wants to defend himself and his country from decay and death. Saleem is one of India's 'Midnight Children', and he is India, map, radio, and even the instigator of language riots. He claims that the whole history is writ on his skin as he was born at midnight on the 15th of August. In this way Rushdie attempts to reach beyond the boundaries of the historical novel.

Like Marquez's use of the word 'shit' for literature, Rushdie's Padma asks, "What is so precious to need all this writing-shiting?" Saleem defies the classification of his writing into generic repertory. Very often he parades the intertextuality of film-script writing by repeating the term 'close up': or exhibiting dates like placards. At one place he tells us how Padma was bullying him "back into the world of linear narratives, the universe of what-happened next" because his writing was "Anglepoise-lit writing" (38). He calls it a story, autobiography, memoirs and what not. He claims that it is his special blend. It is the "pickling process". There is "the feasibility of chutnification of history" (548). For this kind of chutnification he makes use of songs (106, 228), Hindi-Urdu words and phrases in the original freely. He does not translate them into English. Syed Amanuddin has complimented Rushdie in the concluding paragraph of his article as follows:

> Although he (Rushdie) told his interviewer that there is sufficient rich material for about twenty novels *on* India, Rushdie is now planning works of fiction on his experience in England. One hopes that he will continue to explore concerns and interests of Third World nations ....A novel such as *Midnight's Children* can be written only once in an author's lifetime, however. It compresses history, legends, myths, gossip, and folklore into some 550 pages. By the process of 'pickling' these experiences in words, Rushdie has caved for himself a permanent place in South Asian and world literature in English (45).

V

The foregoing discussion has made it clear that only such novels, which boldly confront the question of what has happened during as well as after the colonial period, seem really postcolonial. Much postcolonial fiction is a searching, critical inquiry into new society that has evolved after the colonial contacts. The writers are conscious of their role as emerging Third World artists. The postcoloniality of their writing will not be counted by their easy name-calling and / or self-congratulatory propaganda. For instance, Mascarenhas's novel shows that as early as 1955, six years before the independence of Goa, a new regime was taking over through the freedom struggle which was opposed by the Goan landlords. Mascarenhas's nationalist use of the fictional discourse as an 'anticolonial weapon' is likely to be considered as propagandist, and to some extent Peter Nazareth hints at this point at the end of his article. Mascarenhas's colonial experience was full of violence; and his patriotism allows him to interpret and represent reality in nationalistic terms. Consequently, he is least conscious of the self-division and neocolonialism which would be continued by the Goan comprador class itself. This other side of the coin is exposed by Naipaul. He is dismissive of the post-independence politics of the Brown. Whereas Mascarenhas writes of the disturbed rhythms of the peasant life in the colonial period, Naipaul's Mr. Biswas is an uprooted person searching for his roots. He does not set out in search of the ancestral home in India, but wants to build one of his own in West Indian island. Naipaul falls short, like Mascarenhas, in exploiting the theory of the creole continuum. Their language is not subversive. They are not conscious of, in terms of Bill Ashcroft and others (1989:40), re-placing language: textual strategies in post-colonial writing.

To be brief, *Mr. Biswas* provides the model of hybridity and syncreticity. These samples exhibit the nature of postcolonial societies in different countries and the types of hybridization their various cultures have produced. New theories in postcolonial criticism have proceeded from these considerations; and Bill Ashcroft and others (34) commenting on Homi Bhabha's reading of Naipaul's novel argue:

> Homi Bhabha has noted the collusion between narrative mode, history, and realist mimetic readings of texts. Taking V. S. Naipaul's *A House for Mr. Biswas* as his example, Bhabha demonstrates the dangers of the way in which readings of postcolonial works as socially and historically mimetic foster their reabsorption into an English tradition, domesticating their radicalism by ignoring the important colonial disruptions to the 'English' surface of the text (Bhabha 1994a).

To the other end, Achebe's *Things Fall Apart* provides the model of the postcolonial African 'black writing.' Its African characteristics are important for comparing and contrasting it with that from Caribbean and Afro-American diaspora. The race-centred critique of Achebe's writing has been influential in the post-colonial discourse. The concept of Negritude asserted qualities of Black culture and identity, and Achebe's fiction demonstrates African view of time space relationship, ethics and aesthetics.

We have juxtaposed *One Hundred Years of Solitude* with *Midnight's Children* in order to point out how the labels such as post-colonial, post- modern and post-structuralist are inconvenient. These descriptive terms cover a wide range of overlapping litera·y and cultural practices. Rushdie's postcolonial fictional text shows how the postmodernist tendencies of dismantling assumptions about language and textuality can find echoes in *Midnight's Children.* Its intertextuality with its precursors, namely, *One Hundred Years of Solitude* and *The Tin Drum* also discloses how postmodern and postcolonial fictional discourses are 'increasingly interactive and mutually influential'. Bill Ashcroft and others have given the rules of 'postcoloniality' (167). According to them, the post-colonial discourse means "to invoke certain ways of thinking about language, about truth, about power, and about the interrelationship between all three." They have explained how the postcolonial writing has not only "radically questioned easy assumptions about the characteristics of the genres but also extended the 'boundaries' of a genre" (181-82). They point out that Rushdie has altered the idea of narrative structure by reproducing the traditional techniques of the Indian oral narrative tradition. Finally they concludes:

> Postcotonial texts like *Midnight's Children* (or Amos Tutuota's *The Palm-wine Drunkard* three decades earlier) have been subjected to a schizophrenic form of critical dismissal. On the one hand, contemporary nationalist critics dismissed the text because in their view they only reproduced in translated or 'plagiarised' form the traditional techniques of narration and so failed the test of 'authenticity' on the other hand, European critics, out of ignorance, failed entirely to record the debt of these texts to African and Indian traditional forms. What neither position did was to engage with the text as an extreme example of that hybridity which is the primary characteristic of all postcolonial texts, whatever their source (184-85).

Thus the comparative critique of the postcolonial fiction provides new insight in rereading of 'canonical' texts in the light of postcolonial discursive-practices. That is not only of great help in judging 'literariness' of the text, but also in evaluating its true 'postcoloniality'.

NOTES

1. A number-of critics from the settler as well as non-settler colonies such as Linda Hutcheon (1989), Edward Said, Albert Memmi Kwame Appiah, Djelal Kadir (1995), Gsyatri Spivak and Homi Bhabha; Bill Ashcroft, Helen Tiffin and Gareth Griffiths (eds. *The Post-colonial Studies: Reader* 1995) and several other have theorised 'post-colonialism; but no Indian theorist's name (except Aijaz Ahmad) appears in this list. Perhaps the Indian 'comprador' upper caste intelligentsia is still under the spell of modernism which is an incarnation of colonialism and fascism.

   Linda Hutcheon, in 'introduction' to *PMLA*: Special topic Colonialism and the Postcolonial Condition 110: 1 (Jan. 1995, 7-12), has explained 'complexities' that are associated with the use of the term 'postcolonial' in different contexts.

   Bill Ashcroft and others, in 'introduction' to their edited collection of critical essays: *The Post-colonial Studies: Reader* (1995, 117) Part IV, have given a brief comparative analysis of two terms: 'postcolonial' and 'postmodernism'. Although these are very overlapping concepts as projects of "the deconstruction of the centralised, logocentric master narratives of European cultures", their claims upon experience are different. According to these editors,

   > . Postcolonialism is not simply a kind of 'postmodern with politics' sustained attention to the imperial process in colonial and neo-colonial societies, and an examination of the strategies to subvert the actual material and discursive effects of the process (117)

   The hybridity of the Indian post-colonial writing has been hardly examined with such "attention to the imperial process", because the majority of the Indian writers in English are great grandsons-daughters of Lord Babbington Macaulay.

2. Lambert Mascarenhas's *Sorrowing Lies My Land* (1955 rpt. 1970) has been totally ignored by the Indian literary criticism in English. Although it was first published in British 'Bombay' and prescribed for the post-graduate curriculum by the Bombay University Board of Studies in English only once, it is a forgotten classic. A comparative perspective on the Indian 'regional' or rural novels in English reveals that it is not only an 'anticolonial weapon', but also the unique first realistic novel of peasant life in the whole corpus of Indo-Anglian fiction.

6

Images of *King Lear* in Marathi

The present paper proposes to discuss some changing images of *King Lear* in India with special references to its translations, adaptations and other offshoots in Marathi, the regional language of Maharashtra State. *Lear* was introduced to the 'natives' mainly through English textbooks by the British, but it was never performed on the Bombay stage in the eighteenth and nineteenth centuries.[1] Although it has given rise to fewer translations and adaptations than other great tragedies of Shakespeare,[2] innumerable allusions to it can be traced in Marathi literature. For instance, Madhav Julian,[3] a romantic poet, at the critical moment in his life, cited the following speech of mad Lear.

> The Userer hangs the cozener
> ... ...
> Arm it in rags, a pigmy's straw doth pierce it.
>
> *King Lear, IV vi*

Madhavrao Patwardhan saw his personal experience reflected in the image of mad Lear facing the storm. Thus the theme of injustice and ingratitude, the history of Lear's spiritual progress, and a number of scenes and characters of the Lear folklore have attracted Indian readers from time to time. Such images as Lear bound to 'the wheel of fire'. Cordelia's sacrifice, Kent's loyalty, Gloucester's blindness, the fool's philosophical speeches which resemble Vidushaka's commentary in Sanskrit drama, and the oft-quoted lines: 'As files to wanton boys', 'I am bound to the wheel of fire' and a number of metaphors and images have found roots in Indian soil. For the purpose of the present discussion we choose the 'mental images' created by *Lear* and their focus on what happens in the Marathi playwrights' mind (effect). We will be examining the versions of *King Lear* in Marathi drama only; and for this purpose, we concentrate on an image as defined by Miss Downey. She says, "The image must not be conceived as: a material copy or thing but merely as the content of thought in which attention is centred on sensory quality of some sort."[4]

Out of five Marathi versions of *Lear*, the earliest one, *Atipeedcharit Natak,*[5] (a drama of one who suffers most), was made by Moro Shankar Ranade (1850-1899), who published it in his *Natyakatharnv* (monthly) in 1881. It was reprinted in book form but never staged. This prose adaptation bears a strong evidence of a stage of the confluence of Sanskrit and English drama in Marathi. From these two different dramatic traditions representing different cultural products of different social groups, we can analyse the process of the transfer of Western literary value to Indian cultural contexts. Ranade's introduction to the second edition of *Atipeedcharit* illustrates the manner in which the English educated Hindu Brahman received *Lear*. The tragic end of the original, which is convincing to Coleridge, Schlegel, and Gervinus, is according to Ranade not convincing, or believable at all.[6] Ranade's moralistic point of view deeply grounded in Indian philosophical and religious thought does not accept *Lear* wholly because it is farthest from Sanskrit drama in its philosophical content. According to him, the presentation of the scene in which Atipeed (Leer) carries the dead body of Mragankamala (Cordelia) to the tent of Khaladarshana (Duke of Albany) may be convincing and proper in view of *rasa* but it is improbable. It is not known what happens to the fool afterwards (Intr. 8, 9). Such observations made by Ranade show his lack of understanding as well as his inability in integrating the elements from European and Indian drama. However, with 'poetic justice' and the happy ending of his version in view, he made the following changes in the original. It seems he used Nahum Tate's altered text for adaptation. There are 352 altered "prompt copies" of *King Lear*.

The names of characters, viz. Atipeed (Lear), Mragankarnala (Cordelia), Chandranana (Regan), Shashikala (Goneril), Khaladarshanrao (Duke of Albany), Sudarshanrao (Duke of Cornwall), Sukhapeedraj (Duke of Burgandy), Marutsen (Kent), Chandwarma (Gloucester) etc., bear allegorical overtones which evoke ethical and religious associations. The Indian setting at Ṣindhudesh, Udasdurg, Karshri Bandar birngs medieval local colour to it. However, the conversion of the farmhouse in the original into a temple presents an idealised picture of the Indian life which suits the adapter's purpose but distorts the thematic structure of the original. The aims of the two civilizations are different and thus devise different images in which each finds satisfaction. The synthesis of the two cultures at this early stage of Marathi drama resulted in a number of artificial and comic situations. For example, in the following dialogues we are told that Goneril and Regan put 'kumkum' (mark with red powder on forehead) on each other's forehead and take leave of each other:

Chandra- *tai chalalis? ag kon ahe ga tikade ?*
Kunkawacha karanda gheoon ye,
Shasi- *tai, ag he nighaichya weli kasale kunku ani*
kasale kay ghuen basali ahes? Jate mi.
Chandra- *ashi kaypan tai agadich utawel kapave?*
bayakanche soubhagya te!

Atipeedcharit III. viii. p. 74.

Consider this Indianized scene in which ladies perform the rite of putting "kumkum" on each other's forehead and Lear chews beetle leaves, in scene VIII of Act IV of *Atipeed.* Here Marutsen embraces and kisses Chandranana *(Antipeed, 102).* Kamalini, a maidservant, is an innovation to serve the melodramatic purpose. Lear's age is reduced from 80 to 60 and he is made to marry thrice for the sake of having a son to inherit his kingdom. *Antipeed* tells us that his wives, namely, Pramati, Wasumati, and Sumati, gave birth to Shashikala, Chandranana and Mragankamala, respectively. They died earlier and don't appear in the play. (It is interesting to note that Ranade provided three wives for Lear even before Gordon Bottomley

(1874-1948) wrote his *Lear's Wife*). We get the picture of a typical Sanskrit tragicomedy in *Antipeed* presenting a universe very unlike that of the original.

Regarding the plot structure, Ranade made a number of alterations in the original in order to make the story end happily with a moral note that truth conquers at the end. Moreover, he simplified the complex texture of the original in such a manner that his version became a play of intrigues befitting the tradition of tragicomedy in Sanskrit drama. According to him, Shakespeare's plot of *Lear* was incomplete, imperfect and inconvincing, so he decided to amend it in a proper way (Intr. 8-9). Ranade has retained the opening of the original in his version but he makes Atipeed wander in the forest and finally Atipeed is taken to Mragankamala, who looks after him. Then both pass through a number of ordeals and are saved in the end. On the other hand, Regan and Goneril are punished for their deliberate hypocriacy and infidelity and die of their own contrivances. In order to present such a moral picture Ranade revised the fifth Act of the original. Three scenes in the original are extended to five. According to him, Shakespeare's Fool and Kent are inactive and the Duke of France should be given equal prominence with the two other sons-in-law. So he brings him back in the fifth Act to rescue his wife and father-in-law from prison by intercepting Edmund's letter ordering Lear's and Cordelia's death. The Fool and Kent help him in this rescue operation. Rajwahan and Mragankamala come to power, virtue is rewarded and the Fool speaks the ending lines of *Atipeedcharit Natak*. H. H. Wilson's observation should be noted here. He comments:

> The absence of tragic catastrophe in the Hindu dramas is not merely an unconscious omission; such catastrophe is prohibited by a positive rule, and the death of either the hero or the heroine is never to be announced.... The excepted topics of a serious nature are, hostile calamity; whilst those of a less grave, or comic character, are biting, scratching, kissing, eating, sleeping, the bath, inuction, and the marriage ceremony.[7]

Atipeed, sandwiched between two great traditions of drama, violated these precepts of the classical drama of India and retained both the terrible scene of the blinding Gloucester and that of the romantic embracing and kissing by Edmund in *Atipeed.* And yet Ranade did not dare introduce Cordelia and Edgar's love affair as Nahum Tate did in his version.

Atipeed raises a question of the medium for adequate and appropriate communication. The contextual and other situational features of play's setting appear to require compatible linguistic resources. Language needs to be consistent with the linguistic sociocultural features to such settings.[8] Here the vernacular, which was in the earlier stages of cross-fertilization falls short in recapturing the poetry of the original. It is full of Sanskritized and anglicized words which make it artificial. When Marathi came into contact with the English language, variation in spoken as well as written Marathi posed a number of problems for the first generation of English-educated writers. Caste, professional, dialect and subsystematic varieties which were impervious to the formation of period style had to be eliminated.[9]

Ranade solved this problem by employing various devices for transferring words, expressions, form of address, songs, praise names, etc. He translated the songs of the original in three dialects, viz, Hindi, Kachi and Marathi:

Madhu *aya ji betal, aya ji betal*
a chol hamal ji kal deta hai hal ||*dhru*||
Atipeed iii. iv. p.65.

This song sung by Madhukar (Edgar) has no source in the original. Urdu and Parsi adaptations of Shakespeare's plays were popular in those days and must have influenced Marathi drama.

For his free translation of the Fool's songs Ranade has used metres such as Abhang, Ballad, Saki, Dindi, Pad, etc. *(Atipeed* p. 26, 27, 28, 29).

Khushamaskarya (the Fool), at the close of *Atipeed,* sings a comic song which has no source in the original text:

yachya galybhowati dori bandhuniya nothya jori,
apuliya samori, phasi dhyavya agodari,
vedya pira, wat mazi paha jara.

Atipeed V.v.

(Let us tie the rope around their neck: Goneril, Regan and Edmund who are dead and kill them in front of us quickly, wait madman, wait and see.)

Thus, *Atipeed* becomes a dance and drama adapted to Sanskrit tradition.

Marathi proverbs and idioms used in this version give it a local colour. It should be noted here that Marathi culture differs both from Panjabi culture and Bengali culture. Although there is a unity of Hindu culture this diversity should not be lost sight of. So Marathi versions of *King Lear* are bound to differ from those which are made in Tamil, Kannada, Bengali, or any other Indian language. It is obvious indicator of native language speech. Since most of them are not translation equivalents, they very often add to or distort the original. A few examples are:

Maru : *sen bhuiwar padale asata te matila gheunach utate. (If the dung falls on the ground it picks up dust with it)*

Atipeed, I. iii. p. 13.

Sashi : *mi ikudachi sarva vyawasthe karate, anakhi gharat*
"Ram Hari ! Ram Hari !" karit bassayala chipalya dete...
(I shall arrange everything here, and give you cymbals to sit in the house lazily saying "Ram Hari! Ram Hari")

Atipeed. IV. ii. p. 80.

Maru : *ya weli he bhayankar Yampash mazya galyabhowati padu lagale ahet.*
(At this time my neck is being caught in the noose of Yama).

Atipeed. V, v. p. 120.

The use of figurative expressions, imagery, myths is also characteristic of Hindu culture. The importance of the linguistic dimension as an aspect of technique in drama is ignored by Ranade. The following rhetorical speech illustrates the point:

> Ati - *he mazya priyakanykano? he shur sardarano!*
> *tasech amache*
> *priya mandalik Khaldarshan aarii Sudarshano !*
> *tumhi sarvajan maze bhasan laxapurvak aika ! ya*
> *Sindhudeshwar aj chalisvarshe paryant mi*
> *aikchhatri*
> *rajya kele? nana prakarachya rajvilasancha upabhog*
> *ghetala va yathas' astra, yathanyara prajapalenhi*
> *kele!*
>
> *Atipeed* I. i. p. 2.

Omission of significant sentences and idioms of the original such as "And laugh at gilded butterflies", "and take upon us the mystery of things. As if we were god's spies", and modification or expansion of some original English lines into many Marathi sentences spoils the poetic texture of the original. For example: 'And tell old tales': *mi tula tuzya lahanpanachi aikck gost athaun sangat jain, ani tuhi tula athawatil tya gosthi mala sang*: "Men must endure/there going hence, even as their coming hither: Ripeness is all." "ha sansar ahe yatale barewait bhog konas sutale ahet .... nasibapudhe konachi dhav chalat nahi."

On the whole, Ranade's prose adaptation projects a completely altered image of *Lear so* that it becomes closer to a typical Sanskrit tragicomedy which aims at spiritual equilibrium. Vinda Karandikar, whose statement echoes Shaw's comment on adapters of Shakespeare, has rightly pointed out that in spite of Ranade's sincerity and missionary zeal in introducing *Lear* into Marathi for the first time, we should say that he set a bad trend of 'improving upon "Shakespeare".[10]

II

"Kanyaparikshan" (a test of daughters), another *Lear* adaptation by G. C. Gore, was staged by Chittakarshak Natak Mandali in Pune in 1913-14. Karandikar refers to a third one entitled *Vikarvihar* (the play of vices) by L. N. Joshi. Both these versions were not published, hence are not discussed here. They are mentioned only to point out that *Lear* occupied Marathi dramatists in the beginning of the twentieth century. Moreover, Pralhad Keshav Atre, who staged *Samratsinh* (The Emperor Lion) a prose adaptation of *Lear,* in 1968, had seen *Kanyaparikshan* (The Test of Daughters) being performed in Poona. Atre tells us in his preface to his version that he liked *Atipeedcharit* but found its happy end disappointing. This remarkable sibling relationship is evident in his adaptation. A close study of the *Lear* adaptations in Marathi reveals the Oedipal strategies by which strong writers deny their relation to their major precursors.

As early as 1929, C.J. Sisson had stated, "The literary influence of Shakespeare in India offers but a mediocre interest for the growth of vernacular literature, upon which such an influence might be exercised, has been understood to be the classical literature in Sanskrit, Persian, and Arabic and for the last hundred years English also."[11]

As our contact with the English language and literature deepened, playwrights felt that Marathi needed a standard version of *Lear*. After a wide gap of 87 years the second version of *Lear* was staged in Bombay in 1968. Meanwhile commercial, political and other existential encounters between East and West had increased. Pralhad Keshav Atre, who adapted *Lear,* had travelled in England. It was expected that his *Samratsinh* (The Emperor Lion) would project the complex vision and poetry of the original in Marathi theatre. Alas! it did not prove that learning and scholarship regarding *Lear* had moved forward in Marathi. Admittedly, Atre grafted his version on Ranade's *Atipeed.* Both Atre and Ranade label their works as translations, but they are pose adaptations thrice removed from the original. Neither playwright furnished any information concerning the *Lear* text which they used for their versions. It appears from their introductions to their works that they read some contemporary Shakespeare criticism and yet failed in rendering *Lear* faithfully. The Europeans had butchered Shakespeare's plays already.

Innumerable arguments can be made for and against their failures. The change of names of dramatis personae which Atre made in his *Samratsinh* shows the Indian playwright's love for abstractions and personifications. He reduced the number of characters to 15 and did not revive Ranade's innovations of Kamalini. Raja (Lear), Meghnad (Kent), Ugrasen (Gloucester), Bujang (Edmund), Soudamini (Goneril), Meghmala (Cordelia), Chandralekha (Regan), Kalingraj (Duke of Burgandy), Chitrasen (Edgar), Sourastraraj (Duke of France), Jambuk (Oswald), Widushak (Fool) are converted superficially to Indian culture.

Although Atre made use of Ranade's version, he did not make as many alterations as Ranade did. According to Atre, two scenes in the original, i.e., Gloucester's inability to recognize Edgar's forged letter (i, ii.) and Edgar taking Gloucester to the cliff (IV, vi), are unbelievable and improbable. One major change he made in the original appears at the close of Act IV, vi which shows how Shakespeare's art of preparation and skill in creating suspense is often beyond the grasp of the adapter's sentimental attitude. Here Gloucester (Ugrasen) recognizes and embraces Edgar (Chitrasena). Quite a melodramatic scene sought to win the sympathy of the Marathi audience. Atre says, "Edgar should have told his blind father who he (Edgar) was, but in the original text he does not reveal his identity. So I have corrected the *mistake* in my adaptation" (emphasis added):

> Ugrasen : *ata mala tilmatra shanka nahi. toch to. (Chitrasen yeto. tyala uddesun mothyane) Chitrasena- Chitrasen-mi olakhi tula! tuch maza Chitrasen! (tyala mithi marun tyachya tondawarun hat phirawito) mala dole nassale tari mazya ya hatana tuzya mudrewaril resha-n resha disate.*
>
> Chitrasen :*hoy Baba, mich to tumacha durdaivi Chitrasen. mala kshama kara*
>
> *Samratsinh* IV. vi. p. 71-72.

It is significant that while Ranade boldly retained Shakespeare's stage directions regarding kissing Regan

(Atipeedcharit v. i.) Atre, who adapted *Lear* for the Marathi stage, conformed to the public taste and deleted the direction in his version. Considering these few changes we should concede that Atre did not transform the plot of the original to the extent Ranade did. However, it should not pass unheeded that Atre copied sentences, paragraphs and some songs from Ranade's version: for example,

Chard: *parantu ti lajja ata chat sari sodun dhyo - vayache tharawil ahe.*

Atipeed, p. 1.

Meghanad :*pan ata matra ti laj chat sari sodun dhyavache me tharavile ahe.*

Samratsinh, p. 1.

Atre dropped a whole paragraph of about 10 sentences that follows the sentence mentioned above. Many such examples can be traced. Vidushak in Atre's version also sings a Hindi song imitating Ranade's Khushamaskarya: "puskal apane pasarakhans, duniyako par kam batana" (I-V. p. 20).

Atre dropped Ranade's Hindi song but copied the following:

ahaha kay tuzya pori
gudgud mawasha
tudtud hudhud, kariti tamasha
chal sara sosa, mukatya basun,
tya tumachya saswa, an turnhi tyanchi sun

Samratsinh ii. iv. p. 34.

gudgud mawasha, tasha tuzya pori
tudtud hudhud, kariti chatori
ata raha tumhi, mukat sosun
tyach tumchya saswa, tumhi tyanchi sun.

Atipeedcharit ii. iv. p. 48.

In short, Atre's style is highly influenced by Ranade's version. The structure of *Samratsinh is* predetermined by the original yet the thematic structure is changed due to major variations. Atre being a professional dramatist made some alterations in the fifth act of the original by dropping the complete second scene of the original. In order to make suitable adjustments he employed a popular Sanskrit stage device by making *Lear* fall down in swoon and shifting the speeches by the characters after Lear's death in the original text. In his version *Lear* then wakes up in delirium, speaks his last six lines and dies.

> Raja : *(ardhwat bhramat uthato sare chapapun mage saratat) chhe, chhe, chhe, he kay jivan ahe? Jagat kutri, manjare.*
> *undir dekhil jagatahet mag hicha swas kuthe gela? to ata kadhini parat yenar nahi kadhi nahi-kadhini nahi kadhihi nahi, are, paha, paha, tichyakade, ti haluch baghate ahe mazyakade...bale Meghanale, amhi alo tuzyamagun.*
>
> *Samratsinh* V. ii, p. 84.

This final speech by Lear is melodramatic and declamatory, thus failing to create the cathartic effect of the original. The original text ends with Edgar's speech which suggests that the order is restored after the protagonist's death. Although Atre tried to revive the tragic ending in this version, his maladjustments and reckless alteration have distorted *Lear's* image by twisting it for the sentimental effect. Atre's *Lear* represents the Indian King who lacks the vitality of the Christian Lear who is more sinned against than sinning. What S.I. Goldberg has observed as to how Christian people react to *Lear* is equally applicable to Maharashtrians. He says:

> It is not hard to see why many people find King *Lear* so unbearable that they virtually reject it.[12]

III

Although *Lear's* tragic vision is 'unbearable', a number of actors in Marathi theatre aspired to play the 'unactable' role of *Lear*.[13] It was Nana Phatak, an eminent actor, who approached V.V. Shirawadkar and requested him to adapt *Lear* for him. Shirawadkar, having a long standing theatre experience of adapting *Macbeth and Othello*, was inspired by that suggestion yet did not adapt *Lear*. Instead, he selected the stock of *Lear* and skilfully grafted Marathi scion on it. Grafting is an ancient art.[14]

Shirawadkar writes in the prefatory note to his *Natsamrat*.

> ... While thinking about it *(Lear)*, in place of the king there arose the great old *Natsamrat* (The Emperor of Actors) in my mind and haunted my imagination. I am presenting that picture for the readers and playgoers here.

Considering *Natsamrat* in terms of a pre-existing image of *Lear* in English and his word picture in Marathi versions, Shirawadkar created a fine *Lear* offshoot surpassing his Marathi predecessors. It is a Shakespearean tragedy in Marathi dealing with the family problems and tragic sufferings of an old retired actor, Appasaheb Belwalker. Conceived in response to *Lear*, *Natsamrat* develops from a more central tension than that Atre could visualise or Ranade could adapt in their versions. The flexible image of the playwright as gardener and his play as a hybrid created by the judicious bringing together of selected stock and scion fits here at almost every point. The investigation of this process of cross-fertilization leads to the following conclusions.

The structure of *Natsamrat* is pre-determined by the structure of *lear* with the exception of the subplot which is totally dropped by Shirawadkar. Both plays are entitled after the protagonists. Shirawadkar reduced the original twenty characters to a dozen. Kaveri the wife of Appasaheb, his son Nandu, his daughter-in-law Sharada, a grand daughter Thami, the farmer and his wife, are innovations. The retired actor, who divides his property, is driven out by his own son and daughter. The charge of theft is brought against him. Kaveri dies of heart attack. Appasaheb wanders on the pavements of Bombay where he meets Raja. Vithoba, the servant, who is an embodiment of Lear's fool in the dress of Vidushaka, accompanies his master. The bootpolishwala Raja, who inherits the traits of Edgar, gives shelter to the emperor of actors in the slums of Bombay. Finally, the son and daughter of Appasaheb come to take him home. Appasaheb dies of a heart attack with the last utterance of Caesar on his lips. As Shirawadkar has eliminated the Gloucester subplot from his play, *Natsamrat* becomes a domestic melodrama of an old actor. Shakespeare's handling of a most complex and intricate plot, which is triumph of symmetry and constructive skill, is wanting in its Marathi offshoot condensed in three acts. The longest period that can be allowed for the action in *Lear* is one month. *Natsamrat* covers more than twelve years.

From this outline we can judge that *Natsamrat* is not a play like *Lear* which is "an unruly chaos of strange and forbidden things where the ground rocks under our feet." *Natsamrat* is, in short, a melodramatic tragedy that has occupied the stage since 1970. We are reminded of H.W. Wells' remark in this connection. "... Thus, torture, disfigurement, purely physical discomfort, as developed to so extraordinary and shocking a degree in the great Act of *King Lear* are unthinkable in the Indian theatre."

Shirawadkar's handling of his more poetic or imaginative character, viz., Appasaheb, is particularly revealing. Shakespeare's Lear has remained alive today in large measures because of his extraordinary imaginative vitality. He produces imaginative speculations, creates illusions, and casts spell over others. Many of the subtle changes Shirawadkar made, by employing a poetic device, selecting an actor as protagonist and by drawing heavily on Shakespearean imagery, emerge out of cultural circumstances. Appasaheb cites soliloquies, poetic speeches and allusions from Shakespeare's great tragedies from time to time. The examples include:

> Mhatara : ... *Ganapatro loshini he ghadyal mazya hatat bandhale hote - Nagapurala amachya Hamletcha gauraw zala tevha (I. i. p. i. 2)*
> *...don porinchyua roopane sara jag sarpasarakha ultalyawar Raja Lear kay mhanala hotsathawatay? (uthato ani Learchya avirbhawat mhanato.)* I. i. p. 12.

Appa : *tumachya Hamlet natakaparyant sar kahi tii kam karate ahes.* (II. i. p. 42, 48, 49)

Appa : To be or not to be that is the question (II. iii. p. 66)

Raja : *an udhyacha khelach nav ahe Julius Caesar* (III. iii)

Appa : *Othello nawacha aik jangali manus asato.* (III. iii. p. 79).

Appa : *Macbeth apalya mitranche khoon padatahet* (III. ii. p. 86)

Admittedly, Shirawadkar succeeded in putting oriental content in "white form". The play won Sahitya Akademi award and its contribution to Indian drama should not be lost sight of. To borrow Ruby Cohn's words, Shakespeare's *Lear* has been "engaging creative artist in dialogue."

IV

A leading Marathi poet and Professor of English, Vinda Karandikar, published his poetic translation of *Lear* in 1974. In his *Raja Lear* he succeeded where his predecessors failed in capturing the essential meaning, the tone, even the sound of the original text. His *Raja Lear* bears strong evidence of his own creative personality, his imaginative gifts to read the *Lear* subtext, and of his views on tragedy. He invented "Chatuskhandi Kutachandra" (free verse with four feet) to convey the blank verse of the original. He discovered the true character of Shakespeare's style. Though certain ideas from Hindu culture which are an inevitable part of Marathi language invariably give local colour to his translation, he has rendered the original faithfully without changing names of places and persons.

Lear : *Kent gapp raha?*
Dragon ani tyacha krodha yanchyamadhye nako yeus. *Raja Lear*, I. i. p. 75.

Lear : *sahavya divasi ti tuzi tiraskrat path pahije walali amachya rajyawar; ho chalata. Jupiterchishapath suryashapath, he nahi kadapisuddha honar raddbatal.* I. i. p. 77.

Lear : *And on the sixth to turn thy hated back Upon our Kin gdom: if on the tenth day following. Thy banish'd trunk be found in our dominions. The moment is thy death Away? by Jupiter, This shall not be revok'd)*

In the translation Karandikar has added an oath by sun and has not translated 'thy banished...thy death'. Marathi is a time-syllabled while English is a stress-syllabled language. In order to transmit the tone of the original Karandikar has skilfully experimented with the use of Marathi words arranged in four-feet free verse.

Lear : *garja, wadalano, thobad phateparyant? kara akrosh he jalstambhano ani tumphanano, soda phootkar amache manore bhijun jai*paryant, amache pawankukkut budepaweto?

Raja Lear, III. ii. p. 127.

Lear : *Blow, winds, and crack your cheeks, rage, blow*
You cataracts and hurricanes, spout
Till you have drench'd our steeples, drown'd the cocks.

Karandikar has faithfully communicated the meaning of the original by interpreting the subtext and by employing all the resources of his language. However, his versions of the songs are more witty and less lyrical than those of his precursors. He is very close to the original in transmitting them.

Vidushak : *Jyachyajawal doke thewayala ghar asate*
tyachech
shirastran uttam samjawe.
dokyasathi ghar nasatahi
ase bhikari lagnanantar
mithimadhye uwa gheti

(*Raja Lear*, III, ii. p. 128)

Fool: *He that has a house to put's head in has a good*
Head - piece.
The God piece that will house
Before the head has any,
The head and he shall louse;
So beggars marry many.

King Lear III. ii. 30

Boris Pasternak's assertions in his 'Notes on Translations of Shakespeare's Tragedies' may be extrapolated to Karandikar's translation of *Lear*. Pasternak asserts:

> We have already said that translations are impossible because the primary fascination of the work of art lies in its uniqueness. How then can this be repeated in a translation?
>
> Translations are conceivable, because ideally they too should be works of art and, in sharing a common text, should remain on a level with the original, through their own uniqueness?

To a larger extent, Karandikar's *Raja Lear* remains on "a level with the original" and projects the images of *King Lear* faithfully for the first time in Marathi.

V

One more Shakespeare avatar, in which *Hamlet, Othello, Macbeth* and *King Lear* are transformed and blended, is Vasant Kanetkar's *Gaganbhedi* (1892). A number of similarities in themes, characters and structure can be traced between *Gaganbhedi* and the great tragedies mentioned above. Shakespearean characters in these tragedies are combined as well as simplified or trundled through new vents in *Gaganbhedi.* They move through a partly non-Shakespearean plot. K. P. Khadilkar put together Hamlet and Iago in his *Sawai Madhavrawacha Martyu* (1906). Kanetkar went a step ahead and fused four great tragedies by grafting non-Shakespearean events onto the Shakespearean frame in his three-act prose play.

Gaganbhedi depicts the life history of the capitalist's son, Vikram, who passes through four successive phases modelled on the plots of *Hamlet, Othello, Macbeth* and *Lear.* The first Act of *Gaganbhedi* presents the abridged adaptation of *Hamlet.* Lalitagauri, Vikram's mother, immediately after her husband's death (murder), marries Priyaranjandas, the manager of Shivashankar's industry. Vikram who passes through this

Hamlet-like phase in his life is quickly transformed into Othello. He marries Jai (Ophelia+Desdemona). The second Act leads us to the condensed version *of Othello* and *Macbeth.* Ambitious Vikram and Jai get Priyaranjan and Lalitagauri murdered. He is jealous of Balaraj (Horatio+Cassio) and tries to strangle Jai who becomes mad due to this shock. The third Act is built on *King Lear.* Vikram suffers at the hand of his daughter Roopali and he dies *of* heart attack.

One cannot believe Hamlet being transformed quickly into Othello or Ophelia into Lady Macbeth. Yet the playwright has transformed the roles of characters as follows:

Vikram	- Hamlet	- Othello	- Macbeth Lear
Balaraj	- Horatio	- Cassiso	- Kent
Priyaranjan	- Claudius	- Lalitagauri	- Gertrude
Jai	- Ophelia	- Desdomona	- Lady Macbeth
Dayalji	- Polonius	- Gloucester	
Roopali	- Regan	- Uday	- Duke of Albany

It is debatable question whether a dramatist should take too much liberty with Shakespeare's plays. We need not delve deep into the controversy. Here we are concerned with Lear's image as it is projected in the third Act of *Gaganbhedi.* Vikram (Lear), an acknowledged emperor of Rajendra Industrial Enterprise and the President of the Chamber of Commerce is a respectable man of 50. He suffers from blood pressure and is also a heart patient. His only daughter, Roopali (Regan), now reigns the industry; and she compels the old man to leave the palace. Vikram stays with Balaram in his farm house. Roopali makes sudden changes in business management and soon becomes a debaucher. Vikram's sufferings are thus multiplied. Jai's suicide draws his death nearer. He dies of heart attack.

Kanetkar's well made prose transformation of four great tragedies has been a commercial success in the Marathi theatre. Compared with *Natsamrat, Gaganbhedi* is a creation of craftsman. It lacks the poetic vigour and complexity of vision. We get distant echoes of Lear's speeches and yet it is wanting, in complexity of conception which brings us through the most varied language of dramatic literature. For example:

> Vikram : *ya ra va? sinh mhatara zala mhanun he pilly tyala panjarpolat thewanar mhane ....ghad vatsaiyachya poti upajate tichach nav krataghnata?*
>
> *Gaganbhedi* III. ii. p. 90-91.

In short, *Gaganbhedi* is a conventional melodrama produced with pomp but it fails to theatricalize Shakespeare's virtual translation of time into consciousness. Lear image is distorted in this collage which claims a new approach as well as modernization of Shakespeare's tragedies. In fact, this approach is superficially socio-political.

VI

This brief investigation of *Lear* adaptations, translations, and transformations in Marathi shows that the Shakespeare tradition continues in post-independence India. *Lear* has provoked criticism. Actors have consistently relished some form of *Lear* as a performance vehicle. It has infiltrated imaginative writing in Marathi. Admittedly, the truth of Jan Kott's observation is confirmed:

> Shakespeare is like the world, or life itself. Every Historical period finds in him what it is looking for and what it wants to see.

Thus, Maharashtrians saw *Lear* through different points of view and *Lear* has become the part of Indian cultural heritage handed down by the colonial past.

Notes and References

1. Kumudini Mehta, *English Drama on the Bombay Stage. In the Late Eighteenth and Nineteenth Centuries* (Bombay: University of Bombay: Ph. D. Thesis, 1960). Miss Mehta explored the dates of productions of the following tragedies of Shakespeare by English amateur and professional dramatic companies touring *Hamlet*

(1861), *Julius Caesar* (1859), *Othello* (1864), *Romeo and Juliet* (1884).

2. Lata Wasadikar, *paschyatyancha Marathi natyasrathivar prabhev* (1850-1950): *Shakespeare* {Aurangabad: Marathawada University, unpublished doctoral dissertation, 1969). Chapters II, III, and also see Arati Havaldar, *Sanskrit ani paschtya natakancha Marathi anuwad:* 1851-1965 (Pune: University of Poona, unpublished Thesis 1970), and V. P. Ginde, *Shakespearcha Marathi natakwar zalela parinam* (Kolhapur, Shivaji University) unpublished Thesis, 1970).
3. S. K. Kanetkar, *Swapnabhumi:: Madhav Julian yanche charitra* (Pure: Venus Prakashan, 1965); p. 93. Kanetkar narrates how M. B. Patwardhan had to tender his resignation to the Deccan Edn. Society due to power politics. It was on the 11th Oct. 1925 the romantic poet met Kanetkar and cited those lines. Patwardhan was a lecturer of Pharsi and Urdu in Fergusson College, Pune.
4. Downey, Quoted in *Encyclopaedia of Poetry and Poets* ed. Alex Preminger (Princeton, New Jersey, Princeton University Press, 1995). p. 363.
5. Moro Shankar Ranade, *Antipeedcharit natak* (Bombay: Induprakash Press, 1881).
6. Ibid, 'Prastavana', p. 4.
7. H. H. Wilson, *Theatre of the Hindus* (Delhi: Indological Book House, Third rept. 1971), p. 13.
8. Alex C. Johnson, 'Creative Tension in West African Drama in English: The Linguistic Dimension', *World Literature Written in English. Vol.* 24, No. 1 (1984), p. 65.
9. B. V. Nemade, *The Influence of English on Nineteenth Century Marathi Prose Style* (Aurangabad: Marathawada University. Ph. D. Thesis, 1981), p. 205.
10. Vinda Karandikar, *Raja Lear:* trans. (Shakespeare's *King Lear* ed. G. I. Duthie and Dover Wilson) Bombay: Mouj Prakashan, 1974). p. 263.
11. C. J. *Sisson, Shakespeare in India,* Shakespeare Association by Humphrey, Milford, O. U. P. (1926), p. 6.
12. S. I. Goldberg, *An Essay on King Lear* (London: Cambridge University Press, 1974), p. 7. cf. Maynerd Mack, *King Lear in Our Time* (London: Methuen and Co. Ltd. 1966). p. 3.
13. See Sarojini Vaidhya, Vasant Phatak, eds. *natawarya Nanasaheb Phatak: vyakti ani kala* (Pane: Suparna Prakashan, 1984), especially the entries in Nana's diary which demonstrate how he imitated the British actors and desired to play the role of Lear before his death, pp. 89, 98, 106, 114, 117, 151, 170. And also see Madhukar Toradmal, *Tisari Ghanta* (Pune: Majestic Prakashan,

1985), Toradmal played Vikram (Hamlet+Othello+Macbeth+Lear) *in Gaganbhedi, Maharashtra Times Diwali Purawani* 11 *Nov.* 1985, p. 11.

11. James Gibbs, 'Grafting is an Ancient Art: The relationship of African and European Elements in the Early Plays of Wole Soyinka' *World Literature Today,* vol. 24, No. 1 (1984), pp. 87-99. The recurring image of grafting and the terminology related to it are based on this article.

7

Bardicide in the Postcolonial Theatre: A Comparative Case Study

This paper examines comparatively the use of William Shakespeare's plays in two post-colonial theatres of different countries and cultures. The use of the word 'bardicide' in its title ironically hints at Richard Levin's (1990, 491-94) critical essay entitled "The Poetics and Politics of Bardicide" which satirizes the current trends in Shakespeare criticism. My concern here, however, is not with those "new critical discourses currently circulating around recirculating Shakespeare's dramatic texts"; but with the measure and madness involved in the appropriation of them in two different languages, and the cultural significance of that theatrical reception.

A study (1993 a, 290-98) of Shakespeare's influence on Marathi drama reveals that almost all Shakespeare versions/offshoots were made by the English educated Brahman playwrights who belong to the minority culture group that consists of 3.5 per cent of the total population in India. Consequently, such a caste conditioned reception of the Bard exhibits its own limitations, and can hardly be considered a representative national or cultural appropriation of his texts. So I have termed this process of his reception in Marathi as a "sacrificial bardicide" for not only perpetuating the higher caste image through the bard's dramatic texts, but also for the commercial "profits" and political gains. It is through these distorted versions that the tales of Shakespeare have penetrated the native drama and other genres. These Indian imitators have never tried to subvert the bard's texts as some of the Black and West Indian playwrights have struggled to reverse the roles. Aparna Dharwadkar (I995 a, 4-21; b, 43-47), in her comparative study of the use of the European dramatic texts by the Indian—especially Marathi and Kannada — and African-post-colonial playwrights, has commented on "both the *antinational* and *intercultural* nature of this textual exchange,'" and also pointed out the significance of the role played "by civilized, upper-caste, domesticated spectators" (a 19) in the reception of such hybrids. Her observation that these alien texts "continue to articulate in post-colonial writing and generate antinationalist rather than anti-colonial dramatic texts" is more applicable to the Marathi versions of Shakespeare's plays. They are practised through, not against the Shakespearean canon.

Therefore, "outrage against the bard" committed in the western world is quite different from the ritualistic reception of his plays into the Oriental culture. We have some glimpses of his reception in the First World theatre, "reflecting at the same time changing attitudes towards his works" (see Draudt 1993, 102; Habicht 1989, 111; Cohn 1976; O' Connor 1979). However, the problematics of transferring his texts to the post-colonial theatres involves several oppositional tensions. What the theorists argue about "the act of writing texts of any kind in post-colonial areas" needs to be modified. For instance, this act of writing, according to Bill Ashcroft and others (1989-29), is "subject to the political, imaginative and social control involved in the relationship between coloniser and colonized," and such writing is syncretic, regardless of language of composition. But the cultural contexts and theatrical hierarchies in Indian culture display more complex internal oppositional tensions. This has made all the difference in use of Shakespeare versions in Indian theatres. Even today, as it is clear from many post-colonial Marathi versions, we may have an inferiority complex towards developed Europe, whose symbol may be Shakespeare. Or some of us use him in order to impose the internalized superiority through Shakespeare texts upon the others among us. Moreover, the Shakespeare reception has something to do with the Indian educational system which is more English than the English one, and the authorial confessions show that the bard was never used for radical purposes but conservative and aristocratic.

I would, therefore, like to examine those assumptions and problems first in the poetic realm and then in the cultural, political, and for this purpose, I focus on only two sample texts, namely Vasant Kanetkar's *Gaganbhedi* (1982) and Derek Walcott's A *Branch* of *the Blue Nile* (1985), that provide contrasting illustrations of these practices in their most highly developed forms. Let us also consider the first as a "weak" intentionalist imitation contaminated by the indigenous cultural politics as well as commercial theatre's demands, and the latter a better counterdramatic discourse. The examples were not selected on the basis of their high or low dramatic qualities but at random from the available corpus of the versions of Shakespeare's plays. It was difficult to get a few versions from the alien post-colonial countries, Although these are two samples form the previous decade.. I believe that the conclusions would apply to other terrains where these practices are appearing, for Shakespeare is not the only "author" to suffer this fate.

It is true that Shakespearian dramatic patterns were largely responsible for the "modernization" of Indian drama and its history of the latter half of the nineteenth century was named after him. The tradition of imperialistic, to borrow Arthur Y. Stavisky's terms (1969, front flap) "gush and adulation" of the bard developed in India. C. J. Sisson (1926, 7) declared from Bombay:

> There is but one country in the world, to the best of my knowledge, except possibly Germany, where the plays of Shakespeare have of recent times formed the safest and surest attraction to the indiscriminate masses who attended popular theatres, where the properties of a theatre *could* count on a profit on *a* Shakespeare production .... (7)

Of course, Sisson was exaggerating the point and what he describes as "the indiscriminate masses" was, in Kwame Appiah's harsh words, "the comprador intelligentsia" which consisted of less than point five (0.5%) per cent of the total illiterate masses at that time. Similar "adulation" of the bard can be noticed in the books and reviews published after the independence in India, and *Gaganbhedi* (piercing the firmament) is not an exception to this bardolatory. However, a few young scholars (Niranjan 1993, 139-50; Patil 1993 a) have been trying to contest the concepts such as "modern" and "culture" in the post-colonial theatre in India. Yet we have neither explored what Jonathan Baldo (1995, 112) calls "exporting oblivion" nor the aesthetics of mataplagiarism expounded by Ellen MaCracken (1991,107) and Marilyn Randall (1991, 225). Furthermore Linda Hutcheon's (1986, 229) axiom that intertextuality is as much a hermeneutic concept as it is a formalist one in which the reader plays an important role as the author needs to be applied to the Shakespeare-offshoots in India.

II

In view of the above statements two sample texts are juxtaposed in order to explicate socio-political, cultural or in Michael Escheruo's (1978, 11) terms "the exo-cultural phenomenon" and heteroglotic features of the post-colonial appropriations of Shakespeare's texts. Kanetkar inherits not only the rich indigenous but also the Eurocentric traditions of drama. On the contrary, Walcott belongs to the Trinidadian group of, in V.S. Naipaul's words, "mimic men" who have lost their indigenous dramaturgy. The first had to wrestle with his predecessors who translated or adapted the bards texts; and the latter to write something new in the language and the tradition to which Shakespeare belonged. A close look at the paratexts of *Gaganbhedi* discloses how this collage of *Hamlet, Macbeth, Othello* and *King Lear* in Marathi has been shaped by, what Escheruo describes as, "the exo-cultural stereotype" i.*e.* a culture conditioned imagination of both author and audience. In fact, the history of the bard's reception in Marathi begins with the literal translation of *Othello* (1868) by Mahadevshastri Kolhatkar and its performances by the Ichalkaranjikar drama troupe. Later on these tragedies were translated, plagiarized, adapted or imitated by a number of writers. There are more than one hundred published versions of Shakespeare's plays in Marathi. None of them parodies the bard's text as Walcott does. The undetected intertextuality of

Shakespeare's texts in the modern Marathi drama is a different topic for the further research. Here we are concerned with the exploration of Kanetkar's awareness of this tradition and his use/ misuse of Shakespeare's four great tragedies.

Kanetkar's 'preface' and the publisher's 'note' are the important poetological documents which establish the continuity of the tradition of Shakespeare worship in Marathi. But they do not show any awareness of the Marathi collages of Shakespeare's great tragedies. This is a fine example of, in Harold Bloom's terms, "the anxiety of influence". *Gaganbhedi* exhibits how Kanetkar had to fight not only with the dead imitators of Shakespeare in Marathi, but also with the contemporary ones. Among the dead Krashnaji Prabhakar Khadilkar was the strong rival. His *Sawai Madhavrao Yancha Mratyu* (1896) — the death of Sawai Madhavrao — appeared in the second phase of Shakespeare's reception after V.J. Kirtane's *Thorale Madhavrao Peshwe* (1861) — Madhavrao Peshwa the elder, — the first historical tragedy in Marathi. Both of them followed Shakespeare's model, but the latter one in the chronological order has its own place in the history of intertextual configuration of Shakespeare's tragedies in Marathi. *Sawai Madhavrao* was the first collage of *Hamlet* and *Othello* inspired by the popular versions of those tragedies in Marathi (see Patil (1993 a, 20611). The use or abuse of history for the collage based on the bard's models was not a novel attempt at that time. A number of plays, which used Shakespearian patterns, were based on the history of Marathas in the nineteenth century. Kanetkar himself had employed the Shakespearian technique in his historical plays before he wrote *Gaganbhedi*. In fact, he has been counting "on a profit on a Shakespeare production" from the beginning of his dramatic career. What led him to 'industrialize' the bard's four tragedies into one prose play?

Perhaps Kanetkar's ambition to write a successful tragedy was stirred by the grand success of V.V. Shirawadkar's *Natsamrat* (1972) — the emperor of actors-based on *King Lear*. It is the haunting problem of the stability of the tragic dramatic genres that has led many Indian dramatists ultimately to the poor melodramas. Tragedy has never enjoyed a good literary fortune in our culture. In a way *Gaganbhedi* is the product of Kanetkar's sibling relationship with Shirawadkar. I have attempted a comparative statement on *Natsamrat* (1986, 11-31). Both the writers belong not only to the same city but also the same subculture group. Both are known for the extreme Shakespeare-worship. The Fanonian critics would be surprised by such a blind adulation and extreme submissiveness which pervades their confessions and statements.

Kanetkar's 'devotion' to the bard is exhibited in abundance from the front to the back of the jacket cover of his play. The page reserved for the dedication displays the sketch of "Shakespeare's head", and the play is dedicated to "the glorious genius of universally worshipped William Shakespeare". His "preface" to the play discloses how he liked the bard's four great tragedies. and considers himself to be the *bhakta* (devotee) of the guru Shakespeare. As a student he was fascinated by these tragedies and believes that Hamlet, Macbeth, Othello and Lear are very "great characters". Furthermore, according to him, these characters in sequence represent four basic "phases" (preface, n.p.) in the mental development of any person. So he thought of compressing Shakespeare's four tragic heroes into one protagonist of his *Gaganbhedi.* This kind of Indianization of the bard's tragic hero does not fit into the patterns of Western metaphysics of tragedy. Although he claims that his play is "born of the Indian soil", we do neither find the indepth analysis of these four imaginary stages in one man's life nor any use of the indigenous- intertextuality of various dramatic genres in it. He has tried to justify the title of his play by stating that Shakespeare's tragic heroes are sky high and they pierce the firmament; and they die! what a great mind is there overthrown: But the dramatic text itself falls short in justifying his claims. As I have pointed out before, the Marathi playwrights had grafted the bard's tragedies on the indigenous Maratha history, and Kanetkar had mastered the technique of commercial drama. He wanted to depict the life of an industrialist which remained unexplored in the Marathi Shakespeare theatre industry. Shirawadkar had made the retired actor divide his property like King Lear and constructed the tragedy in the previous decade. But Shakespeare's plays were not modernised till that decade by introducing the family drama of an industrialist in the Marathi theatre. Moreover, the collage of four great tragedies of Shakespeare was an innovation for the craftsman like Kanetkar.

Not only the newspaper advertisements and placards but the publisher's "mujara" (salutation), which precedes the author's "preface", also reveals several features of the bardolatry in the commercial theatre. He proudly claims that Kanetkar has "broken the record" by not only getting his play produced and performed at Shakespeare's birthplace but also by releasing its printed copy at Stratford-upon-Avon.[2] This can be interpreted as an act of commercialization of the bard for the intercultural literary hegemony or as a mark of colonial heritage of the bourgeois class. According to the publisher, it is a great "victory" in the history of Marathi drama. It is interesting to note that the name of the tragic protagonist is Vikram that means great score or great victory. Kanetkar, who has written more than two and half dozen plays, and the publisher, who is known for publishing plays, have acknowledged the debts of the renowned actor (ex) professor of English and playwright Madhaukar Toradmal in writing this play. But they have not mentioned whether it was co-authored also. Toradmal has a different story to tell about the process of the modification of the stage version of *Gaganbhedi*.

With the help of Kanetkar's "preface" one can easily reconstruct the outline of his play. It shows how 'the tales from Shakespeare' have significant after life in the memory of the English educated Indians: and how they are used without subversion for creating another dramatic text. Kanetkar himself has explained his creative process in the "preface". He frankly admits that his thirty plays are more or less influenced by Shakespeare's texts. He wanted to repay "this debt by writing *Gaganbhedi*". He wanted to present four tendencies or states of mind, which are symbolically represented by Hamlet, Macbeth, Othello and Lear in one lonely man. He finally arrived at a formula that the protagonist was ruined by his mother, wife and his daughter step by step. Consequently he conceived the plot which logically incorporated the select events and characters from the bard's tragedies. His protagonist Vikram (Hamlet) hails from the author's own subculture group of Brahmans. Vikram's father became a big industrialist. He rose to heights from the poor family of mendicant, but died in an accident in his factory. Vikram's mother married the general manager — Priyaranjandas — of Rajendra Industrial Complex. Vikram had returned from abroad, and his friend (Horatio) informs him of Lalitagauri's (Gertrude) second marriage 10 months after the death of Shivashankar. Kanetkar has employed the epistolary device instead of the Ghost of Hamlet's father to tell Vikram the tale of his father's murder. *Hamlet* is used superficially to structure the first Act of *Gaganbhedi*. Vikram treats both Jai (Ophelia) and his mother as Hamlet does Ophelia and Gertrude. His father's ghost prevents him from doing any harm to Lalitagauri. The first Act which consists of three scenes is completely governed by the source text. According to Kanetkar, its content represents the first phase in man's life.

To be brief, the thematic patterns in *Gaganbhedi* can be discerned as follows:

Act 1 Scenes 3=*Hamlet*	1st Phase	*Gaganbhedi*
Act 2 Scenes 3=*Macbeth+Othello*	2nd & 3rd Phase	
Act 2 Scenes 2=*King Lear*	4th Phase	

Vikram becomes ambitious like Macbeth and develops his own industry. Jai is transformed into Lady Macbeth first and then into Desdemona and finally she becomes mad like Ophelia and dies. Vikram's ambition represents the second mental stage in his life. In the third phase he suspects Balaraj (Horatio in the first Act now transformed into Cassio) having illicit relationship with Jai, and his family life is headed to the tragic end. Finally like Lear he is fooled by his only daughter Roopali (three into one: Cordelia-Regan-Goneril), and he is shocked by the morally corrupt daughter's pervert life. His daughter decides to send him to the Old Men's Home, but Jai's suicide serves the last blow. Vikram dies of the heart attack. Balraj has already appeared to restore the order.

A diagram showing the graft culture of characters and structures:

Kanetkar's	Shakespeare's plays and characters adapted in phases		
Gaganbhedi	*Act I*	*Act II*	*Act Ill*
Vikram–Hero	Hamlet	Macbeth +	King Lear Othello
Balraj – friend	Horatio	Cassio	Earl of Kent
Jai – wife	Ophelia	Lady Macbeth	Mad Ophelia + Desdemona
Dayal – Jai's father	Polonius	Partly Iago	Duke of Albany
Lalitagauri–mother	Queen Gertrude	Queen	–
Priyaranjan–manager	Claudius	Duncon	–
Roopali–daughter	Cordelia	Regan	Goneril
Uday–Balraj'snephew	–	Duke of Burgundy	Burgundy
First servant	Rosencrantz	–	
Baliram –servant	–	–	Lear's fool

Since Shakespeare's four tragedies are, thus, compressed together there is no space left for the comic relief. Lalitagaurx's ghost is a new addition to the other ghosts from the source texts. The weird witches in *Macbeth* are transformed into the male fortune teller, Rudreswar (44). Along with the appropriations, as shown above, of the structural and thematic elements, a number of Shakespearian dramatic devices such as asides, five soliloquies (1, 99.7,30; Up. 46,64; III p. 91) and Jai's single song show how Kanetkar is wholly dependent on the source texts. The only modern device is the use of telephone instead of Shakespeare's messengers! The choice of anglicized Marathi family seems to have helped this incongruous transformation of characters and dramatic episodes. The characters use not only the Anglicized Marathi language but also English words and complete sentences in Marathi prose dialogues. What is missing in it is Shakespeare's vision of life and Shirawadkar's poetry. As a result it becomes a "popular" drawing room drama. Here "popular" means a play which satisfies the taste of the minority elite class (5 per cent) in multicultural Maharashtra. It does not mean that such fully anglicized or Westernized plays are received well by the multidialectal "indiscriminate masses" in Maharashtra. Shakespeare was deeply rooted in the folk tradition of drama in his land; but unfortunately he met all the Brahman imitators who were alienated from the caste confined Marathi folk arts. In addition to this, Kanetkar seems to be unaware of Kenneth Muir's (1972, 12) observation that "(T) here is no such thing as Shakespearian tragedy: there are only Shakespeare's tragedies"; and also of the truth pointed out by drama critics that it is not so easy to tamper with them. Till date the same trend continues.

III

It is incongruous to juxtapose a poor pastiche like *Gaganbhedi* with an innovative seriocomedy: A *Branch of the Blue Nile*. It is a post-colonial cultural paradox in the theatre that displays varieties of the bard's use according to its specific needs. In this sense the *avatars* of his plays in the post-colonial theatres show how the use of current vocabulary such as imitation, emulation, parody, pastiche, collage, combinations, appropriation, intertextuality and so on neutralizes the contradiction of fakedom and literary plagiarism. True enough, these post-colonial tendencies or trends are outgrowth of the historic process and these efforts do in a measure display various features of the bardicization of drama of different cultures. For example, *Antony and Cleopatra*, the most sexy play by the bard was adapted only once in British Bombay, but *Romeo and Juliet, Julius Caesar, Hamlet, Othello, Lear*, even *Macbeth* enjoyed greater literary fortune in the Marathi theatre. It was Vasudev Balawant Kelkar who first adapted *Antony and Cleopatra* for the Shahunagarwasi dramatic troupe in 1893. His *Veermani ani-Shrangarsundari* (a brave man and a beauty) was a free stage version which did not run successfully. Kelkar chose pseudo historical background for its setting: but V. V. Shirawadkar grafted it on the history of Marathas in his *Dusara Peshwa* (1947) — Peshwa the Second. However,

Shirawadkar also cou'd not revive the romantic and Roman spirit of the source text in the Marathi offshoot. It became a poetic melodrama which suits the Indian dramatic taste so well. Perhaps the Marathi folk dramatist would have boldly adapted it, but they did not have any access to the English education. It means that Shakespeare's reception in Marathi is determined by, to use Levin Schucking's (1944, 75) phrase, "particular taste upholding type" culture group. Both Kelkar and Shirawadkar belong to such a single "taste upholding type". I have critically examined Shirawadkar's *Dusara Peshwa* from this point of view (1993, 259-61).

The foregoing discussion, reveals that the spirit of a particular culture-caste group is more important in reception of Shakespeare rather than "the spirit of the age". It is "more reasonable" to look closely "at this group before bowing to its demands". In this respect Walcott's use of *Antony and Cleopatra* provides a contrasting aesthetics of reception to the Marathi versions of Shakespeare's plays that is parallel to Walcott's postmodern parodic use of the bard's text. So Kanetkar's *Gaganbhedi is* more useful for sharpening the differences between the aesthetics of submissive reception and the aesthetics of resistance. Although Kanetkar used four texts of Shakespeare, the true voice of the bard is rarely heard in his collage but it looms large in *A Branch.* In the first the bardolatry dwarfs the dramatist's vision, in the latter the firm subversive position liberates it to some extent. Walcott's dramatic talent favoured the modes of comedy and farce. Kanetkar created a melodrama by putting four tragedies into one; but Walcott structured a seriocomedy by using only one historical tragedy. The first is least worried about establishing a sociopolitical or personal identity; but it is a recurring theme in Walcott's poetry and plays. It does not mean that Indians are not facing the problems of identity at all. Whereas Kanetkar simplifies problems and sentimentalizes issues, Walcott ends his plays with unresolved solutions. While commenting on Walcott's plays Patrick Colm Hogan (1994, 10-19) writes:

> ...And the anatomy we have sought to abstract from his work should be of value not only in understanding other

> literature, but, one might hope, in conceptualizing and responding to the far more important issues of social and personal identity in the real world—the issue towards which, after all Walcott sought our attention and inspire our action.

Gaganbhedi is a Shakespearian tragedy in the Marathi dress of only one small-caste culture group; but *A Branch* is the network of complex cultures. The first continues the colonial as well as intra-colonial hegemony; on the contrary, the latter, according to Stephen P. Breslow (1993, 267-71), continues the black/white, coloniser/colonized cultural reversals. Profound ironies quickly mount up within his intertextual matrix. The intense multicultural consciousness in A *Branch* is not to be found in *Gaganbhedi.* Walcott is ideologically committed to "the exploration of purely regional Caribbean themes of racism, and discrimination, of the lowest as well as the highest strata of society" (Breslow, 268). Kanetkar is committed only to the "high culture", especially of his caste group; and ignores the black colour of Othello which does not become his Vikram. Kanetkar's use of multitext is neither heteroglotic nor multicentred like Walcott's. *A Branch* shows "a dense cross-road of human differences", sometimes hilarious in their juxtapositions and interrelations.

The comparison of the opening scenes of these plays clearly brings out the "international" and "intercultural" difference of the textual exchanges. The West Indians mostly live in the borrowed culture, but Indians claim to have their own distinct culture. It is rather difficult to trace the Marathiness in *Gaganbhedi.* Its opening is full of mere echoes of *Hamlet.* Even the stage directions are derivative. It opens:

> Balraj: Vikram, I have asked to take all your bag and baggage to the room specially prepared for you only.
>
> Vikram: (engrossed in thought, looking far away) Balraj my friend, what is going on here? What is this decoration meant for ? This orchestra... this laughter... is a lawn party in the bungalow nearby? (Act I, Sc. I; p. 1)

Then Balraj unfolds the story of Lalitagauri's second marriage. The whole first Act is based on *Hamlet* only. It is derivative.

On the contrary, A *Branch* opens with the ending of *Antony and Cleopatra.* Shaila, who is acting the role of Cleopatra speaks:

> Give me my robe, put on my crown .....

Harve, the director, advises her:

> What is all this sexual hesitation, Shaila? You know how sensual his corpse is to her? (p. 213)

Thus, the Trinidadian actors are rehearsing the bard's play for their production. Slowly they themselves get involved into the real drama of their personal relationships. For instance, it is suggested that Harve is a homosexual. From the outset several kinds of intertextualities are skilfully multiplied. They include actors' responses to Shakespeare's text, their "real life" etc. The interanimation of various texts is the basis of *A Branch.* The use of generic mixtures breaks Shakespeare's conventions.

The characters read parts of Chris's — the actor — playwright — three postmodern plays. These plays consist of a farce, a dramatization of their life and the tape recorded rehearsals and conversations.

After this opening, Harve asks Shaila to "play what you feel about Chris, not Antony". (213) This play within or theatre in theatre gives greater scope to cross-pollinations, satire and subversion in A *Branch;* and the source text provides contexts for them. On the contrary, Kanetkar simplifies the intertext of *Hamlet* by leaving out its play within. The role transfigurations in *Gaganbhedi* are the mergers of the heterogeneous characters from the source texts; but Shaila's role shifts in A *Branch* are intended to contribute to the construction of a parody of the pretext. Shaila leaves the theatre in order to join the church. Her association with Brother Jon gives scope to the hitting satire on the religious sects. Then there is Harvey's new "dialectal" version of the source text with a new heroine, Marilyn. Chris's dialectal plays are interspersed with the bard's standard text:

> Marilyn/Cleopatra: Hast thou the pretty worm of Nilus there. That kills and pains not.
>
> Gavin/Clown:Madam, I have him, but 'tain't go be who ask you handle him, because one nip from this small fellow and Basil is your husband; this little person, will make marriage, in poison and in person, but the brides who go to that bed don't ever get up (262).

Baliram in *Gaganbhedi* uses standard Marathi prose. It is clear that Kanetkar lacks the mastery of folk dialects a^ all other adapters of the Shakespeare's texts in his culture group. But he has forgotten Vidushak (clown) from Sanskrit drama.

Finally the performance of *Antony and Cleopatra* fails, because by mistake the scenery prepared for Chris's play is put up for it. Through Gavin's speeches Walcott ridicules the language of newspaper criticism. The ending depicts self-revelation of the black actor Gavin, Shaila's conversion and Chris's dejection. The significance of the title of the play is made clear with comic touches. Chris goes to Barbados to open a new restaurant which he names "A Branch of the Blue Nile". When he returns to Trinidad, he explains its several allusions. They refer to Cleopatra's river, to his earlier comments on the post-colonial culture and so on. Like Antony he returns to his white wife, and yet tries to seduce Shaila by writing a new play. But the whole actor group splits. Marilyn migrates to New York, Harvey to London to die of AIDs, Chris to his restaurant, and Shaila is left alone on the stage. The text of Chris's play performed by Iris and Wilfred is heard on the tape recorder. The play ends with entry of a fool, Phil. He exhorts Shaila: "Continue, Do your work." This reminds one of the ending of the bard's text.

Walcott's characters represent heterogeneous cultures on the western islands, but Kanetkar's is only a subgroup in one culture. Walcott's characters are more complex and realistic; but Kanetkar's are stereotypical arid idealized. Walcott represents the recurrent themes of the emergence of colonialism with a mixture of texts. Kanetkar combines Shakespeare's texts in order to create new one which may be considered a "Shakesperian tragedy" in his language. He enjoys less freedom; but Walcott freely draws on the technique of the *picong,* the satiric song duets and many other multicultural dramatic devices. Such a folkloric intertextuality is absent in *Gaganbhedi.*

By adopting the Bakhtinian viewpoint, Breslow states:

> Walcott has said *(at a* recent conference in Florida) that North American society contains a multitude of cultural/ linguistic hybrids but that its theatre is unfortunately lacking — if he were to use Bakhtin's terms — in "interanimated, heteroglotic hybrids." *A Branch of the Blue Nile* brilliantly begins to fill this gap (*DI.* 49).

It can be safely concluded that the Marathi avatars of Shakespeare's texts lack "interanimated, heteroglotic hybrids" and also the renewal of the established literary tongue "by drawing on the fundamental elements of Marathi folk language."

IV

Both the sample texts illustrate the connections and boundaries between the literary influence and intertextuality. Since we can easily sort out various elements of the bard's four tragedies in *Gaganbhedi,* his influence is not deeper or assimilated. It is centripetal and dominant like a destiny. In contrast to this, :the rich intertextuality in A *Branch* comprises of allusions, quotations, parody, plagiarism, and influence also. It is a game, even a joke and it serves several functions: renewing the dramatic genre, parody of shakespeare's tragedy and so on. The first is a complete text. It rewards the reader's knowledge of influence. Its genealogy can be easily defined and it can be appropriately placed in the tradition of Shakespeare's reception in Marathi. Kanetkar's exhibition of the influence awareness tells us the way influence functions in his text. The affinities are strong and the healthy influence very weak in it. By contrast, A *Branch* is an incomplete text whose meaning is dependent on the reader's knowledge of it together with *Antony and Cleopatra.* Intertextuality makes it meta-criticism which demonstrates how a new text recycles the old text, how the dramatic production resembles bricolage. Thus, self-reflexivity is the common area to both the sample texts; but there is not only the difference of its degrees but also of kinds. And this difference of attitudes to the cultural hybrids can be revealed in the comparative study of Kanetkar's authorial statements, for example, his prefaces to his plays, and "The 1992 Nobel Lecture" by Walcott (1993, 262-67).

This scrutiny of only two samples shows ambivalence in the reception of Shakespeare in the post-colonial theatres and it will continue with simultaneous affirmation of heterogeneity. The spectator in drama and many other factors might determine it. But we have to take into consideration, what Pierre Bourdieu (1986, 485) describes as "the indivisibility of taste" in Shakespeare's reception in alien cultures. The scope and nature of the response to his text may change according to the degrees of postcoloniality in different countries. The post-colonial contexts are changing in the process of globalization. Arif Dirlik (1994, 356) asks to drop out Appiah's adjective "comprador", which I applied to the Marathi intelligentsia, and suggests a modification: "intelligentsia of global capitalism". This new intelligentsia will take the contrapuntal view of the poetics and politics of bardicide in the post-colonial contexts. This is why there is a need of evaluation of Shakespeare's ritualistic reception in Indian theatres. A comparative study of the Indian versions of his texts in Indian languages would throw more light on the Indian "sacrificial bardicide". The findings of my case study can be confirmed on the basis of that comparative study.

Notes

1. Shakespeare criticism in Marathi as well as in English is derivative of the Western drama criticism. M. G. Watawe's (ed.) *Roopakam: Shakespeare Khand* (Mumbai: Marathi Natya Parishad, 1969), Henry W. Wells and Aniah Gowda's *Shakespeare Turned East* (Mysore: Prasaranga University, 1976) are the representative examples. Regarding the responses of the reviewers to the English production of Shakespeare's plays see the column "Last Month in Delhi" in *Enact*.
2. When I met Roger Pringle, Dy. Director of Shakespeare Centre, at Stratford-upon-Avon in *1986*, these claims were not confirmed by him. The placard newspaper advertisements contained these references to the bard's birthplace.

8

Contemporary Marathi Literary and Cultural Criticism From a Comparatist's Perspective

This paper presents a contrapuntal brief account of the major trends in the post-independence Marathi literary and cultural criticism. The term 'contemporary' is used to indicate the post-independence period. In a way, it is an attempt to compare the colonial and postcolonial critical discourse in terms of its postcoloniality.[1] The adjective 'post-independence' is replaced by the word 'contemporary' in order to suggest how the politics of 'post' in the postcolonial matters most in our literary culture. The post-independence Indian literature may not be really independent but only 'postcolonial' in the historical sense of the term. Moreover, the tremendous growth of the post-independence Marathi criticism in the neo-colonial situation may be mere continuation of the traditions introduced by the earlier rulers from Europe. That is why it is necessary to test how far our critical discourse today is 'postcolonial' in the real sense of the term.

The domestic colonialism in literary culture needs to be explicated in the context of 'culture and imperialism'. No postcolonial literature can be free from cultural cross-pollination. In order to understand the present crisis in our critical thought, we have to interpret this hybridity[2] with comparative perspective. The formula: Literature= Comparison, is accepted as a ground for the study of contemporary Marathi criticism. This is not an exhaustive account of all the 'Marathist' critical as well as theoretical positions in vogue today.

'Marathist' means an intellectual who claims to be the 'specialist' of Marathi language and literature. 'Marathiwadi' or 'Marathiwala' of the language dispute 'border' may not be such a specialist. So we must distinguish between a Marathist and a comparatist. Their relationship is always conflictive; and the latter has had no space in our literary culture.[3] Our monoliterary histories of literature and of criticism show how Marathists have been busy drawing up, with impressive skill, registers and balance sheets, synthetic account and full fledged histories of literature. But it is necessary to project our literary as well as cultural criticism of last 50 years against the backdrop of the entire twentieth century by adopting ultra national perspective. So far our literary and cultural criticisms are compartmentalized fields dominated by the 'star-critic system'. As a result there is neither the development of comparativism nor any shift (Pamela L. Caughie's concepts — see *PMLA* 112-1 Jan. 1997:26-27), of emphasis from the traditional literary studies to culture studies. On the contrary, the specialists have been striving to produce a master list of great critics which would include other lists: important / unimportant authors and so on. Here we have critical lists based upon unquestioned assumptions, for example, Gangadhar Gadagil's extremely individualistic *aswadak* (impressionistic) criticism. In such lists of *Marathi's mandand* (standard writers) we notice the distinctive phase of the same cultural parade determined by caste-*varna* system in Indian society. This parade of perpetual Marathi criticism fits into Lord Macaulay's ill famous theory of the colonial education through downward filtration in this hierarchy. So the roots of our contemporary criticism need to be traced in this anthropology wherein lie its strengths and limits.

The Indian critics are now facing not only the problematic of Macaulay's Minutes, but also the complex process of the 'mandalization' of Indian 'literatures'. Not only the trends and movements in the post-independence Marathi criticism reveal the changes as predicted by Macaulay, but the literary awards also exhibit the journey from centre to periphery.

We have experienced both colonization and modernization, and are trying to find liberation from those vestiges of European imperialistic colonization in the 50th year of our independence. Yet we are falling back into the invincible, pernicious netting of global neocolonialism. The domination of Westernized Mardhekarian aesthetics in Marathi for the last fifty years is a fine example of this strong current. It demonstrates how modern Western criticism has displaced several indigenous critical traditions. The present crisis, which has been aptly pointed out by Makarand Paranjape in his statement on the theme of the National Seminar (Nov. 1998) on Indian literary and cultural criticism; has acquired new dimensions at the turn of the present century. There are innumerable demands not only for 'alternative' aesthetics but also for 'oppositional' aesthetics, nativistic critique and so on. This crisis in the contemporary Marathi criticism can be described in Mark Antony's words of comment on the Roman civil war in William Shakespeare's *Julius Caesar*:

> Either there is a civil strife in heaven, Or else the world, too saucy with the gods, incenses them to send destruction (1, iii, 11-13)

Are all indigenous critical traditions completely destroyed by alien cultural conquests? Aren't there some attempts at revival of the sense of the awareness of the essence of indigenous cultures? What is the nature of hybridization of our literary culture? Will 'new' culture studies displace the 'old' cultural studies overshadowed by the colonial Indology? How are we going to extend the concept of 'criticism' in the 'increasingly complex world'? What 'interdisciplinary' and 'cooperative intellectual modes' (see *PMLA* 23 March 1996 'Forum') should be developed to cope with the pressures of the age of information. Today such questions cannot be answered by mere superficial comparative study of the Sanskrit and Greek poetics. They are deeply concerned with the Modern Marathi language, its dialects and 'literatures' as they exist today. A comparatist has to adapt too wider criteria to cope with them. First, the century or half a century should not be envisaged as the usual type of subject for investigation. Second, we should try to understand how contemporary Marathi 'literatures' have been dialogueing with the worldwide network of literatures, and also test if it possesses the adequate idiom or the idioms to conduct that dialogues. Without a reference to the global cultural contacts ii is rather difficult to see whether our contemporary Marathi criticism is really 'postcolonial' or merely historically post-independence. In fact, the Fanonian canon is unknown to it and it seems to be dependent more on the few outmoded quotes from the obsolete Euramerican criticism. Even a few names of the non-Euramerican postcolonial critics such as Edward Said, Gayatri Chakravorty Spivak, Homi K. Bhabha, Aijaz Ahmad, Bill Ashcroft, Benita Parry etc., are not yet known to Marathi. It has not yet learnt the adequate terminology to understand innumerable Western critical theories introduced during the course of the 'theory revolution' which took place in the second half of the twentieth century. Under such circumstances, we have to take the stock of our post-independence contributions to the critical discourse in Marathi.

II

A comparative resume of the colonial and postcolonial developments in Marathi criticism does not display much resistance to the European theories; but the number of contradictions, paradoxes and ambivalent attitudes have been increasing. During the last phase of the freedom struggle modern Marathi literature did not become nativistic as it should have become in the wake of nationalism. It did not break away from the British Romantic tradition because the anglicized critics from the upper *varna* clung to the white master's critical tools to maintain their traditional literary hegemony. All along they had acquired some critical competence by writing through the European critical texts. During the colonial period there was the revival of the Sanskrit poetics, but they were hardly used to construct a critical counter-discourse. Writing through the indigenous texts against the European 'Master narrative' in criticism was one way of decolonizing the critical canon. But we have the towering figure of the most Westernized / modernized Marathi critic who overshadowed the Marathi criticism for half a century. The history of Marathi criticism has failed to explain how the borrowed modernism of the Mardhekarian critical theories is the armed version of alien as well as domestic colonialism. Before Bal Sitaram Mardhekar (1909-1956) was well known to the Marathi readership as a poet and critic, his first critical book titled *Art and Man* (1938) was published in England. Like Eliot and Yeats, he started writing from the centre of the empire and not 'back' to it.

He attended poetry writing workshops for his ICS exams. Eliot did not have deep roots in America, but Yeats was associated with the Celtic revival. Yeats alienated himself from the Irish rebels, Mardhekar did not represent the violent phase of the national freedom struggle. As a poet he became a frustrated pessimist. It is a remarkable paradox that the most "experimental' poet, who turned to the rebel poets of the *Bhakti* movement for models and meters, ignored all indigenous critical traditions in his English and Marathi critical books. It may be conceded that his aesthetics was 'new' in Marathi; but it was mostly the assimilation of the Western, British, theories, for example, Clive Bell's theory of significance and I.A. Richard's theory of communication. This is not only the excellent example of colonial ambivalence in critical thought but also of the production of the "oppressive present". His derivative modernism cannot be defended as an attempt to nativise alien theories, because a single reference to the art of Ajanta Caves in his writings is not enough to represent the indigenous traditions of aesthetics and philosophy.

It can also be argued that Madhekarian aesthetics and later on New Criticism were novel versions of domestic neocolonialism in the 'post-independence' literary culture. Ganesh Devi (1992, 119) described Sri Aurobindo and B.S. Mardhekar as "two prototypical modem Indian critics". Further he pointed out how Mardhekar's criticism lacked the context of the tradition and spirit of revolt of the *Bhakti* poetry. Among several samples of pseudo-theorizing in the colonized literati

Mardhekar's theorizing suited the elitist literary taste for a long time because it was the weapon in the hands of the small taste-upholder type group to prove its cultural supremacy over the masses influenced by Gandhism. It may be conceded on the historical ground that he was the first poet and critic who boldly 'modernized' poetry and criticism which was stuck in the mire of European romanticism and Indian moral preaching. His concepts such as "rhythmic pattern of harmony," contrast and balance, aesthetic judgement, aesthetic emotion, aesthetic experience and several others are still being paraded in the classrooms. His proud pleading for assimilation of Western literature to make Marathi literature strong cannot be defended at all in terms of postcoloniality. If his literary contribution is revalued in terms of postcolonial criticism he will seem to be, like Eliot and Yeats, the victim of the politics of poetry at the centre of the capitalistic culture and imperialism.

By the 1950s a strong Mardhekarian School in the 'gate way of India' became so dominant that even at the turn of century a traditional 'biographical' criticism of Mardhekar's writings, which was original Ph.D. thesis by Vijaya Rajadhyaksha, was awarded the central Sahitya Akademi Award in 1991. Gangadhar Gadagil was the staunch supporter of Mardhekar and has been fighting egoistically the loosing battles against the left wing and nativist critics. As mentioned before, his extremely impressionistic views appear to be too ridiculous in the age of deconstructionism and post modernism. Late W.L. Kulkarni and Madhav Achwal were two more shinning stars of so-called New Criticism who did not know that the Americans had developed that brand as a component to distinguish their literary texts from the European ones. D.B. Kulkarni and several other Kulkarnis and Deshpandes went to such extremes in defining the greatness of work of art that they did not believe that the text is never born in a vacuum. Literary greatness was defined in terms of autonomous form, This textualism of the Mardhekarian star critic system soon produced different counter discourses which will be discussed later.

During the colonial period there was a weak tradition of juxtaposing Sanskrit poetics along with the European traditions in order to avoid total alienation. It was the weak native pull which became a little stronger during the nationalistic freedom struggle. But it was always elbowed by different alien pulls, and the British Romanticism was one such influenza of Marathi criticism. This trend was strongly represented by S.K. Kshirsagar, R.S. Walimbe and a few others even after the independence. The first bombshell was thrown on this pseudo-romanticism by the angry young men who 'looked back in anger' in the 1960s with their 'little magazines'. Bhalchandra Nemade who soon proved opportunistic nativist, wrote his very first critical article to ridicule the writings of the star' romantic critic S.K. Kshirsagar in the 1960s. Ashok Shahane, Raja Dhale and many other rebel writers of the little magazine vehemently attacked the strongholds of our literary establishment. But it does not mean that the little magazine movement was totally an indigenous innovation. It was born in Bombay which was the counterpart of the centre in Europe. Of course, it exhibited a few features of nativism, especially in stray article written by Nemade. Later Ganesh Devi proved how Nemade had partly voiced nativism in Marathi which acquired the national distinction in the 1990s (see Paranjape, 1997).

The third influential trend was set by the introduction of the Marxist criticism and progressive movements in the 1930s. In fact, Mahatma Phule's writings and B. R. Ambedkar's dalit movements had prepared a fertile ground for the progressive thought. D. K. Bedekar, like other Indian socialists, tried to blend humanitarianism, autonomy of art and Marxist thought. He went a step ahead in interpreting the *rasa* theory in Marxist terms. Sharadchandra Muktibodh, a Marxist poet and critic (Gajanan Muktibodh's brother), stands in contrast to Mardhekar. His *Srasthi, Saundarya ani Sahityamuly* is a significant contribution to the Marxist criticism in Marathi. His poetry and novels also show how he practised what he preached. From the above discussion we can trace the replicas of the famous 'cold war' in our criticism.

The Sanskrit poetics has been the think tank of a few pandits since its revival after the British contact. However, its application to the modern literary texts has always remained very limited. It has been used to parade the pride of glorious cultural past. Its paradigms are not modified for interpreting the anglicized texts. G.T. Deshpande, R.P. Kangle, R.S. Jog and other Sanskrit scholars introduced ancient aesthetics into Marathi. Its exhaustive treatment by Deshpande opened new vistas for developing indigenous criteria for judging a text. Jog applied some of those paradigms in interpreting contemporary literary texts. His judgement of the Marathi literary taste is also guided by those norms, but it lacks the sociological contexts. On the whole, their critical discourse is elitist, universalist and marginal. It ignores the *desi*-folk traditions which are deeply rooted in our soil.

Is it the coincidence that the 'theory revolution' was taking place in the major centers of imperialism in the 1960s and 1970s? Perhaps it was the result of the 'domestic strifes' between the mainstream literature and minority discourses. The pluralism gave rise to, in W.J.T. Mitchell's (Ashcroft, eds. 1995 : 477) words, "dissonance between post-imperial criticism and postcolonial culture." According to him, "the most important new literature is emerging from the colonies" and "the most provocative new literary criticism is emerging from the imperial centers that once dominated them." As it is true about the European centre of the empire and its colonies at the peripheries, it is more true about our cultural centers of domestic colonization in Bombay and Pune and caste-*varna* based colonies-islands, as Daya Pawar said. In order to dominate the 'emerging new literatures, such as *gramin, dalit, janwadi* etc., there was a flood of books on aesthetics from the elitist centres in Pune and Bombay even after the demise *of* Mardhekar. It can be described as a pseudo-theory revolution in the sixties. For example, Prabhakar Padhye ransacked the western aesthetic theories which were left out by Mardhekar. A kind of dictatorship of the elitist aesthetics was established. The applied criticism mimiced the jargon borrowed from it. The review of a text was more obscure and difficult than the text itself. Out of dozens of books and hundreds of articles on aesthetics not single one staunchly resisted that Euramerica centricism. How can we explain this literary neocolonialism on the socio-cultural ground?

The individual isolated attempts were made to resocialize literary theories. R.B. Patankar took the all comprehensive view of the major alien as well as indigenous aesthetic theories in his *Saundrya Meemansa* (1974). But he ignored the anti-colonial Black aesthetics. He juxtaposed them by keeping universalism at the centre of his critical thought. His study of Kantian aesthetics dominated his applied criticism too much. He shows his faith both in Marxism and universalism, humanism and colonialism. He lacks the comparative perspectives and the distinctive force of the Fanonian vision. He reinterpreted Mardhekarian aesthetics and placed it in the hierarchy of the alien and indigenous theories. Broadly speaking, he presented a moderate survey of elitist theories of aesthetics at home and abroad. It is a moderate text which does not bear witness, like postcolonial criticism, in the words of Homi K. Bhabha (1984:171), "to the unequal and uneven forces of cultural representation involved in the contest for political and social authority within the modern world order.... They intervene in those ideological discourses of modernity that attempt to give a hegemonic 'normality' to the uneven development and the differential, often disadvantaged, histories of nations, races, communities, peoples. They formulate their critical revisions around issues of cultural difference, social authority, and political discrimination in order to reveal the antagonistic and ambivalent moments within the 'rationalizations' of modernity." It would be interesting to examine the central Sahitya Akademi Award winner critical books in Marathi in the light of these views. Although those awards have been bestowed upon the critical books the project has not yet succeeded in evolving, what Bhabha describes as, "forms of dialectical thinking that do not disavow or sublate the otherness (alterity) that constitutes the symbolic domain of psychic and social identifications" (173).

From this view point, the critical writings of so-called secular and progressive critics in Marathi, for instance Narahar Kurundakar, would seem most regressive and imperialistic parrotry. A comparative analysis of the relationship between culture and imperialism as studied by Kurundakar in *Dhar ani Kath* (1972) and by Edward said in *Culture and Imperialism* (1993) might bring out the difference between the colonialist and anti-colonialist approach to fiction. Teaching a text like *Dhar ani Kath* in a free democratic country known for diversity in unity is itself the sign of domestic colonialism in the modern literary culture. The postcolonial perspective forces us to rethink the profound limitations of "a consensual and collusive 'liberal' sense" of our Marathi cultural community. It insists that our cultural and political identity are constructed through a process of alterity. The questions of *jati-varna* and cultural difference overlay issues of gender, and overdetermine the social alliances of class/caste and democratic socialism. The time for 'assimilation' of Marathi minorities to holistic and organic notions of cultural value has dramatically passed after the *mandalization* of Marathi literature. So the very language of our cultural community needs to be rethought from a postcolonial perspective. Since such critical problems have been neglected, the post-independence Marathi language and 'literatures' are supposed to be on the death-bed in the age of globalization.

This leads us to the discussion of cultural criticism in Marathi. There is a long standing tradition of distinctly compartmentalized literary and cultural studies in the traditional sense. The study of folk or elitist tales and arts, rituals and myths, legends and logus is a part of anthropology introduced by the European missionaries and rulers. The folklorists from Sarojini Babar to Durga Bhagawat, from Madhukar Wakode to Dnyaneswar Khaire, Prabhakar Mande to Gangadhar Morje and R.C. Dhere are many. Most of them are collectors and interpreters of the folk literature. These are not the 'new cultural' studies in the postcolonial sense. We will discuss the current concept of 'cultural studies' a little later. Let us note one post-independence cultural paradox. A symposium on "Mass Culture, Language, and Arts in India" was held at Duke University in the USA. and the collection of research papers presented at it was published in Bombay (1970). Its editor Madhav L. Apte writers at the outset of his 'Introduction':

> Indian society and culture have intrigued Westerners for a long time. There are both scholarly and popular writings that deal with numerous facets of India. However, in this huge mass of literature there does not exist any discussion of the concept of mass culture as it relates to India (1).

The non-resident Indian anthropologist has taken a very objective view in pointing out the limitations of our elitist cultural studies which help to revive so-called glorious ancient culture and ignore the living culture in daily life in the street or at home After reading such research papers by the Indian immigrants an *adiwasi* Madhukar Wakode or the man of the border land Laxman Mane or a tribal poet Vaharu Sonavane would ask: "About whose culture are these Sahebs talking?" One is reminded of the opening sentence of Lesley Johnson's *The Cultural Critics from Mathew Arnold to Raymond Williams* (1979: 1): He asserts:

> The history of the concept of culture is complex and tantalizingly ambiguous...

Thus, the cultural studies, as defined by Simond During, (Introd. 1993:1) "the study of culture or more particularly, the study of *contemporary* culture", is not known to Marathi. The interdisciplinary studies such as film and literature, law and love poetry etc. are unheard of. We need a Cornell West (During ed. 1993:217) who pleads for the case of the "demystificatory criticism":

> The time has come for critics and artists of new cultural politics of difference to cast their nets widely, flex their muscles broadly, and thereby refuse to limit their visions, analysis, and praxis to their particular terrians. The aim is to dare to recast, redefine, and revise the very notion of 'modernity', 'mainstream', 'margins', 'difference',

> 'otherness'. We have now reached a new stage in the perennial struggle for freedom and dignity . (217).

This is one way to get out of the present crisis of the want of cultural relativism in our literary culture. In order to emphasise this aspect of the dilemma let us take resume of some of the post-independence movements in Maharashtra.

III

Our literary movements are also overdetermined by the colonial contexts of place-centre, caste and creed. New trends and movements give rise to a new critical writing which supports it or prepares the ground for them. Very good creative writers are frog-marched into the movements by their supporter critics. Many of the sectarian anti-establish movements produce critical counter-discourses. It is believed that the movement changes the face of literature, but very few critical writings on it expose the contradictions in it. Three major post-independence movements have given rise to several critical books and some of them have been controversial. They are too local to understand internationalness in a text.

In the pre-independence British period Marathi literature was believed to be monolithic with capital 'L'. It was being standardized and 'modernized by the traditional upper caste *Shastris* and white *Sahibs*. With the spread of education Macaulay's Indian grand children from the lower castes began to express the voice of dissent, for example, in the literature produced by the pioneers of the *Satyashodhak* movement. As the British rulers had used ordinary English literature as, to borrow Gauri Vishwanathan's title, 'masks of conquest', the literate among the ruled struggled to imitate the 'white' masters. The historical infighting of the caste fractions has been always appropriated with the help of European critical theories. The *grameen* and *dalit* literary movements are the fine examples of theoretically manufactured consents.

The *grameen*, *dalit*, *janwadi* and other epithets are supposed to be the post-independence labels given to the fractions which symbolize the return of the mass cultural repressed. Before independence in the 1920s a group of romantic writers had adopted the Irish mode of the romantic nativistic writing. The American face of modernism later changed its direction. Till now our literature is considered to be an embodiment of classical caste confined bourgeois culture. There is the difference of degrees in their resistance to the anglicised upper *varna* domination. A comparative study of the critical writings of the leaders as well as patron critics of these movements exhibit various facets of the politics of caste difference and literature.

Anand Yadav, the leader of the grameen literature movement and some of his followers wrote critical books overshadowed by Mardhekarianism. Sharad Patil's *Abrahmani Sahityanche Saundryashastra* —Aesthetics of the non-brahman literatures (1988) is the Marxist interpretation of the Indian traditions. Soon the dalit literature movement acquired distinct identity in the 1960s. Like the Negro Black Panthers, the dalit panthers poured fires on the uppercaste domination and exploitation of the down trodden. The dalit critics from M.N. Wankhede, who was educated in the US., to Gangadhar Panatawane are many. The common factor in these movements is that they were patronised by the Kulkarni critics and appropriated in the cultural politics of difference. In Nemade's words, the dalit literature movement was over-patronised by the Brahmin critics for political reasons *(Teekaswayanvar).*

On the whole, this 'civil strife', as described in Shakespeare's blank verse before, brings destructions to us and prevents our literature and criticism from becoming truly 'postcolonial'. This is one more crisis Which does not allow our criticism to become too negative to be aesthetically original and creative. This problematic of the aesthetics of resistance/ oppressed is being debated, but with least awareness of anticolonical theories, now with reference to these movements (*Asmitadarsh* 4 Oct. 1996, *New Quest* 120 Dec. 1996). The battle of critical books has now acquired a new dimension because not only the Jain, Christian, Muslim and other religious groups have started a cultural politics of difference but the OBC groups are demanding the 'reserved space' in aesthetics and criticism.

This pluralism shows dissonance between post-imperial Marathi criticism and postcolonial culture. Gangadhar Gadail's current gloomy comments on the casteism in literature reveal transference and reconfigurations in our literary culture. Neo-conservatives like him react to the rural and dalit or women writings by declaring, just as an American elitist scholar's reactions to the African-American, Native American, gay and other writings are reported by Mitchell (Ashcroft 1995: 477), "the barbarians are in our midst". Similarly the contemporary criticism, which claims that 'no bias, no merit' and the rhetorics of literary greatness, discloses how the orthodox neo-colo ıial literary as well as cultural empire is on the verge of decline. The transformations in the elitist image building culture industry are brought about by one more contemporary literary movement in which the caste factor was less important (see Dhasal 'Interview' in *Anusthubh* July 1997:47-74). It was the little magazine movement that tried to cleanse the rotten literary culture in the 1960s. It emboldened the writers from remote corners of Maharashtra.

The Little Magazine Movement led by the angry young men such as Bhalchandra Nemade, Ashok Shahane, Raja Dhale etc. was a strong reaction which resulted into cremation of *Satyakatha* (magazine) which was the symbol of the established systems thinking at that time. It was followed by the mushroom growth of little magazines from *Vacha* to *ABCDE*. Three critical essays written in protest are considered to be the bombshells thrown on the strongholds in the sixties. They are:

1) Ashok Shahane, 'Marathi Sahityavaril X-kiran' (963) – X-ray on Marathi literature
2) Bhalchandra Nemade, 'Lekhakacha Lekhakrao Kasa Hoto?' (1964) – How does a writer become a snob?
3) Raja Dhale, '*Satyakathechi* Satyakatha' (1969) – A true Story of *Satyakatha*.

But they seem "childish" in terms of theories of colonialism. A collection of Raja Dhale's creative and critical writings mirrors not only the spirit of revolt of the disillusioned youth after the war with China and defeats of development plans, but also the first phase of the panthers' dalit literature. All writing in the little magazine was not guided by any specific ideology, but it challenged the pseudo-modernism of the 'star system' in the establishment represented by the periodical *Satyakatha* in Bombay. *Satyakatha* was the organ of the private publication firm which spread Mardhekarian modernism. This dominant group preached 'arts for forms sake' cult and American type of 'New Criticism'. It was a literary neocolonialism which gave rise to the counter-discourse in little magazines. Yet the overestimated contribution of the little magazine movement was not fully anticolonial in the global sense. A glance at any language and literature in India of the 1960s, for instance, Hindi *Sachetan* led movement, reveals similar products of the PL 480 in criticism. The little magazine movement was not free from the alien influences. Most of the rebel critics were more influenced by the European existentialism rather than the Russian Marxism.

The Indianised form of existentialism found expression not only in poetry and fiction but also in criticism. It discloses how Indian criticism is Euramerica centric, but I would prefer to call it 'anglo-window centric'. We receive only such Western philosophical or critical theories which are translated/mediated through the English language. It is doubtful if any Marathi critic had ever studied Jean Paul Sartre or Albert Camus in original French. A significant aspect of this reception of new brands is chiefly to imitate alien models for power and cultural hegemony. So our critics hardly struggle, to use Bill Ashcroft and others' words in *The Empire Writes Back* (1991 rpt. 194), to "produce powerfully subversive general accounts of texturally and concepts of 'literalness' which open up new areas of concern." The example of Albert Camus's warm reception without criticism shows the neocolonial contradictions in the family romance of our writers. It is a paradox that our bourgeois writers' mimicry of existentialism was lauded by the elites. From Ashok Shahane (1963) to Vijay Tendulkar (1971) several rebel writers were much impressed by Camus's *Outsider* or its film version *A Stranger*. One may now laugh at their childish fascination for Camus's writing. Marathi criticism needs an Edward Said (1993:203-24) to expose the domination of French 'culture and imperialism' in Camus's writings. Why did .the Marathi youths in the 1960s identify themselves with Camus's fictional protagonists? Was the existence of the upper class/ caste threatened by the lower class/castes empowered by new democracy? The dialogue of the Marathi existentialist critics and researchers is very limited.[4] They discuss the philosophy of existentialism more than its impact on literary works.

There was a thin stream of the Marxism from D.K. Bedekar and his son to Digambar Padhye which counter checked the existentialism in Marathi criticism. G. V. Karandikar's essays in criticism show how Marxist criticism is weak in Marathi. We have .already made a reference to Muktibodh's contribution to it. But innumerable strands in the East European critical theories are still unknown to us.

The foregoing discussion shows how the colonial erasure of the local could go unchallenged for so long because it was assumed that reality exists in great books. From the colonial vantage, the mission of a literary education in Marathi is to take the locals elsewhere. Broadly speaking, colonialism operates where local voices are systematically muted, and especially in our social caste hierarchy they are more silenced at different levels. The domestic colonialism prevails wherever local subjects are de-realised in the name of literature that displaces common culture. There were caste-oriented literary movements but never the nativist one of the African kind. Comparative study of Western influence on the Marathi drama (Patil) strengthened this trend. Nemade's famous essay on 'nativism' was inspired by the writings of Ralph Linton and Edward Said. It forced us to acknowledge that modernist literary language can never be autonomous and self-referencial but must face the task of conceptualizing non-Western customs, native aesthetics, and ideological values against the background of a Euro-American tradition. But it did not evolve into a theory, because he is an opportunist nativist.

Nemade preached the cult of 'new' morality and nativism sans practice. Like Raymond Williams, he reinterpreted the tradition of Marathi fiction and tried to undermine the

Mardhekarian School of westernized aesthetics. Later on Ganesh Devi carried that cross to the national level and Makarand Paranjape (1997) placed it in the context of the Indian literary criticism. Now a number of essays are being published on nativism in Marathi. Although it is not a movement as such, its territories will be mapped by the budding talents which are strongly reacting to literary criticism's restricted specialization. That domineering specialization has remained Unchallenged even at the height of the influence of the Mardhekarian 'theories' a few years ago. Despite the opposition of the dalit fractions to nativism on the basis of suspected orthodox Hinduism, the search for nativistic intertextuality .is certainly going to be the fertile field for the new comparatists.

The critical practices are not so wide ranging to cover all superspecializations developed, in the Western' world, with innumerable canonical texts. Yet antispecialization current is not clearly visible in the Marathi criticism at the turn of the century. Individual attempts such as Gangadhar Patil's archetypal criticism and structuralism, M.S. Patil's semiotics, Mr. and Mrs. Dhongades's stylistics and feminism respectively, Ashok Kelkar's linguistics etc. are guided by the Western models. The reader response, reception aesthetics, comparatism, deconstructionism, post-modernism and many other Western theories are not yet systematically introduced. Even if someone tries to bring some of these 'travelling theories' they may appear obsolete now. The 'theory' revolution ran its course in Europe in the 1980s. Unfortunately, Marathi has not yet produced a Gayatri Chakravorty Spivak to translate Jacques Derrida's *Of Grammatology* from the French into English and Bengali books into English with a comparative perspective. However, there still continues the colonial tradition of quoting the Western critics in vogue. It does not mean that Marathi literature is able to hold dialogue with the Western criticism on an equal footing. Even the current names dropping shows how it is determined by the 'global English'. Our critics rarely state with confidence: 'says Tuka' or observes M. T. Vasudevan Nair, but will proudly record what says Jacque Lacan, Michael Foucault and so on.

In the current decade anti-theory and anti-literature movements are on foot in the Western world (see *PMLA 112-1,* 1997:7; special topic: "The Teaching of Literature"). It is the decade of uncertainties. The Western world dreams of the neocolonial conquest of the whole world through the 'Global English' (see *Critical Quarterly* 39-1: Spring 1997; the special topic: "The Future of English"). They are planning 'the future of English. We have been holding the Seminars on 'The Future of Marathi' believing that it is on its deathbed. In this situation we cannot think of Marathi criticism without the global contexts. It has become more difficult to run the journal which creates a space for the novel critical thought. The editorial note of *Yugawani*, yearly 1997 reveals how literary periodicals of the reputed forums are slowly passing away. It means the dictatorship of the borrowed alien theories and our overdetermined literature have produced counteractions.

Both literature and criticism have become irrelevant. The absence of true interdisciplinary and dialogic education in the megadiverse situation has led us to the dead end. Literature is taught to us as if it were independent of historical and social forces. A complacent and compromised bourgeois humanism that makes universal claims has come under the onslaughts of the downtrodden classes/castes. *We* are placed on the horns of new dilemmas. The fear of death of the Marathi language and the love and attraction of the 'global English' are the two extreme points which show how meaning is produced, transmitted and interpreted in our community. It means we have to institutionalize new critical practices. It is a time to turn our critical skills to the cultural artifacts, such as print media; television, advertising and films that are becoming the principal modes through which various narratives of self, other, nation, and the world articulate *in* India. This is not to argue for the retirement of literary analysis but suggest a way out of the present crisis in our criticism.

IV

Thus, at the turn of the century, there is a lot of confusion in our criticism which is clearly reflected in the more confused

"Interview" by Namadev Dhasal (1997). The writers belonging to different literary cults such as Vilas Sarang, and others have declared openly that there are neither critics nor critical theories in Marathi. The dalit writers have been continuously making claims for an "alternative" aesthetics unsuccessfully. The great gulf separates the Marathist mono-literary 'star' stalwarts and the multilingual English teachers-critics in their interpretation of the same text. The process of globalization has unsettled the concept of old nationalism. The rush of information technology has threatened the 'star system' which is no more effective. A conflict between the introduction of the global higher cultural unity and attempts to maintain all cultural differences of minorities has given rise to creative tensions. 'Think globally and act locally' is the slogan of the time. In the age of multiculturalism there is a greater need of new cultural literacy and team work in critical ventures. We do not have our own centres of literary authority. John Oliver Perry (1992) has commented on the issue of 'absent authority in contemporary Indian English criticism'. It is rather difficult to create such a central authority which will hold all cultural groups together. Now we are used to the coalition government of more than a dozen political parties at the centre. Similarly we have to adopt a supranational approach to literature. From my research as well as creative writing experience in Marathi, the remedies for the present crisis in our criticism are:

1. Comparative Literature
2. Culture Studies
3. Postcolonial Criticism

Comparisons are more odious in our hierarchical social structure. To be international implies an appreciation of one's cultural deliminations and ex-centrity. The recent responses to the American Comparative Literature at the turn of the century (1993), show how comparative literature is becoming "the site for powerful intellectual renewal in the study of literature and culture". The utopian views of Complit as "a theoretical free space and a more cosmopolitan environment for multilingual and multicultural community" go a long way toward making comparative literature into the "humanity's counterpart to international relations" (see *World Literature Today* 69-2 Spring 1995). The process of perception begins with comparison. We cannot deny that the basis of knowledge is comparison. As pointed out before, the presence of literature is being eroded by cinema, television, electronic media, etc. It is a paradox that literature has never enjoyed greater interdisciplinary prestige. Interdisciplinary thought is the name of a new discipline. In the Indian context comparative literature is more important as a discipline of the encounter, a movement toward other texts and cultures. We have not yet studied comparatively how our people have confronted the texts of other culture and other people. Thus comparativism is not a theory but it is a practice. The metaphor of the pyramid of similitude and difference is used for it.

Comparative literature has its own limitations, but I (1998) have pleaded its case for decolonizing the canon. Now its popularity is threatened by the new brand of cultural criticism to which we have already made a passing reference. In Marathi cultural and literary studies are still strictly isolated, distinct and antagonistic. They create cognitive dissonance in a reader. The mental impasse of such a reader leads him to suggest a tentative blueprint for the constant merging of the literary and the cultural in the postcolonial criticism. The Complit comes in conflict with the cultural studies because of the methodological emphasis (see *PMLA* 112-2 March 1997:281). "The differential methods in the best cultural studies work displace the fundamentally comparative approach that undergird traditional literary studies". David Lloyd has further pointed out the basic differences in these disciplines. He argues:

> ... While differential methods tend to situate and even disperse their objects among the systems and networks of cultural signification, teasing out the dynamics of complex and often incommensurable relations, the comparative method tends to require the stabilization of its objects. That stabilization is either hierarchical works are judged in relation to canonical touchstones or developmental, as in the assimilative and evolutionary model of European comparative literature that extends into discrete national

> traditions. In displacing the traditional hierarchies and canons of literary studies, cultural studies addresses more adequately, concretely, and inclusively the actualities and genealogies of cultural phenomena, for these phenomena do not send themselves to hierarchization or comparison (281-283).

Some scholars consider comparative literature as 'comparative exile'. This 'exilic aura' is its distinguished past. By contrast to the founding fathers of Complit in America and other converts to the field the current generation of exilic critics are 'often deeply antithetical to their European counterparts, non-German speaking, non-metropolitan, non-white, antipatriarchal, and, in varying degrees, hostile to elite literalness." This generation of postcolonialists such as Bhabha, Spivak, Said, Kwamy Appiah, Sara Suleri, Rey Chow etc., is regarded as normative for the 'new' Complit. The major objection to the colonial tradition of comparison is that it conflates two modes of comparison, qualitative and quantitative and produces a version of incommensurability. Such comparison cannot measure because its equivalencies do not unify.

Above all, now it is the time for postcolonial criticism which inherits "the mantle of comparative literature's historical legacy". It interrogates cultural subjectivity and pays attention to the tenuous bonds between identity and national language. We have to understand how the cultural power of colonialism lives on in language. Postcolonial criticism has emerged as a distinct category only in the 1990s. Its major canonical texts are in the European languages (Peter Barry 1995:191-201). They are neither translated nor introduced methodically into Marathi. Perhaps it is a new threat to the universal claims of 'satyam, shivam and sundaram' in our literary tradition. Reading literature with the perspective of Edward Said's 'Orientalism' in mind would make us, for instance, critically aware of how Anglo-Indian and Marathi writers provide images of East and West respectively. The first characteristic of postcolonial criticism is an acute awareness of representations of 'Other.' It traced the ways in which colonizer's language is permanently tainted, and how the writer's identity is doubled, or hybrid or unstable. It helps us to interpret literature with three key concepts: adopt, adapt and adept. To be brief, our postcolonial criticism should be a good detective story; but our post-independence critics are very bad detectives! Recent critical approaches have challenged the role that the literature has played in definitions of literature as a humanistic discipline. As a result comparative/cultural/postcolonial studies are generally furnishing new approaches to literature. Of course, they threaten the autonomy of literature and are likely to meet with the greater resistance in our static Marathi literary culture. So I borrow George Bernard Shaw's famous ending couplets of the epilogue to his *Saint Joan* and pray:

> O God, who madest this beautiful Maharashtra State
> When will it be ready to receive thy saints,
> Detective critics, comparatists, and culturalists
> How long, O Lord! How long!

Notes

1. The term "Postcolonial Criticism" is not yet familiar in Marathi, albeit two Marathi speakers: Nemade and Devi-are considered to be the stalwart nativists as postcolonial critics (Makarand Paranjape ed. *Nativism: Essays in Criticism* (1997): Preface ix-xvi, 129-152). Even the implications of the hyphenated and unhyphenated prefix "post" in "postcolonial" are not yet made clear in Marathi. Two translations of this term are "adhunikottar" and "uttaradhunik", but they are used indiscriminatingly, almost in the historical sense: For detail discussion of this concept see(1) Bill Ashcroft et, al. eds. *The Post-colonial Studies: Reader* (1995) Introd. 7-10,119-147; (2); Linda Huteheon ed. *PMLA* 111-1 (Jan. 1995) Introd. 7-14; (3); Ariel 20-4 (Oct. 1989): Post-colonialism and Post-modernism.

   For a short note on the salient features of postcolonial criticism see Peter Barry, *Beginning Theory: An Introduction to Literary and Cultural Theory (1995).*
2. See Anand Patil, 'Kadambaritil loksahityashi sambadhit antarsanthita', *Anusthubha* (Jan,. 1995)*:*37-52*:* and in a book titled *Taulanik Sahitya: Nawe Siddhant ani Upayvjan* (Aurangabad: Saket Prakashan, 1998).
3. My argument in this paragraph is based on Armando Gnisci's "Contemporary Italian Literature from a Comapratist's Perspective" *World Literature Today* 71-2 (Spring 1997) 248, 250. The phases

in the development of Italian literature from 1900 to 1970 mentioned by him surprisingly correspond more or less to similar stages in the history of modem Marathi literature. Eurocentricism rather than geo-politico-ethical factors has brought about such similarities and parallels in many literatures all over the world. Gnisci has exposed various limitations imposed by that Eurocentricism on Italian literature and also on Italian Italianist scholarship.

4. Compare Nada Elia, "In the Making: Beur Fiction and Identity Construction", *World Literature Today* 71-1 (Winter 1997): 47-54. "Bear" is the label used to refer to the children of North African (Maghrebi) immigrants to France, previously known as "second generation immigrants." Among them, those who fought against their own people in the Algerian freedom struggle are called 'harkis' In all the immigrant Muslim Arabs in France are one and half million in number. The word 'Beur' is a distortion of 'arabe' read backward. In the last decade and half they have produced mainly fiction in their hybrid language. The dominating theme in their novels is the sex, violence and anti-racism. The White race has not assimilated them into their culture. There is a strong anti-Beur movement. It is a paradox that Camus's *Outsider is* set in Algeria and Mehdi Charefs *Tea in the Harem* (1983, trans. into English 1989) the bestseller is set in Paris. In Charefs second novel *Le harki de Meriem* (1989) he has further elaborated on the cultural homelessness. Thus Beur literature constitutes one of the most recent developments in postcolonial writing. Elia pleads:

   ... It is now up to postcolonial scholars to familiarize themselves with this body of work, in order better to engage with the multitude of "minorities" that make up the Majority World (53, 54).

9

Can Subaltern Writers Write or Rewrite?: A Case Study of the Literary Representation of Marathi Subalterns

The first part of the doubledeck title of this paper is meant to exhibit the intertextuality of such pretexts as Gayatri Chakravorty Spivak's (*PSR* rpt. 1995:24-28) "Can the Subaltern Speak ?" mainly and half a dozen essays and interviews on the same polemical topic: Margery Fee's (*PSR* rpt. 1995: 342-43) "Who Can Write as Other?", Werner Sollors's "Who is Ethnic?" (*PSR* rpt. 1995:21-222) and many other writings on, in Arun Mukherjee's (1994) words, 'Oppositional Aesthetics: readings from a hyphenated space.' Her introduction to *Towards an Aesthetic of Opposition* reveals various aspects of "a painful and difficult process of decolonization" and records "the dialectics of that struggle" in her postcolonial education in India and Canada. Going by the caste hierarchy in India she is an immigrant "elite" but in the international postcolonial context a subaltern, especially a gendered subaltern. She believes that a similar collective struggle (is) being waged in the hearts and minds of all Third World people. She writes from the Canadian 'hyphenated space' about the effect of Western education on her:

> Thus, a canon made mostly of a histroical and apolitical Anglo-American texts was presented to me as the epitome of what constituted literature. It did not educate me in anything and alienated me from my reality ....
>
> My Canadian education did not remove any cobwebs .....

> Obviously, the themes of history, conquest and subjugation, anticolonial struggles, racism, sexism, class conflict are all absent from this worldview. Hence, the works that deal with this worldview are also largely absent from the curricula of Departments of English in Canada... (1-4).

S. Sankar (1994 : 479-88) has aptly described such Third World postcolonial intellectuals educated in the First World as modern Eklavyas who have lost their thumbs to the First World institutions. This is why African Ngugi wa Thiong'o (1992 rpt. *PSR* 1995:438-47, also see Anand Patil 1995: 1-21) pleaded "On the Abolition of the English Department". If we juxtapose the critical prose writings of Bhalchandra Nemade and Dilip Chitre with Arun Mukherjee's essays, we reveal similarities as well as several differences in their construct of 'oppositional aesthetics' in the international context. In Indian context Nemade and Chitre are not subaltern by caste or class, but they are subaltern as creative writers in the international context. Compared with the anticolonial theories of other Third World postcolonial critics, their oppositional aesthetic exhibits very feeble resistance. It means we have to develop different categories of Marathi subaltern writers and examine the changes in their representation of the subalterns and also their own performances as subaltern writers. The dalits would classify B.S. Mardhekar as a Brahman, elitist or modernist Marathi writer, because the Mardhekarian maze of aesthetics has bismeared the literary culture for a long time. But no Marathi critic has ever placed him in the colonial context which makes him a subaltern of a different kind.

Thus, postcolonial perspective on Indian literatures, Indian writing in English included, discloses real dangers in representation of indigenous 'peoples' in popular discourse. "The Brahmanical Indian literatures" (Meenakshi Mukherjee's concept) and the media claim an 'authentic' voice. Such claims of 'bourgeois nationalism' ignore the actual complexity and differences and continue the colonial process in the neocolonial world. The result is crippling to the efforts of subalterns to evolve an effective strategy of recuperation and resistance.

Perhaps these are the reasons of the demands for the 'non-brahmanical' (Sharad Patil 1985), 'alternative' aesthetics (Pradnya Lokhande) or 'the dalit aesthetics' (Sharankumar Limbale 1996) needed to interpret texts which are written in a language called Marathi. The problematics of the subaltern consciousness in Marathi is well illustrated by staging the most imitative and derivative anglicized Marathi writer like P. L. Deshpande as "Maharashtra Bhushan" (Ornament of Maharashtra). In terms of Fanonian canon Deshpande's creative writing would be considered as a part of the colonial imperial project which thrives on mimicry. Nemade's label for him i.e., "the clown" is befitting in the literary context. It is the pan-Indian scene that such pro-establishment literary works as are derivative and intertextually linked with the works of the Western European tradition are recognised for the highest literary awards. In terms of anticolonial aesthetics such Third World writers cannot write with 'authentic voice'. In Spivak's words, they cannot 'speak', and according to Andre Lefever (1987: 55-68) they are "rewriters". In order to probe deeper into these problems of literary colonialism and of identifying sites of counter-discourse, let us first address to the debate on Subaltern Studies and then analyse some sample cases.

I

It is a neo-colonial paradox that the First World critical texts have allotted the 'space' of one separate Chapter for the Third World "post-colonial" criticism (see Peter Barry 1995 191-201), but in Marathi criticism we can hardly trace a single article which demonstrates methodical resistance to colonialism at both levels: internal and external. We have neither created adequate space for comparative literature nor yet defined, in terms of Jenny Sharpe (*PSR* rpt. 1995:99-102), "figures of colonial resistance". According to Sharpe, the first figure is that of the "mimic man" or "colonial subject" — the Western educated man "who simultaneously reenforces colonial authority and disturbs it" (99). Further she points out several contradictions of colonialism and reads the 'cotton weaver' and 'untouchable' as the mimic man's shadows, in order to demonstrate the class and caste determinants of colonial as well as postcolonial relations. By extending Sharpe's metaphor, it can be said that Shanta Shelake a weaver by birth, is the shadow of Ravikiran Mandal poets basking in Wordsworth's Lake District. Anand Yadav and R.R. Borade, peasants by heritage, are shadows of Gangadhar Gadagil and B.S. Mardhekar who are in turn shadows of James Joyce and Henry James. Namadev C. Kambale, the dalit by caste, is the shadow of S.N. Pendase who stands upon the shoulders of N.S. Phadake and V.S. Khandekar in order to look at *The Mill on the Floss* in England. These are the results of lord T.B. Macaulay's theory of infiltration of the Western education to the lower castes/ classes as implied in his famous *Minutes*. Even in the postcolonial Marathi criticism the doctrines of American New criticism rendered by a W.L. Kulkarni or a Bombay-based anglicized high caste lecturer were instrumental in canonizing the works of the "rewriters" mentioned above.

It should be noted here that Sharpe refers to the colonial scene in India. Of course, the dalit literature has answered, to some extent, the internal "colonizers back" with the borrowed American Black modernism. Yet it does not mean that the subaltern Marathi writing exhibits adequately "a critical awareness of colonialism's effects". Sharpe argues that 'none of us escape the legacy of colonial past and its traces in our academic practices,' and concludes:

> The 'success' of our critical work depends on the recognition that the subaltern is irreducible and yet ultimately irretrievable. Our models remain inadequate. In the absence of that failure we run the risk of imitating successful historical records and subordinating the subaltern (102).

Such acute awareness of the effects of mimeticism and colonialism blocks the creative process of a writer who faces the problem of, in Canadian writer Dennis Lee's (1974 rpt. *PSR* 1995: 397-401) words "writing in Colonial Space".

> The colonial writer does not have words of his own. Is it not possible that he projects his own condition of voicelessness into whatever he creates that he articulates his own powerlessness, in the face of alien words, by seeking out fresh tales of victims? ... Perhaps the colonial imagination is driven to recreate, again and again, the experience of writing in colonial space (399).

In other words Homi K. Bhabha (1985 rpt. *PSR* 1995:29-36) explains the effects of the English book on the colonized Indians. According to him, "the discovery of the English book establishes both a measure of mimesis and a mode of civil authority and order". Further he comments on "signs taken for wonder' as 'texts of the civilizing mission" and observes:

> In the doubly inscribed space of colonial representation where the presence of authority the English book is also a question of its repetition and displacement, where transparency is *techne*, the immediate visibility of such a regime of recognition is resisted .... It is the effect of an ambivalence produced within the rules of recognition of dominant discourses *as* they articulate the signs of cultural difference and reimplicate them within the differential relations of colonial power—hierarchy, normalization, marginalization, and so forth ...(33).

Benita Parry (1987) has discussed problems in current theories of 'colonial discourse' developed by Gayatri Spivak and Bhabha. According to Parry, their different discursive practices "constrain the development of an anti-imperialist critique" (36). So their theories need to be supplemented by Fanon's theory in order to liberate Marathi literature by developing the subaltern counter-discourse.

The history of Marathi literature is written "from above" and subaltern voices are hardly heard in it. It is the "shadow" of the Cambridge models of colonial historiography, hence not more important, for the subalterns, than a telephone directory. What Ranjit Guha (1982:1) writes of the historiography of colonial India is equally true of the historiography of 'modem' Marathi literature. Guha states at the outset of *Subaltern Studies* I:

> The historiography of Indian nationalism has for a long time been dominated by elitism-colonialist elitism and bourgeois-nationalist elitism. Both originated as the ideological products of British rule in India, but have survived the transfer of power and been assimilated to neo-colonialist and neo-nationalist forms of discourse in Britain and India respectively. Elitist historiography of the colonialist or neo-colonialist type counts British writers and institutions among its principal protagonists, but has its imitators in India and other countries too (1).

These varieties of elitism share the prejudice that the making of "modern Marathi" literature and the development of literary taste were predominantly elite achievements and R.S. Jog's *Marathi Abhiruchiche Vihangamvalokan* (Looking back at Marathi taste, 1959) is a typical example of this trend. In the colonialist and neo-colonialist literary historiographies these achievements are credited to British colonial rulers, policies and culture; in the nationalist and neo-nationalist criticism to native elite personalties and institutions. The majority of the fathers of the modern "hybrid" Marathi literary genres are from the Brahmin elite class/caste: Vishnudas Bhave-drama, B.S. Mardhekar-poetry, Gangadhar Gadagil-short story, to name a few fathers. Now the feminist list of mothers of Marathi literary kinds is certainly going to be elitist, because it has never linked its agenda with the down trodden dalit or peasant literary movements like the Western feminists. So a literary movement of killing the colonial "fathers" in Indian literary history would be the prime objective of undertaking subaltern studies.

This demonstrates how the heterogeneity of the colonized subaltern *subject* is suppressed in literature. Guha's definitions, derived from Antonio Gramsci's writings, imply non-elite or subordinated social groups by the term "subaltern". He uses it as a synonym of the word "people(s)". His classification, which is given below, helps us to deconstruct the history of Marathi literature.

1. Dominant foreign groups.
2. Dominant indigenous groups on all India level.
3. Dominant indigenous groups at the regional and local levels.

4. The terms 'people' and 'subaltern classes' are used as synonymous throughout by Guha. The social groups and elements included in this category represent *the demographic difference between the total Indian population* and all those whom we have described as the 'elite' (8).

II

Let us examine, in the light of the preceding discussion, if Marathi writers see their positing of "a theoretically and historically possible subaltern consciousness" as a form of "strategic essentialism". Do they write as if they are aware of the complicity with subaltern insurgency? Do they make "strategic use of positivisitic essentialism in a scrupulously visible political interest?" Does gender and the figure of woman operate in unexamined ways in the Subaltemists' texts? Do they make start on a particular decolonization of the mind? Are there any collective literary projects of Marathi subaltern writers? Theoretically and archivally speaking, what is their contribution to the subaltern studies? The list of such questions is not exhaustive, albeit the answers to them might be more in the negative.

The history of the protest literature of the subalterns is traced back to Jotiba Phule's works. This pioneer rebel writer was the first spokesman—person of the subaltern during the colonial period, but his 'internal' counter-discourse was determined by the British imperial policies. Even Tarabai Shinde's essay on the suffering of women, which may be considered the early feminist writing in Marathi, was also the product of the colonial metaphor of the relationship between the colonizer-male and the colonized-female. In those days imperialism's 'epistemic bellicosity' had been decimating the old culture and left the colonized without the ground from which they could utter confrontational words. Their resistance was directed more against internal colonialism rather than the external.

Apart from the colonial binaries such as master-slave, white-black and so on. As long as English language and *jati-*

varna caste hierarchy does not leave us, people will never cease to be subalterns as Spivak dreams them to be. Partha Chatterjee opens his article:" Caste and Subaltern Consciousness" (*SS* VI: 169) with the following statement:

> It is now widely recognised among social anthropologists of India that the religious beliefs and practices of subordinate caste groups are quite often based on principles that are contradictory to those of the Brahmanical religion, The question that is raised for us is: what do these observations mean for a description of the consciousness of the subaltern classes? Even at the surface level we can sense the importance of these findings, for no matter how we choose to characterize it, subaltern consciousness in the specific cultural context of India cannot but contain caste as a central element in its constitution (169).

But showing caste consciousness is considered to be an extra-literary sin in Gangadhar Gadgil's impressionism. Now a days he confesses that the creative writers of his generation were never caste conscious. Are the social anthropologist wrong? Why has V. Geetha published the polemical article: "Re-writing History in the Brahmin's shadow: and the Modern Historical Imagination" (1993: 127)-151)? It is one more example of how Subaltern Studies meet with failures and "how subaltern cannot speak."

Take one more illustration of the immigrant subaltern. Arun Mukherjee in her essay: "Race Consciousness" of a South Asian (Canadian of course) Female Academic (1994:9) writes about her race consciousness in a white county where being "just Canadian" is the privilege of only white people and others are 'tagged with identity cards.' Her total life experience is determined by that fact and she writes:

> .... Moreover, "non-white" is only one aspect of my multiple identities, for I am also a woman of colour, a Third Worlder, a South Asian, and an east Indian, an Indian, a Punjabi, and a Mukherjee (my patronymic caste marker). What term I use to describe myself and my subject matter

> depends on who I am speaking to and what I am talking about... (10)

Now take a contrapuntal review of what Vilas Sarang writes in his "Confessions of a Marathi Writer" (1994:309), of course, from Kuwait:

> At the same time, I have always thought of myself belonging, in my small way, to an admittedly some what nebulous-international modernist tradition. It is also, should I say inevitably, a Western European tradition I have imagined myself as working in the context of writers, I have admired most: Kafka, Hemingway, Camus, Beckett, et al. Marathi literature is so hopelessly mired in the stick-in-the-mud middle class ethos and reflexes, with its peculiar literary style (laden with exclamation marks!) that would appear antediluvian in English, that, from the beginning I refused to have any truck with the sensibility it represented. The narrow and subtly caste-marked, paths of Marathi literature I saw as something to avoid at any cost... (309).

After these representative examples of the 'contradictory consciousness' of caste at the international cosmopolitan level, let us consider some samples of the indigenous subaltern writers. They explain how 'subtly caste-marked' literary kinds are produced by them in their, in Spivak's words, "upward, downward, sideward, backward mobility" in literary career. The canon of modern Marathi literature is formed by not true subaltern writers as such but by those upper caste English educated elites who belong to, "the floating buffer zone of the regional subaltern elite" remotely controlled by the colonial counterparts of the metropolis. A comparative study of the development of Ranjit Desai and Viswas Patil as fiction writers reveals how caste conditioned imagination of a Marathi writer plays the 'in-between' role to cater to the literary taste of the canon makers' uppercaste readership, and, to use Raymond Williams terms, "cultural industry". As Werner Soller (1986 rpt. *PSR* 1995:119-22) has demonstrated in case of America, the ethnic historiography of literature is of great help in interpreting "boundary-construction processes which function as cultural markers between groups" (220), For instance, the ethnic name-calling also signifying simply 'men' or 'first men' and to regard alien as something 'less than men' or by some derogatory term and tags such as 'barbarians' *(rangat, mattya* for Maratha, *shamalu, shelpat; kapati* for Brahman, *gavandhal, untouchable,* son-in-law of government for a *dalit, landa* for a Muslim etc.) 'greaser', 'nigger', 'thug' are universal. Perhaps this is why Indian writers prefer 'forewords' and 'prefaces' written by the stalwarts of different caste, if possible from the member of the higher caste culture-bearing stratra. Similarly the hegemonic upper-caste culture industry lures the select talents from the lower-castes, like the European colonizers, as comprador sub-subalterns to support the discourse of the culturally dominant upper caste groups. The emergence of divergent culture groups on the literary scene compels the theorists "to rethink the definition of subaltern" in this specific context.

Both Desai and Viswas Patil are of the same caste but with great differences in their subaltern status. To deny that all Marathi writers write as people whose consciousness has been formed as colonial subject is to deny our history. Their consciousness as colonial subjects might be modified in correspondence with one's own experiences in the colonial as well as caste hierarchy and the relation they establish to our intellectual tradition. Sumit Sarkar (*SS* VI 1989:273) employs the "term" "subaltern" as a convenient short-hand for three social groups: tribal and low-caste agricultural labourers and share-croppers, landholding peasants, generally of intermediate-caste status in Bengal (together with their Muslim counterparts); and labour in plantations, mines and industries (along with urban casual labour)". In these terms Desai and Patil, as their sur names signify the ruling class of exploiters, belong to the category of the indigenous elite kshatriyas of two subdivisions. The first is an aristocrat-landlord with relatively autonomous political domain and the latter from a family of the marginal farmer. Both were brought up in the same district and educated in the same city: Kolhapur which is known for anti-Peshawa-Brahmin socio-cultural-political movements. Both began their career by writing short stories depicting the rural subaltern consciousness. Patil dared construct the anti-colonial fictional discourse in his first novel: *Krantisurya* (The Son of Revolution) based on the life story of the famous communist leader and freedom fighter, who formed alternative government-*patri sarkar*, Nana Patil. But the elite taste did not extend the boundaries of their canon of the "Great Tradition" to include or at least to recognise this subaltern consciousness.

Then both the 'post-independence' Maratha writers preferred the pre-British Peshawa Brahmin regime, of which history was documented by elite historian, as subjects of their historical novels. Both were guided and helped by the publishers in Pune. Perhaps, a story from King Shivaji's epoch did not fit into Maharashtrian nationalist paradigms, but the Peshawa history was fictionalized to create image and locate cultures, usually by defining a national culture that selects some aspects of history and symbolism, but sidelines others. The use and abuse of history by our novelists is a separate topic of usual debate, and we are not going to evaluate here Desai's *Swami* (1962) and Patil's *Panipat* (1991) as models of fundamentalist projects of producing pseudo-historical detective fiction that mimics white master's models, especially Walter Scott's novels. It is just like Doordarshan's serialised drama which depicted Chanakya as hero of the Maurya empire, instead of Chandragupta or his grandson Ashoka. In fact both Maratha novelists in their "upward mobility" were in V. Geetha's terms, "rewriting history in the Brahmin's shadow." Soon they were rewarded not only by State level decorations, but also by the central Sahitya Akademi Delhi awards and 'honours'.

By the way, it is interesting to compare the transfer of culture and literary awards from former internal as well as external centres of imperialism to former colonies at the periphery. W.J.T. Mitchell (1992 rpt. *PSR* 1995:475-78) observes that "the former imperial centres today excel in criticism while former colonial nations are producing the most exciting literature" (475). In support of his statement this comparitist has quoted the names of recent non-Euramerican Nobel laureates, and of the non-English winners of the Booker Prize. Similarly, our literary map is in greater flux; but we fail to read it in global context. The subaltern *dalit* and *grameen* writers have surpassed the elite writers at the metropolitan cities like Bombay and Pune. Thus the "balance of *literary* trade has shifted from the First World to the Second and Third Worlds", and similar shifts are seen today in Maharashtra.

This does not mean that the above mentioned novels display "the total absence of colonial provinciality", and the presence of a sophisticated cosmopolitan awareness, including an awareness of "contemporary criticism" which one finds in the Latin American novel. Dipesh Chakrabarty (1992 rpt. *PSR* 1995:383-88) has rightly problematized the idea of 'Indians' 'representing themselves in history'. He has explained 'postcoloniality and the artifice of history' in India and asked: 'Who speaks for India's Past?' He calls this the project of provincializing 'Europe', the 'Europe' that modern imperialism and (third world) nationalism have, by their "collaborative venture and violence, made universal" (385). These samples do not subvert history but rehabilitate elitist myths. This kind of "storying" does not call for a redefinition of the "dialetical relation between writing, history and ideology". In order to explain this point let us discuss only one crucial site of contestation in *Swami*. Bhalchandra Nemade (1990:195, 202-4) rightly exposed the socio-cultural politics which conditioned this pseudo-historical romance written in an unheroic age. It is a neo-colonical contradiction in the subaltern consciousness that the ending of the novel, which depicts Ramabai's death as, in Spivak's famous words, "an ad hoc, subaltern rewriting of the social text of *sati suicide*." Desai glorified it despite the long history of reforms and ban on *Sati*. In several essays on feminism Spivak repeatedly states

> .... subaltern insurgency, and this is the moment of that, is an effort to involve oneself in representation, *not* according to the lines laid down by the official institutional structures of representation. Most often it does not catch. That is the moment that I am calling "not speaking",

> distinguishing it from the general condition of subalternity where all speech acts exchanged in subalternity are only accessible to oral history, or a discursive formation different from the investigation (*SR* 1996: 306).

But such deconstructive practice and feminist critique is certainly beyond the present boundaries of neo-colonial Marathi criticism which has not yet acquired the status of postcolonial criticism. It is not a coincidence that two elitist writers in two countries and cultures react to the subaltern historiography and post-imperial critical trends in the similar vein, Compare the following:

A) Gangadhar Gadagil stated in a public speech in Bombay:

> In the prime period of reading our literature, as it is today, was not fragmented into different fractions such as the *dalit*, feminist, progressive etc. There were no separate divisitions, and no politicians had thrust themselves into it as they do today. So leaders committed to different ideologies frankly debated the issues, on one platform. They were so intimate to sit at one table for the dinner. Now a days because of different divisions monolithic Marathi literature is at great loss. Moreover, those different sections also bear the loss (*Maharashtra Times*, 15th Nov. 1936).

B) Mitchell writes in "Post-colonial Culture, Postimperial Criticism" (*PSR* 1995:477):

> When the neo-conservative National Association of scholars reacts to the emergence of ethnic and women's studies by declaring that 'the barbarians are in our midst,' we recognise the hysterical rhetoric of an empire in decline. Allan Bloom's characterization of Afro-American studies as 'the Little Black Empire' plays on similar buzz-words, simultaneously denigrating the value and inflating the threat of the barbarians by projecting imperial *ambitions* onto them (477).

The emergence of *grameen* and *dalit* texts in the university production of knowledge is also considered by our neo-conservatives as 'the presence of barbarians among us'. The number of 'little' subaltern empires is multiplying in Marathi literati. However, subaltern writers have not yet explored the innovative possibilities of representation of the contradictory consciousness. The investigation of true subaltern would revolutionize writer's own literary consciousness. Most of the literary works display that subalterns are not represented adequately. A comparative study of the portrayal of the subaltern consciousness by the colonial anglo-Indian writers such as Rudyard Kipling, E.M. Forster, and others and our Marathi writers from Hari Narayan Apte to Sadanand Deshmukh would not reveal much differences. It is true that a number of dalit writers from Annabhau Sathe to Daya Pawar have tried to construct the anti-domestic-colonization discourse, but with less awareness of global imperialism.

The subaltern mentality is characterized by two elements. In Gautam Bhadra's (*SS* VI 187:54-90) view, 'Submissiveness to authority in one context is as frequent as defiance in another'. Because of this combination the oppressed have made "voluntary sacrifices in favour of the rich and the dominant, at least as often as they have rebelled against the latter" (54). He suggests to separate "the idioms of domination, subordination and revolt" in order to analyse the literary work. The process is 'marked by struggle and resistance'.

The purpose of analysis of a poem is 'to highlight some of these tensions with reference to a particular text.' Besides such linguistic makers of the subaltern 'mentality' we have to analyse subaltern writer's consciousness in choice of themes and forms which reveal the tensions in their creative process. The dalit autonarratives or self-writings/self photo-narratives soon became stereotypical. On the whole, the *grameen* and *dalit* literatures are blocked up in repetitive patterns of mimicry of the elitist modern Marathi literature which is the shadow literature of the West. Narendra Jadhav's *Amacha Bap Aani Amhi* - Our Father and We (1993) and Kishor Shantabai Kale's much politicised *Kolhatycha Por* - a Kolhati boy (1994) or Namaeo Kambale's elitist *Raghavwel* — The dusk time (1994) show how our literature needs new break-throughs. The latter two are examined less critically by the elite critics, but are being reviewed more sincerely by the dalit interpreters (see

Ashmitadarsh July 1996). The latter two can be criticised from the nativistic point of view to show how these are not true *dalit* texts with specific cultural intertextuality.

Historically and archivally speaking, at a first glance the markers of the ambivalence and contradictions in the creative process of the writer-spokesman for the subaltern become apparent in Jadhav's text, and its paratexts. For instance, its title *Amacha Bap Aani Amhi* sets the dialogic tone of the Mahar dalit narrator who immediately transforms himself into a Sanskrit Shastri while penning the dedication. Even the intertextuality of sketches and paintings is post-modern. This is the triumph of technology but the writer hardly knows the technique of representing the subaltern father's and his children's subalternity without the domination of the colonial master narrative. The contrast between the father's experiences in the Bombay Port Trust and of Narendra in the Mantralaya of Bombay as a secretary are blurred by the linguistic elitism of the narrator. The son improved upon his less educated father's auto-narration. The English educated and America-returned Narendra refers to Ambedkar's impact on them but the text neither does exhibit the intertextuality of Ambedkarian ideology nor of the Black aesthetics of oppression.

The line on the back leaf of the blurb of the second edition advertises that five thousand copies of this book were sold in eleven months. It is one more proof that the elite dalit writer's subaltern father 'cannot speak'. He is made to use a learned scholar's language on one page and the idiom of the defiant worker and nearly illiterate villager in the next paragraph on the same page. It is this elitism which caters to the upper-class-caste literary taste. So the majority of self-writings cum auto-fiction cum detective stories of subalternity are very popular today. It does not mean that they are representing the subaltern consciousness with true consciousness of internal or external colonialism.

III

Thus, examining Marathi literature in the light of contemporary "postcolonial" theories is one of the means to make it really "post- independence/postcolonial" in the real sense of the term. The foregoing discussion of the theories of post-colonialism in the first part and the analysis of the samples selected at random for comparison in the second leads us to the conclusion that the deconstructive practices and subaltern historiography would turn the traditional Marathi criticism, as it is practised today, upside down. For example, if a researcher explores the contemporary extraliterary documents related to the village life of communities and places so-called milestones in *grameen, pradeshik,* even dalit-*grameen* literature in the perfect historical context, the masterpieces will be reduced to the level of best-sellers and vice versa. The scrutiny of the sample texts revealed that Marathi literature is on the whole neocolonial literature but not necessarily postcolonial 'Marathi' subaltern literature. There is more rewriting because no space is created for the subaltern writer who can 'write' with some authenticity. The absence of awareness of postimperial Third World criticism has caused the absence of the subaltern aesthetics of resistance in 'minority Marathi literatures'. Hence subaltern studies in Marathi literature would definitely bring about revolutionary changes. Let the subalterns 'speak' in their own voice.

10

Beyond Modernism: The Aesthetics of Resistance

I

This is partly a comparative study of major tenets of the aesthetics of resistance as revealed in Marathi "literatures". In order to suggest some means to go beyond modernity the so called literatures of protest viz., *grameen* and dalit are juxtaposed with Black aesthetics. The demand of "an alternative" aesthetics is ill-informed and meekly differentialist. No one has defined the "otherness" in Marathi language and literary culture in terms of the aesthetics of resistance 'based on caste conflicts' as some black theorists have done. Moreover, the salient features of "modernity" introduced into them after the colonial contact with Europe also remain unexplored. Consequently, there is little awareness of striking new paths to overcome the dead-ends effected by half-baked modernism which is closely connected with colonialism and fascism.

The caste conditioned world-view complicates the issue still further, and the beginner is baited by the nylon net of mimeticism. The literary minority discourses become ambivalent as regards the imitation of the metropolitan centre, both indigenous as well as alien. Although prestigious awards are being bestowed upon writers at the periphery, their works are not free from the colonial curse of dwarfing mimeticism. Modernity, coloniality, "post" and multiple combinational possibilities of these terms have not yet held much of our academic discourse in the regional languages. We designate the issues implied in these terms as postcolonial or, in a more misleading term, post-independence: what are we after?

One of the colonial Indian vernacular literatures in British Bombay Presidency was considered as monolithic Marathi literature. Now it is split into half a dozen fractions, namely, the *grameen,* the *dalit,* the *janwadi,* the Jain and so on. Is any one of them, including mainstream, really postcolonial? Where do our writers speak from? The word 'literatures' is used ironically to point out the caste, subculture, region and religion based plurality of Marathi literature. This kind of inter-determining condition has barred it from the wide frame of reference which is effectively used by anticolonialists. For example, in the review of Derek Walcott's play Patrick Colm Hogan (1994, 110) argues:

> The reactionary nativism is a rejection of colonial racist ideology which presupposes the acceptance of that ideology. Put it differently, reactionary nativism is obverse of mimeticism—mimeticism being the formation of one's identity in terms of the concepts and values ascribed to one's oppressors. Mimeticism is what leads to racial despair to the sense that one has no value, as well as to the imitation of white culture, devotion to white law and rule, white idea and language (i.e. ideas and language which are categorized by whites as superior and as their own—even when those ideas had their origin outside Europe).

These lines can be rewritten adequately by inserting the casteist terminology which dominates the literary scene in India. Whether spoken of in terms of decolonizing, decasting, *vidrohi* (protest), or "negritude", defining one's social and personal identity has been a central task of literary artists from Saint Tukaram to Dilip Chitre. A few current examples of the under class-caste protest include Baburao Bagul's *Sood* (Revenge), P. E. Sonkamble's *Athawaninche Pakshi* (Memories with Wings), Shankar Gaikwad's *Shudra.* But do these works resist the forms of "master narratives"? The answer is negative. Modern Marathi literature is already over determined by European "modernity" which can be described, in Ashish Nandi's words, as "the armed version of colonialism". In order to "break through" it, indigenous aesthetics is one of the remedies. It can be linked with postmodernism also. To belong to the Third World is to accept an identity with the "wretched of the earth" spoken for by Frantz Fanon. So I have shifted the critical axis slightly away from these usual caste marked local debates to the subaltern writer's role in the neo-colonial situation.

II

Very few of our writers have chosen to look at the issue from the other side, examining how the *jati-varna system* undermines cultural identity, retains the hegemony of one caste or other and favours alien literary influences by relegating the indigenous ones. The impossibility of assimilation, as in case of Whites and Blacks, which gave rise to the theme of intercaste marriage in *Tethe Pahije Jatiche* (Caste Determines All), has added new facets to some literary works. The exponents of different positions among these fractions have arrived at the conclusion that neither the Euramerican nor elitist indigenous critical theories practised at present can help any interpretation of literary works produced by underprivileged writers at the periphery. Out of nearly two dozen Marathi books on aesthetics, not a single one represents the resistance to the Euramerican theories which dominate our curriculum. A few of them are critical of the anglicized brahmanical Marathi aesthetics. Some of the more obvious instances from the postcolonial canon would include Bhalchandra Nemade's single article on nativism, M.N. Wankhede's (1981) essays on the dalit protest literature. Sharad Patil's (1967) *Abrahmani Wangmyanche Saundaryashastra* (The Aesthetics of Non-Brahmin Literatures), assimilationist comprador Anand Yadav's (1979) *Grameen Sahitya* (The Rural Literature) and stray articles by the young rebel writers. They display more of the age old "in-fighting" rather than conscious revolt against Euramerica-centric literary imperialism. The absence of "a Calibanic Tempest" and the lack of adequate introduction of various models of Black Aesthetics in Marathi make much difference in the degree and kind of resistance to the European master narratives.

The sub-title of this National Seminar is now a misnomer. Marathi dalit writers prefer the lebels such as "Ambedkar/ Phulewadi" or "panther". U.R. Anantha Murthy devised two terms: "Frontyard" and "Backyard" cultures, but I come from "agriculture" which offers an indigenous aesthetics of plant culture and graft-culture. Our literary works are battle-grounds of such cultural strifes. Hence the title of this paper: "The Aesthetics of Resistance". The dissenting voices from Dnyaneswar to B.R. Ambedkar are many. From M.N. Wankhede to Anand Yadav the dalit and grameen movements have taken paradoxical turns. Gangadhar Pantawane's attempt to develop the aesthetics of *Nav-Boudha* dalits through the periodical *Asmitadarsh,* and the writings of Janardhan Waghmare and Kashinath Ranveer on the American black literature exhibit the possibilities of protest. But the "post-coloniality" as such is not yet adequately debated by any fraction among the oppressed. The elitist Marathi mediators of the Western cultural imperialism are least bothered about nativism, and Gangadhar Gadagil's writing reflects the ambivalent attitudes of this comprador class. Let us illustrate this point to show the relationship between caste hierarchy and Lord Macaulay's famous famous theory of filtration of Western education and culture in India.

Namdev C. Kambale, the first dalit novelist to win the Sahitya Akademi Award for his *Raghavwel* — The dusk time (1996), confessed that he is an active member of Bharatiya Janata Party and would not like to be frogmarched in any dalit movement. It is an intra-cultural contradiction that the dalits themselves demonstrated by leading *morchas* against him and condemned Kambale for projecting false images of both the *Mang* (caste) females and Maratha males in his novel (see *Ashmitadarsh,* June 1996). This explains how our postcolonial writers are placed on the horns of a dilemma when they employ an alien form to represent indigenous reality. The poetics and politics of representation of reality reveals writer's divided loyalties. Such gestures need to be interpreted in terms of the writer's class/caste position in the hierarchy of a largely illiterate population, lure of recognition and publication offers from Pune and Bombay. These are indirectly linked to

Euramerican centres via the Gate Way of India. Aime Cesaire, Octave Mannoni, Albert Memmi, Edward Said and many other non-white theorists of anti-colonialism, who plead for the recovery of the "national" or "native" voice in literary discourse, can hardly dream of strange cultural contradictions in our literati. At least we have a Saneguruji to argue in favour of "authenticity" and cultural nativism in literature. But we have to define our literary post-coloniality in concrete terms and practice what we preach.

Officially colonial rule has ended, but the historical, political and cultural effects of an alien empire still do persist. Post-colonial writing has to position itself in this international context as a broad anti-imperialist emancipatory project. The term "post-colonial" and its categories have created complications that involve the historical and national contexts. For some, the prefix *post* is premature. It means the possible displacement of other critical procedures. It may create "new Orientalism". To the other extreme some observers claim that it is the "space clearing gesture" of an oppositional "counter-discourse". The politics of constructing a counter-discourse is implied in this poetics. Some of the pre-occupations of post-colonial theory intersect "problematic theoretical discourse such as postmodemist, feminist, lesbian, and gay or queer studies" (see *PMLA,* Jan. 1995, 9). Even as generic label, *post-colonial* may be misleading, but has never been discussed in Marathi thoroughly. "Post" means "after", because of and even inclusive of the colonial. It signifies resistance and opposition, the anti-colonial. On the whole, we fail to find such agenda in any *Sahitya Sammelan* (Annual Gathering of writers or Seminar in Marathi).

The real "post-coloniality" reacts to the Euramerica-centric mimeticism rampant in the comprador intelligentsia created by the former colonizers in their own image. Our ill-informed underclass writers blindly imitate the literature of the Westernized upper class-caste. True, the dalit literature, the gift of so called progressive Maharashtra, challenged the status quo and demanded new aesthetics. Any claims about such postcolonial texts must be negotiated through an intricate mapping of social and cultural conditions that accompany the production of a particular text. A common history of economic and cultural bondage has resulted in similar political and cultural expressions. For instance, the dalit auto-memoirs/self-writing has become stereotype now. In this way, the underclass writers, and projects contribute to a broader understanding of writers for whom the rereading and rewriting of the upper-class-caste historical and fictional record remains a vital task. The dalit writers have been struggling to revive the Boudha narratives, but are not yet free from the labyrinth of westernized historical and fictional record.

The deep-rooted colonialism is reflected in literary culture and careers of our writers. Anand Yadav's rural literary movement was more Mardhekarian because it had nothing to do with the ideology of protest developed by the reformers from Jotiba Phule to Bhaurao Patil. This is why Shankar Patil failed to write a novel on the life of Shahu Maharaj; and he regretted it till he breathed last. The impact of Gandhian movements and the politics of the Congress party weakened the anti-Brahmin stance. On the contrary, the Grand Debates since the 1960s marked dalit writer's revolt against the Vedic Hindu tradition so much so that Namdeo Dhasal asked to dump all the Hindu saints into the gutters of Bombay. Although dalit literary movements got more momentum than the rural ones, as Nemade (1990, 135) has rightly pointed out, they were "politicized to encourage casteism" and over-patronized to suit vested interests by the "brahmin dominated print-media". In brief, the writers' consent was skilfully manufactured by the fully anglicized upper-*varna* "modernist" formalist school guided by American "New Criticism" which was irrelevant in India. Such developments can be analysed as a natural result of borrowed "modernism" and inherited fascism in the given culture.

The search for distinct literary identity has not yet acquired right position and direction. Literary anarchy is evident in separate annual gatherings of the writers belonging to Jain, Muslim and other fractions. One centre cannot hold them together. They face the danger of romanticizing their own group and denigrating the culture of the other. All of them are least aware that various sets of Eruamerican literary myths have been operating to extend their culture institutionally to India. So our literature in any Indian language is not really "postcolonial". What do they resist to? Do they misuse alien narrative forms which exhibit the negative influences of the casteist infighting?

That is a dilemma which the Third World intellectuals have not yet solved. S. Sankar has interpreted it in the international context by using the metaphor of the story of Ekalavya (1994, 481). The lack of resistance to Euramerican texts also means continuation of the story of Indian Ekalavya. In contrast to this, the post-colonial black writers have reacted more vehemently against cultural imperialism and literary colonialism. Bill Ashcroft and others (1989, 156) confirm:

> In fact, the history of literary and critical movements in the twentieth century is, as one might expect, deeply determined by art interaction with imperialism. Indeed such interaction is characteristic of oar century (156).

Similarly, the misuse of Euramerican texts by our writers is one more common characteristic of our generic repertory. See *Critical Practice* (Oct. 1996) for the study of the differences between the reception of Shakespeare's plays by Indian and "black" Caribbean or African writers. Generally, Indians have used his texts, V.V. Shirawadkar and Vasant Kanetkar included, for making "profits" in Indian theatre. This process can be described as a "ritualistic bardicide" and submissive hero-worship not only for commercial "profits" but also for retaining theatrical hegemony. We do not have a single Indian Aime Cesaire, or a Derek Walcott who parodies and subverts Shakespeare's plays in order to create a new dramatic genre which "constitutes a detailed condemnation of imperialism and racism" (Porter 1995, 362). The survey of Indian appropriations of the Bard's plays exhibits no subversion but only versions by upper-caste English educated writers made for conservative cultural purposes. No "anti-colonialist discourse" can be traced in them. This international "intentional and intercultural nature of textual exchange" is never systematically analysed in Marathi criticism. Aparna Dharwadkar's (1995 a, 4-21; b 43, 47) comparative study of use of alien plays by Marathi, Kannada and African writers fully corroborates the findings of my (1993, 272-77) influence study. She rightly holds the "civilized, upper-caste, domesticated spectators (1, 19)" responsible for that kind of colonialist intertextuality in Marathi adaptations. Her more objective observation that the alien texts "continue to articulate in post-colonial writing and generate anti-nationalist rather than anti-colonial dramatic texts (1, 6)" points an accusing finger at P. L. Deshpande's *Teen Paishacha Tamasha* (based on *The Three Penny Opera)* and Girish Karnad's *Tughlaq*. In short, all major English educated as well as less educated writers write "through" Western texts and not "against " them. In fact, they should "write back" to the empire, but they have failed in it because of the collaborationist stance of the upper-caste-class writers.

Major differences between our and black writers are many. Like "blacks" Indians do not have a common ground of "colour" to stand united to resist "an intimate enemy", i.e., colonialism. Thousands of caste barriers do not bring all Indians at one centre. A single slogan: "Black is Beautiful" attracts all Negroes all over the world. As a result they are more resistant and more eligible for Nobel laurels and Olympic awards. Their Afrocentricism makes them more regional, but our writers are never truly "regional", because they do not have one centre of authority to hold them together. Even the emigrant of "the wounded civilization"—V.S. Naipaul—could not outgrow the inherent Indian conservative culture in Caribbean islands. On the contrary, the black Derek Walcott won the Nobel Award as predicted by Stephen Breslow (1993, 267). Walcott proved his Caribbeanness by ironically hinting at the *Ram Leela* performance at the outset of his Nobel lecture (1993, 261). As Naipaul looks down upon Indian folk culture, Kishor Kale fails to assimilate any rhythm of a *lavani*-song which might have enriched the intertextuality of his much "modernised" and anglicized (even more politicized) *Kolhatyacha Por* (1995) — a son of the Kolhati. This kind of cultural "double exilement" of our writers deprives their texts of and rich interanimating network of intertexts and colourful heteroglossia. This leads us to the discussion of multi-colloquialism and acceptance of "difference" in construction of "the aesthetics of the oppressed" in general.

III

Edward Kamau Brathwaite's (1992) search for Caribbean aesthetics stands exactly at the opposite pole from the Indian confused strifes and selfish metaplagiarism. He staunchly opposes everything that is non-Caribbean. Indian writers get more prestigious awards mostly for their innovation and experimentation inspired by Euramerican models. However, young talents, like Tejaswini Niranjan (1993), in India are contesting the concept of "culture" and "modern". Marathi comparative studies also disclosed generic confusion and the problem of neglecting the identification and naming of forms indigenous. For example, we do have various forms of folk dramas which show a very good "communal critical awareness of the essence" of the concerned culture groups. A select few may claim the mastery of Sanskrit lore. The only way out is the acceptance of caste "differences" on equal footing and the construction of "a subject on the equal footing". But it is very difficult to liberate our arts from caste confinements. Even the conversion to Christianity in Goa has not liberated *tiatr;* like *tamasha,* from these barriers. It means that the labels such as *grameen,* dalit, regional, Goan etc. do not show any value related judgement.

The contrapuntal view of current Marathi writings reveals a rich variety introduced by the first generation of writers belonging to innumerable tribes and castes. Laxman Mane's *Upara* (The Outsider) demonstrated for the first time how, albeit very limited, Kaikadi code languages can add new dimensions to tribal life-writing. Similarly Madhukar Wakode has explored the "brave new world" of the *adivasi* (tribes in jungles) people. Baburao Gaikwad's (1994) assessment of the contribution of non-*dalit writers to* dalit literature also reveals the problematics of creative process. Neo-*Bouddha* writers have been negating traditional caste confined folk arts. Thus the warring fractions have not yet mastered the art of speaking intertextually "through" multicultural secret languages of masses. The new Indian aesthetics would take its own shape if they succeed in, to use Mikhail Bakhtin's terms, "creating a heteroglot novelistic language".

Our dalit writers were exposed to the American black aesthetics superficially. The varieties of black aesthetics are not introduced adequately into Marathi. The African models are also useful for us. But their extension to many other post-colonial countries has "never been enthusiastically embraced by critics out side the African diaspora" (Ashcroft et al., 21). Even the Latin American or Caribbean reactionary theories might have provided better models which would have checked the incessant process of stereotypical mimeticism. Like all other minority literatures of the oppressed, literatures of varied culture groups are marked by the rise of poetry first and then auto-confessional-self-writing modes. It must be noted that any literature in India is a "minority discourse". But our literature rarely claims a distinctive Indian view of time-space relationships, and an aesthetics which separated itself from the supposedly "universal" values of European or anglicized upper-class/caste literary taste and style. Modern Marathi "literatures" could easily be reincorporated into Europeanized brahmanical model. Although M.N. Wankhade (78, 86) pointed out this risk, he meekly introduced T.S. Eliot, Walt Whitman, William Shakespeare and other Euramerican men of letters as universal models without much understanding of the relationship between culture and imperialism. Albert Memmi (1974, x) has explored various features of this "love and hate' relationship between the colonizer and the colonized.

Like "negritude" the ideology of Phule and Ambedkar has been largely influential; but it finds expressions through inadequate derivative forms. Other backward classes are also trying to assert their distinctive features. Yet none of them has produced texts which could be "read by the illiterates". The result is the same: the claim to a literature which stresses a shared suffering and resistance to the indigenous oppressive hegemony over shared biological heritage. The dalits are suspicious of nativism because they fear a revival of orthodox Hinduism. Like Negroes they do not return to caste compartmentalized folk traditions. Perhaps, owing to the caste barriers, the political agenda of dalits and feminists has not been linked together like the Black and feminist aesthetics in the West.

It is clear that a culture/caste based aesthetics seems to stand on more sure grounds than a gender-based one in Marathi. Even to claim that the *dalit* aesthetics is grounded in culture and not in politics is to stand on more shaky ground. The bywords for their writings are *gramya* (obscene), *vidrohi* (protest) etc. It may be conceded that the most revered canonical works in our tradition very often arose out of a tradition of "negative aesthetics". Such problems of the classic dialectic of marginalized discourse need to be remedied by the acceptance of differences. We must consider the claim that each group has to play its part. The upper-castes and their lower-caste "OTHERS" are related not as superiors but as contemporaries. To minimise caste distinctions is to deny difference. As such, oppositional caste politics is an intrinsic part of the present literary discourse. Our anti-dialogic education provides us with ready-made "foreign" theories which create hosts of mimic men. The "consciousness industry" supported by the system allows no space for a strong indigenous counter discourse.

IV

Thus our "literatures" have arrived at crossroads where critics are roping together alien structuralism, post-structuralism, post-modernism and several other "posts" which reach through "Air Mails". As a result the subaltern writers are always subject to the activity of the dominant culture group even when they rebel. Their subordination has not been broken by the "permanent" victory of literature of protest even after political independence. More or less similar crises can be noticed in the new literatures of the formerly colonized countries. Even the settlers' colonies are setting their images straight. The Canadian resistance to American domination is illustrated by H.W. New (1989). He states:

> For the writers and artists who would subsequently emerge in Canada, one of the greatest challenges they would face was to work out their own connections with these stereotypes. They would accept the implicit (and often explicit) hierarchies of culture that derived from Europe—accept the idea that European standards were universal, and write or paint or compose in a way that would primarily seek European approval. They would claim indigenous cultures as their cultural roots. In time, they would mimic other models, borrow American culture, and seek American approval as an alternative to things European. Or they could, whether consciously or not, adapt their art to their own place and time, devise methods of telling their own stories, and develop an eclectic culture of their own (23).

This is fully applicable to Marathi literature produced after the colonial contact. The final mode suggested by New leads to the new aesthetics of resistance based on nativism which has been occupying some space in Indian critical thought today. We have not yet applied these new tools in practice, but the Black theorists do use them effectively. As mentioned before, Patrick Hogan (1992) has classified nativism as follows:

1. Romantic Nativism of the pre-independence period.
2. Opportunistic Nativism in its anti-popular or individualistic form.
3. Sectarian Nativism which affirms narrow linguistic., religious and ethnic identities.
4. Neo-colonial Nativism which celebrates indigenous traditions in order to advance their own interests.

There are many kinds of nativisms, and their full length discussion is not intended here. The title of Gervais's recent book *is Literary England: Versions of Englishness in Modern Writings,* It speaks volumes for the centre of European "master narratives".

A number of contradictions in the aesthetics of resistance should be pointed out before making valid prescriptions to the "Protestant" Marathi writers headed towards the twenty first century. Belinda Edmonson's comparative study of various types of Black aesthetics and feminism throws light on some contradictions. According to her (1992, 1994), the formulation of blackness as well as Afrocentricism differs in degrees and kinds. Similar reversals car be found in the concepts such as *grameen,* dalit and so on. The reliance of our writers on alien form shows how they seek reentry in middle class/elite Westenrised theories. In Black aesthetics they privilege the illiterate community over the literate one. This negates the presence of the artist which is more important in the autonomous theory of literature. A colonialism begins with literacy. The ambiguities give rise to creative tension. The tension also resides in the stabilizing theories of oppositional discourse.

Finally, a working model of the Indian aesthetics of resistance can be developed on the following lines:

1. Rely more on privileging Marathiness in general over Euramericanism and universalism.
2. Replace anglicized Marathi and its alien narrative strategies by the use of indigenous polyglossia and narrative techniques.
3. Use socio-aesthetics in representation of the reality of the double colonized life. Guard against extreme caste-centricism that would fall victim to massive oversimplification.
4. Subvert alien texts as well as indigenous decadent forms of dominant master narratives.
5. Establish links with resistance writers of all castes who operate in direct opposition to Eurocentric or decadent Sanskritic epistemologies.
6. Employ politics and poetics of representation of reality in order to establish a regional, cultural and national identity against something that is imposed.
7. The basic prescription: The culture of the downtrodden illiterates is the "authentie" culture, and "authentic" literary work is indicated by its utilization of the dialect and certain principles of orality.

8. Revive folk rhythms, folk music and structures which can compete with alien elements of master narratives.
9. Develop critical terminology drawn from indigenous resources of traditional crafts, arts and aesthetics. For example, the critical vocabulary drawn from agriculture or from the weaver's craft could be more relevant than the alien theories of "deconstruction", "reader response" and reception.
10. The presence of the writer in the expression of the collective is meant to eliminate "chaos" and "alienation" which are hallmarks of European modernism, privileging indigenous worldview.
11. Provide alternatives to the European romanticism, Victorianism, modernism and several other "isms" which still operate among us.
12. A "Marathi" text should use a "myth-based" non-Western time and worldview. It may receive such alien elements which suit its blood group and may not stunt its growth.
13. Make the literary work accessible to the uneducated "reader". It should not employ any of the "elitist" stylist innovations of the modern or post-modern schools.
14. Resist all forms of European narratives and their Indian *avatars*.
15. Renaming literary kinds in indigenous terms which would be understood by the majority.

This list is not exhaustive.

11

"Re-visioning" Intertextualities in R.K. Narayan's Novels: Comparative-Cultural Critique

ABSTRACT

The concepts of revisiting, redoing, rethinking, re-imagining, re-visioning, rereading, reinterpreting, rewriting etc. imply improvisations or new dimensions added to the earlier knowledge. The wavering loyalties of the colonized reader are not yet theorized in India (see Nancy Hogley). So reading *A Passage to India* or *The English Teacher* in the light of post-colonial or cultural theories will certainly not only deconstruct but discard hegemonic intra-colonial judgements of Indian comprador class of imitators of Anglo-American New Critics. R.K. Narayan is the cultural product of Anglo-American "regional modernism", British colonialism and indigenous elitism.

Reading of Edward Said's *Culture and Imperialism* or Homi K. Bhabha's *Nation and Narration will* lead us to new comparative perspectives on RKN's fiction. It is not an accident that similar Brahminical "innate nativism" (see Chomsky) can be traced in *The English Teacher* and "distand Diaspora-immigrant nativism" in Vidyaprasad Surajprasad Naipaul's *The House for Mr Biswas* Not only poetics but also international cultural politics of recognition has influenced the selection of *The Guide.* To be brief, rereading of RKN's fiction with rich? Interdisciplinarity and multiple approaches will certainly produce new knowledge. Does Narayan really "write back to the empire"? Why? W.B. Yeats wrote, "What Next? asked Plato's Ghost." The seminars and conferences are meant to debate such questions.

Keywords: Revisit: meant to look at the same object after some period with new perspectives and historical contexts. Intertextuality is a new concept used to analyse structures of the text at the microscopic level. The other terms such as interculturalism, *internationalism*, etc. are used to undermine the outdated concepts such as influence, imitation, originality, autonomy, authenticity etc. *Comparative cultural study* is the American concept, but comparative culture criticism is the British one. It reveals the Janus face of Indian fiction. "'Family Romance" is the Freudian concept in psychology. It is a metaphor of "love and hate" relationship of writers writing in the same language. *Castealization*: I have coined this term after theory of "racialization". It helps us to theorize "self and other" in literature on the basis of caste-*varna* system..

> Time for a pause, right there, I'm beginning to do exactly what I've always criticized the Naipauls for doing: drawing grand, sweeping conclusions from the flimsiest of anecdotal evidence. After all, one cannot be unaware that in trying to paint even an impressionistic portrait of contemporary Indian society and culture, one is recalling a concept to undefinable that T.S. Eliot was curious enough to call his book on the subject: *Notes Toward the Definition of Culture* and George Steiner, two and half decades later, could do no better than subtitle *In Blue-board's Castle* as *Notes Toward the Redefinition of Culture*. I have neither the desire nor the ability to attempt to define or redefine this slippery term; one cannot entirely forget the pro-Nazi poet Harms Johst's declaration, "When I hear the word 'culture', I reach for my gun."..

Shashi Tharoor. "India at Forty-nine: Notes Toward an Impression of Indian Society and Culture Today". *Midnight to the Millennium and Beyond*, New Delhi: Penguin Books, 1997:278.

Much water has flown under the bridge than what Tharoor means by "Indian society and culture" in terms of "the social heritage and contemporary life of Indians". Tharoor's title exhibits the echoes of intertextuality of Salman Rushdie's controversial *The Midnight's Children.* Moreover, revisiting any colonial text from the postcolonial comparative cultural perspectives would reveal a number of unexplored contradictory aspects than what is seen through the elitist "blue" eyes of Tharoor in *Midnight to Millennium,* R. K. Narayan in *The English Teacher* and Meenakshi Mukherjee in *Realism and Reality: Novel and Society in India* or M.K. Naik in a host of articles and books on Indian writings in English. Tharoor's sibling relationship and "family romance", in Sigmund Freud's famous terms, with Naipaul's *The Area of Darkness* or *A Wounded Civilization* and Rushdie's *The Midnight's Children* is apparent in this essay. Similarly the fiction of the first famous trio, i.e., Raja Rao, Mulk Raj Anand and Narayan needs to be "revisited" with not only new strategies of reading their texts as a symbolic, 'casteist' political unconscious act but also as products of Western, in Edward Said's phrase, "culture and imperialism." Stepping back and looking comparatively with post-colonial and postmodern perspectives at R. K.Narayan's fiction and contemporary reality after nearly 70 years is more or less similar to, what Chinua Achebe did in his "An Image of Africa: Racism in Conrad's *Heart of Darkness*" (1972) and Henry Louis Gates in his *'Race', Writing and Difference* (1995). Elsewhere I (2011) have coined the term "castesalisation" based on Western "racialization" of literature to study national and international affiliations of intertextualities in Indian literature.

So concepts of revisiting, redoing, rethinking, re-imagining, re-visioning, rereading, reinterpreting, rewriting etc. imply improvisations or new dimensions added to the earlier knowledge. In Harold Bloom's terms all reading is misreading and revisions lead to new creations. Intertextual relations are determined by the anxiety of influence and in Sigmund Freud's concept "the family romance of writers". The pre-text makes the post-text possible. The author child is the father of stalwart "writerly" writer. Which R.K. Narayan do we want to revisit, from which perspectives? Does he represent the rich, in Bakhtinian terms, "carnivalization and heteroglossia", of diverse Indian cultures and languages? For whom did he write? In order to answer such pertinent questions we have to take the descriptive term "revisiting" to the deeper analytical conceptual level. For the intellectuals undernourished by colonized traditional curriculum of mono-literary studies it is still a greater challenge to reinterpret colonized texts with pseudo-secularism and cultural illiteracy without Raymond William's vision and commitment to challenge Leavisian Great Tradition of critical thought. In the new millennium of internationalization of literatures it demands postmodern interdisciplinary approaches; but our criticism is stuck in the mire of Anglo-American modernity. See the simple dictionary meanings of the word "revisit" in the title of the theme of the seminar. The dictionary meanings are many: To visit again, A second or repeated visit. (*The American Heritage® Dictionary of the English Language*, Fourth Edition copyright © 2000 by Houghton Mifflin Company. Updated in 2009. Published by Houghton Mifflin Company). revisit (Verb) – visit again; "We revisited Rome after 25 years", return – go or come back to place, condition, or activity where one has been before; "return to your native land"; "the professor returned to his teaching position after serving as Dean" (Based on WordNet 3.0, Farlex clipart collection, ©2003-2008 Princeton University, Farlex Inc).

Our "revisit" to Narayan with ideology of Namwar Singh's preaching to decolonize Indian mind and prior to him Ngugi wa Thiong'o's battle cry for decolonizing African mind would certainly bring new revelations and rewards. It is Ngugi's "homecoming" (1972) and the agenda of "abolishing Departments of English" (1976) that might help us more than our too subjective and impressionistic caste conditioned Indian criticism. It should be noted at the outset that the wavering loyalties of the colonized reader are not yet theorized in India (see Nancy Hogley). In "re-examination" of Narayan's *The English Teacher,* 66 years after its birth, by the post-independent Indian readers fed on Anglomerican postcolonial theories and affected by indigenous, in Edward Said's word, "affiliations" of regions, religions, class and caste, needs new cultural approach today. For example, reading *A Passage to India* or *The English Teacher* in the light of post-colonial or cultural theories again enriches our understanding. But for this we have to read Harold Bloom's "introduction" to the first and compare the latter with Naipaul's A *House for Mr. Biswas* in Fanonian terms. Such revision is bound to deconstruct and discard hegemonic intra-colonial judgements of Indian comprador class of imitators of Anglo-American New Critics; but also take us to their resistant counterparts in black aesthetics. In fact, R.K. Narayan's oeuvre is the cultural product of Anglo-American "regional modernism", British colonialism and indigenous elitism. In this sense, Meenakshi Mukherjee's Brahmanical concept of "twice born" fiction falls short in *contrapuntal analysis* of cultural hybridity in any Indian English novel. It is confined to, in Edward Said's term, the "worldliness" of the earliest sociological twin process namely. Anglicization (modernization) and Sanskritization (Brahmanization) used for analysing the process of acculturation after the elitist cultural contact with Europe. But why only "twice born"? Has it not projected the monolithic Brahminical image of Indian literature to the Western world? What, about indigenous "native" cultural tranaformations? Why are they excluded both from *Kanthapura* and *The English Teacher,* albeit both are set in the villages? Hence the cultural representation of "the Other's double" in Indian English fiction is yet to become the subject of discussion. In this cultural sense the terms such as "Indianness", "Indianize", "nativize" etc., are very deceptive. We may be able to trace how old wine in new bottle may be more poisonous, if we understand why Americans always condemn the French theories of structuralism, deconstruction and intertextuality as "poisonous".

Moreover, in our literary image building cultural industry, to use Fanonian theory, "the battle for reciprocal recognition" is determined by hierarchical cultural capital and degree of illiteracy. Consequently, this dominant Orientalist (British-Brahmanical) image of earlier Anglo-Indian, later Indo-Anglian Commonwealth and the latest Indian writing in English by the Indian elitist writers with traditional, in Pierre Bourdeu's sociological concept, "cultural capital" must have led the German scholar Hyacinth Cynthia Wyatt to undertake the research topic for the doctoral degree "R. K.Narayan as a

Brahman Novelist" submitted to Universitat Rovira I Virgili in 1997. We hardly find such cultural materialism and semiotic approach in our double colonized Indian critical thought. No one can dare to think of such inflammatory cultural area of research where devils fear to tread in a pseudo-secular environment. This shows how and why the term "culture" is considered not only the most difficult word among three English terms but also the most inflammatory of all as demonstrated by George Huntington in *Cultural Clash*. It is necessary to study any Indian literary text as a Walmikian as well as Homerian cultural battlefield. In the tsunamis of globalization it is a right time to rethink of not only the relevance of true contributions of our stalwarts but also device new strategies of rereading colonialisms of various kinds and replacing literary theories for survival in the new competitive literary market of the global village. I hope this Seminar is a welcome beginning in this direction. But we should think of its concrete returns in terms of marketing new knowledge by producing books to be sold all over the world. Of course, there is the ending in the beginning itself. As a creative writer and comparatist-culturalist, I limit this discourse only to the intercultural and international intertextualities in two novels.

It is necessary to demonstrate comparatively, with the help of theory of intertextuality, how literature in all formerly colonized countries is Eurocentric, two-toned, multi-faced, and multi-layered. Owing to the, in Michael Escheuro's words, "culture conditioned imagination" in a peculiar Indian systemic way, a researcher is the victim of Anglo-American critical theories, and local structures of culture and imperialism. Let us juxtapose two samples of the titles and conclusions of the Doctoral theses carried out in the same year in India and Germany. Ramesh Dnyate's "The Novels of R.K. Narayan: A Typological Study of Characters" (1996) was completed in University of Pune under the guidance of a " reputed Marxist interpreter of literature" and published with a bibliography which includes only 80 books but not any periodical. The contents do not show least awareness of interdisciplinarity and the conclusions remain at very superficial levels. The final paragraph runs as follows:

> In short, the typological approach may be regarded as a strategy focus on the essentials in the craft of Narayan's novel. The essentials seem to have been reflected (a) in Narayan's presentment of the epic of the ordinary conceived on the stage of the middle-class Malgudi; (b) in his bifocal vision of comic irony perceiving the essentially illusory nature of the life and (c) in his positive vision of life despite its predestinate or karmic conception (170).

This title seems to be a misnomer and we do not know how Narayan's characters are "cultural products", which are determined by double binds of imperialism. The majority of Indian doctoral works on Rao and Narayan, excluding Anand, exhibit salient features of "culture and imperialism" and project the image of their novels as "prose epics of India" (see M. K. Naik). Elsewhere, I (1997) have demonstrated how *Kanthapura is* "a bogus prose epic" of anglicized elitist India. What is consciously or ignorantly ignored by Indians is objectively analysed by the foreigners. Hyacinth Cynthia Wyatt's "R. K. Narayan as a Brahman Novelist" (1997), in Germany, is a simple cultural study, which demonstrates once again how foreigners have studied Indian languages and literatures better than Indians. We cannot imagine of the first paragraph of the conclusions in this work in any caste and culture conditioned Indian criticism. The first paragraph runs as follows:

> Throughout this study, it has been shown that Hindu culture and Narayan's Brahmanical beliefs and preparation constitutes the substratum of his novelistic work. This study has also called attention to the strong presence of Narayan's Brahmanical heritage and erudition as revealed by the recurrence of cultural symbols and allegorical tendencies that appear at different levels of understanding in all his novels. It has been demonstrated that the myths and teachings continually influence the psychology and behaviour of Narayan's protagonists, many living out roles similar to the mythological, some even with the same names, such as Chandran in *The Bachelor of Arts* (the myth of the King Chandran), Savitri in *The Dark Room* (the myth of Savitri), Vasu in *The Man Eater of Malgudi* (Vasu, the King of the Sudras). (172).

Now crossing the boundaries of one language and literature is inevitable in anglobalization. Let us study comparatively Narayan's *The English Teacher* and Naipaul's *A House for Mr. Biswas* to illustrate interculturalism and both poetics as well as politics of culture in fiction. What structures of literary feelings did go in making of Narayan's and his counterpart immigrant Naipaul's novels? Naipaul's *A House for Mr Biswas* is a fine example of continuation of "distant nativism" of a different kind by the immigrants, especially diaspora writers of the original Brahman caste in majority. The names of his characters such as Mr Mohun Biswas, Shama, Tulsi, Ganesh, Jairam, Govind, Leela etc., have distinct myths and legends associated with them and they are deeply rooted in Indian ethos. Even the names of houses, places and stores such as a Hanuman House, a Tulsi store, a Tulsi shop etc., remind us of, in Derek Walcott's compliments used in his Nobel lecture, "the fragments of the great epic culture" on that distant island in the British colony. William Walsh has cited Gordon Rohlchr's observations to show how: "The book can be interpreted on several levels. There is the obvious surface level where Biswas can be seen as a second generation Indian who, although rebelling against his own decaying Hindu world, cannot compromise with the Creole world of Trinadad' 65). Walsh has not commented on the impact of British "high" culture and literature on Mr. Biswas. As an outsider, Walsh cannot claim adequate cultural literacy of India also, but recommends it as Naipaul's masterpiece and further points out:

> . . . The members of the community in *A House for Mr. Biswas,* even those like .the Indians who were exempt from formal, historical slavery, carry about with them in their attitude and posture, in their management of life and feeling, the indelible mark of the slave, who is supremely the unnecessary man... Mr. Biswas constructs the proof of his necessity ...that he becomes a model of man, just as the history and situation which formed him are seen to be a metaphor of the process which constitutes any man (30-31).

It is not the coincidence that Nayarayan's protagonist is constituted in the same mould of the Brahmanical Vedic culture with very few local differences. I (2005) have demonstrated how a single "sign" like "bell" plays a significant semiotic role in the cultural structure of a novel. Wyatt has analysed Narayan's protagonists in terms of four *ashramas.* Like his Raju (*The Guide*), Raman (*The Painter of Signs*), Mr Biswas acquires knowledge through books and learns to help people as well *sarvadharma.* Mr Biswas represents *grahstha* also. But he is the product of more hybridized culture which is reflected in a ritual meal described by Ganesh:

> 'Open a tin of salmon, Ramlogan ordered. 'And get some bread and butter and peppersauce and some avocado pears'. And he went himself to look after the preparations, saying, 'We have a author in a family, a man, girl..." After quoting these lines Theorux writes, 'In the first year of their marriage Ganesh beats Leela considerably. No brutality is attached to beating; on the contrary, they are a source of pride for traditional Hindus. Mr. Biswas, not a wife-beater reflects ....' (58).

The interdisciplinary exploration of such Hindu culture specific structures in both the novels and the degree of Westernization illustrate the significance of comparative culture studies. The problem of creative tension in ,representation of the colonized needs to be studied with reference to theories expounded by Frantz Fanon, Edward Said, Homi K. Bhabha and others. For example, Said argues:

> Think the narratives through together within the context provided by history of imperialism, a history whose underlying contest between white and non-white has emerged lyrically in *the new* and more inclusive counternarrative of liberation. This, I would say, is the full situation of postmodernism, for which Lyotard's amnesiac vision has been insufficiently wide. Once again *representation* becomes significant, not just as an academic or theoretical quandary but a political choice.
>
> How the anthropologist represents his or her disciplinary situation is on one level, of course, a matter of local,

> personal, or professional moment. But *it is in* fact part of a totality, one's society, whose shape and tendency depend on the cumulatively alternative or deterrent and oppositional weight made up by a whole series of such choices .... The main point is that anthropological representations bear much on the presenter's world as *on who, or* what is represented (224).

The sources of this interculturalisrn and internationalism should be traced to the Anglo-American project of high modernism and aestheticism. The Joycian trend of modernization of myth had reached the Gate Way of India as well as shores of West Indies along with other western, to use Edward Said's term, "travelling theories" of novel. The Anglo-American "Project of Modernity and Aesthetic Experience" was designed in the 1920s immediately after the First World War. Narayan wrote his fiction in the next decade. Of course, he amalgamated Indian reality and "cultural heritage" in Western technique. Apart from Narayan's alien technical devices, Wyatt's mastery of deconstructing "Indian" myths from Vedas to modern "Bharata" can be hardly found in the corpus of Indian criticism on Narayan's novels. So his objective semiotic cultural interpretation of Narayan's novels is a novel intervention in Indian critical thought. Albeit not comparative, his cultural materialistic approach is so neutral and scientific that there is not a single casteist tinge that spoils the image of any caste. It is a very illuminating thesis of less that two hundred pages and not voluminous duplicate compilation like any doctoral thesis in India: "A Critical Study of R.K. Narayan's Life, and Works." If similar myth making is traced to in V. S. Naipaul's *A House for Mr Biswas* set in a village in the West Indies, it will be more revealing and rewarding comparative cultural study. The semiotics of names of persons and places carries with it not only their religion, markers of identity; but also history, politics and what not. Perhaps Shakespeare wanted to ignore them when he said "What is there in a name?" His characters and plots of the plays were structured by the western culture and society. It matters most as to how the creative writer uses or misuses/subverts these classical texts in his own fiction. Walsh has explored several "personal matters" in Narayan's life which reveals the texture of hybridity of Indian and Western elements of culture. His wife used to play tennis with white women in the club. Walsh observes:

> An Indian child of this class and caste was introduced to the classical Indian tales, myths, and Vedic poetry very early in life (11).
>
> ...He went first to the Lutherian Mission School (Madras) where he was one of the few non-Christians and the only Brahmin boy in his class. Scripture classes were devoted to lampooning the Hindu gods and ridicule was poured on the Brahmins, who, it was said, while claiming to be vegetarians sneakily ate fish and meat in secret and were probably responsible for the soaring prices of those commodities (12-13).

All such autio/biographical references helped the earlier comparatists in traditional studies of literary influences, imitation, mutation, echo, adaptation, translation, offshoots, plagiarism„ and so on. But in new comparative cultural study it is more important to analyse the structures of writer's literary feelings in terms of the interculturalness, interliterariness, internationalness and intertextualities at the microscopic levels. The concept of regionalism in *The English Teacher is* guided by contemporary "aesthetics of regionalism" depicted by William Empson in the essay of the same title. Our comparative culture criticism has to give equal importance to the study of both poetics as well as politics of cultural productions. In the age of information traditional umbrella term "autobiographical approach" has taken a new avatar of "literary biography" In the introduction to a recent book aptly titles as *Built of Books: How Reading Defined the Life of Oscar Wilde*, Thomas Wright observes:

> Wilde's reading was the chief inspiration for his writings. He was essentially a pre-modern author who adapted and conflated the books he read, rather than a Romantic writer concerned with originality and self-expression. His works are saturated with allusions from his vast and

> miscellaneous reading: they form a little library of exquisite echoes ....Wilde knew how to use books the traditional symbols of authorship and learning in Western iconography — to convey his culture and his literary achievements. (6-7). Wilde devoured and luxuriated in books . ...Wilds talked of books and often talked like books; he talked so well that he seemed to talk books away. He told stories based on books and countless anecdotes and jokes about them; in his writings, his characters are frequently compared to kooks... (7).

Narayan (and also by 'heritage of loss' Naipaul) belonged to the priestly class and culture traditionally known for monopolized classical learning. He was a son of the Headmaster of the Secondary School, and William Walsh, like Wright, has used Coleridge's famous phrase, a true 'library cormorant' to show how was fed off a varied diet of books in the school.

Certainly the above cited references, albeit exclude any reference to Indian books; have contributed to the shaping of spirit of *The English Teacher* (1945) which we will consider later. In addition, a comparitist, like monoliterary critic, should not believe the authorial confession cited by Walsh as follows:

> After Scott I picked up a whole row of Dickens and developed his London and the queer personalities therein. Rider Haggard, Marie Corelli, Moliere and Pope and Marlowe, Tolosti, Thomas Hardy- an indiscriminate jumble; I read everything with the utmost enjoyment (14).

It is very interesting to compare literary intertextuality in these sample texts. Narayan's protagonist is a teacher of English in the pre-independence phase of the freedom struggle, which gives rise to the resistant literature of, to use Fanon's phrase, "fighting phase". It is neither the product of Fanonian violence nor of Gandhian non-violence but rather of a priestly ideological "return to the village", especially Malgudi coloured by American aesthetics of regionalism. Krishna is a college teacher, but the literary intertextuality is neither exhaustive nor illusive in Wildean sense. The absence of Indian texts, both *deshi* and *margi,* shows how Western cultural imperialism had been alienating our intellectuals from their own roots. It is the first person narrative which reflects the dialemma of Krishna caught between two pulls indigenous rustic and alien modern. His family is in the village and he stays in the college Hostel and engages four lectures per day. The colonized life is full of paradoxes. Krishnan who once "devoured" English books and hopes to write poetry and later fiction by following British models and by reading books on creative writing in English, now beings to hate the white master's language and literature. This Prospero-Caliban Complex needs to be illustrated in detail. The monotony of this exercise in, to use a strong term in Black aesthetics, "daffodilization' of minds and dislike of teaching profession strikes the reader in the opening paragraph itself: "some sort of vague dissatisfaction; a self rebellion" (5). Like *Mr Biswas*, the dominant presence of British texts in his consciousness is noticed in the next paragraph. The married teacher tells:

> I took stock of my daily life. I got up at eight every day, read for the fiftieth time Milton, Carlyle and Shakespeare, looked through compositions, swallowed a meal... (5).

He teaches *King Lear* to B.A. junior students. Four lines from the stormy scene are quoted. The teaching of grammar and composition provides another butt for a mild satire. He writes further:

> I spent the rest of the period giving a general analysis of the mistakes I had encountered in this batch of composition — *rather* very, as such for hence split infinitives, collective nouns, and all the rest of the traps that the English language sets for foreigners .... Then I set men on Exercise in essay writing on the epigram' 'Man is the master of his destiny'. "An idiotic theme," I felt, "this abstract and confounded metaphysics"' but I could not help it." I had been ordered to set this subject to the class (5, 6).

Further there is a pun on' 'Kant' and 'can't', American spelling and domination. The father in law of the protagonist provides one more model, for him to rise up in arms against the British education system and tender the resignation to return to the village. He brings out the contradiction in the life of his father in law: "He was a B.A. of the olden days brought on Pater, Carlyle and Scott and Browning; personally looked after by Dr. William Miller, Mark Hunter, and other eminent professors in Madras... refused to enter Government service, settled in village.. " (19).

Two theoretical aspects might explain some aspects of intra and international colonialism and imperialism. The love and hate relationship with the ruler's culture and education takes us to the sources of comparisons in *Miseducation of Negroes, The Pedagogy of the Oppressed, Masks of Conquest: Literary Study* and *British Rule in India.*

Unlike Rao in *Kanthapura,* Narayan has not mentioned M.K. Gandhi's name that was the fountainhead of nationalism in those days. Here steps in the intra cultural clash in India. So the resistant elements in this novel need to be studied at two levels: national and international. The latter is illustrated by the following intertextuality: "I picked up *Taine's History of Literature* and leaned the glass against it." 'Thine every time', I muttered" (22) . But it is a very meek resistance which fits well into the pattern of the flexibility of the comprador class. Later Jane Austen's *Pride and Prejudice* is mentioned as a text for non detailed study. However, nowhere there is a deeper psychoanalysis of such literary responses. It seems that Narayan consciously guarded himself against British stream of consciousness techniques which had penetrated into Rao's novels. For locating such elements in a text we have to take into consideration several factors such as place of writing, implied readers, publishers, critics, local creative tensions etc.

Krishna's creative urge is the only oasis in this desert. When he becomes introspective he thinks loudly: Nothing to do. Why not write poetry? Ages since I wrote anything? My conscience had the habit of asserting itself once in six months. Some pieces written in English and some in Tamil. ... (He hopes to publish them. Wordsworth's "She was the phantom of delight' and Keats' 'A Thing of Beauty"... are cited. 'The Ode to the West Wind' gives the ironic touch to the letter of resignation submitted dramatically to Mr. Brown. The intertextuality of

Golden Treasury (p.47) opens the Pandora's Box of pre-independence plagiarisms in Indian poetry. Finally, before protagonist's declaration in the resignation that "I am up against system"... "The whole system of education" "insensible Shakespeare's sonnets or the ode" are referred to in passing. The soft corner for the twin process of Anglicization and Sanskritization does not allow Narayan to resist the Western tradition of education just like Achebe in Africa and Braithwaite in Caribbean islands. There is some nationalist spirit which entered through the freedom struggle movement. But it remains at the superficial level.

Although the similar names of both protagonists invoke cultural signs associated with Lord Krishna, the degree of their literary acculturation differ in few ways. But similarities are many. Hindi texts and Jairam's teaching influence Mr. Biswas less, but British texts play vital role in making him a journalist of *Trinidad Sentinel. Bell's Standard Education. Volumes of Comprehensive Knowledge, Collie's Clear - Type Shakespeare* other Western, especially British, texts mentioned by Naipaul speak volumes for his more dialogic imagination and richer cultural hybridity in his novel. Paul Therous writes:

> His marriage is not a secret in Oagotes, he is welcomed tearfully by his mother, pestered for details by his relatives, who have the same awe for Mrs. Tulsi that Joe Gargery has for Havisham in *Great Expectations.* Mr Biswas's confusion (how to explain to these simple people the ways of those in that great house?) is similar to Pip's, but he must admit to himself that what he has done cannot be undone: 'He was married. Nothing, now, except death, could change that" (62).
>
> Mr. Biswas, reading the *Meditations* of Marqcus Aurclius and Samuel Smiles, is trying to be different from the Tulsis, from the people he knows, from his own parents. He is trying to escape from tedium (64).

In this way, both the protagonists "rise up against" two distinct systems in two different regions of the British colonies. Yet the structures of their literary feelings are not much different like those in the French or Portuguese colonies.

What changed Krishna's love of European literature into hate of Western education and dislike to enter into the machine of otherness and made Krishna resign the post of the teacher of English in a college in the nineteen thirties? Narayan graduated in 1930 and after his M.A in literature made "half-hearted effort to teach". This "love and hate" relationship needs to be studied in terms of Albert Memmi's *The Colonizer and The Colonized* (1957). He has theorized how the slave slowly internalizes the master's model and becomes Europe-America-centric. His resistance to the colonized wears different masks. For example, the colonisers always create the class of bourgeois of their own colour, taste and culture 'from among natives'. Frantz Fanon in his revolutionary *The Wretched of the Earth* and *Black Skin, White Mask* presented the psychoanalysis of their violence which led to the apartheid movement in Africa as well as the Black Panthers' movement in the States of America. We cannot imagine the violence of that kind in the Gandhian era of non-co-operation and non-violence in which Narayan conceived *The English Teacher* and other novels. Thus the major theme of resistance and nationalism, which is much hyped by formalist critics,, needs to be reconsidered. "The White Man's Burden" was shifted to the "whitish/ wheatish" highest class/caste among browns in India. Narayan's writings represent that bourgeois class/ caste which must have provoked "leftist students at Madras", as Walsh reports. Narayan's as well as Raja Rao's elitist nationalism in their novels needs to be reinterpreted in terms of the literary representation of the subaltern. Ranjit Guha opens his article," On some aspects of the "Historiography of Colonial India" as follows:

> 1.The historiography of Indian colonialism has for a long time been dominated by elitism-colonialist elitism and bourgeois-nationalist elitism. Both originated in the ideological product of British rule in India, but have survived the transfer of power and been assimilated to neo-colonialist and neo-nationalist forms of discourse in Britain and India respectively. Elitist historiography of the colonialist or neo-colonialist type counts British writers and institutions among its protagonists, but has its imitators in India and other countries too. Elitist

> historiography of the colonialist type or neo-colonialist type is primarily an Indian practice but not without imitators in the ranks of liberal historians in Britain and elsewhere (1).

According to Alpana Sharma Knippling, the period of the 1930s and 1940s display how "the alliance of nationalism and colonialism" produced India's modern moment 'and now the writing of a certain kind of fiction participated in this inauguration of modernity' (170). Further she observes:

> R.K. Narayan (b.1906) and Raja Rao (b.1908), two early Indian writers in English, productively demonstrate how the literary project participated in the' modern 'moment' inaugurated by the complicitous embrace of the discourses of nationalism and colonialism. Narayan's *The English Teacher (1945)* and Rao's *Kanthapura* (1936) are novels produced at a time when the most volatile political imperative concerned the need for Indian subjects to position themselves vis-a-vis British colonialism and Indian nationalism. But with the exception of *Waiting for Mahatma,* neither colonialism nor nationalism occupies a central position in Narayan's novels of this or for that matter any later period. Conversely, questions regarding colonialism and nationalism do occupy a large part of Raja Rao's *Kanthapura,* but they are treated in such a way that they are deterred rather than addressed in both Narayan's *The English Teacher* and Rao's *Kanthapura,* the, aspects of colonialism and nationalism are engaged in a sidewise fashion, indirectly and obliquely (170, 171) .

She has pointed out how *Kantthapura* does a lip service to Gandhism, it fails to explain: why did it happen? Why did M.K. Naik laud *Kanthapura* as "a prose epic of India"? How to decolonize such extensions of Anglomerican projects of modernism and aesthetics which demand, in Immanuel Kant's words, production of "ignorance' for retaining hegemony of aesthetics of "forms and culture." Our colonized curriculum produces much ignorance. It is necessary to take into consideration the second part of Kantian aphorism for gaining better comparative perspectives on all "Indian Writing in

English" and the big process of internationalization of literature. My (1999) works have brought out some hidden aspects of this intra- as well inter-colonialism. The different nature of colonialism and imperialism in Portuguese Goa still awaits explorations. Hence I am asked to translate my Marathi book *British Bombay ani Portuguese Govyateel Wangmay* (1999) into English (literature in British Bombay and Portuguese Goa) by the German publisher. In order to understand this complex creative process we have to master Bloomian aesthetics of influence, Venetian theories of intertextuality, recent medical concepts of "textual intercourse" and K.K. Ruthven's long list of terms such as faking; remaking, retailoring, prefabricating, etc. In addition to this it is necessary to define double colonized Indian reader as Nancy Hogley had done in case of Irish reader from the new historicist perspectives. It is necessary to trace the significance of the relationship between culture and imperialism in Indian fiction. Since this talk focuses on intertextualities in a novel on the English teacher it is befitting to cite some lines from Ngugi wa Thiong'o "The Writer in a changing Society" (1969). He himself is a committed writer and a teacher of English. He writes:

> I too must have changed since I started writing in *1960. I was* then a student at Makerere University College ....I had read a number of writers, African and West Indian, and I knew that what they told, the song they sang, was different from what I had heard from the British writers who had been crammed down my throat in schools and at the University ....I grew up in a small village ...One day I heard a song. That song I heard as a child then spoke of things past and things to come. I was living in a colonial situation but I did not know.... I believe that African intellectuals must align themselves with the struggle of African masses for meaningful national ideal ....Perhaps, in a small way; the African writer can help in articulating the feelings behind this struggle (7-50).

I believe our revisit to RKN and his Malgudi threatened by the Special Economic Zone in Americanization "can help in articulating the feelings behind this struggle". Keep it up.

While keeping up with the tremendous changes in concepts of literary genres and theories in the electronic age, it is a right time to take the stock of reception of western texts in our culture from the comparative perspectives. If they are used as weapons of re-colonialisation, one has to resist that cultural imperialism. This should be and is the motive of re-visiting the pioneering novelists of the colonial period and not only to discard their works merely as a "tourist fiction": Seminars encourages both the 'academic tourism' and 'travelling theories'.

12

Literary into Comparative Culture Study: Internationalization of Faking Translation

Over a ten year period from 1897 to 1906, Marcel Proust set aside his varied ambition as a writer in order to enter into a "novitiate" under John Ruskin, a writer who would have a decisive influence on his subsequent career as a critic and novelist. Beginning in 1900, the year of Ruskin's death, Proust undertook the task of translating into French—two of Ruskin's works, *The Bible of Amiens* and *Sesame and Lilies. I do not wish to critique his translations as such, in the traditional sense of comparing original to translation and finding passages to praise or to find fault with.* Rather, I hope to demonstrate the extent to which Proust *both absorbed and resisted the aesthetic doctrines of an author* to whom he surrendered entire decade of his life. By examining the ideas at work in these two books and Proust's own engagement with them as both a devotee and critic of his master, I intend to elaborate the grounds for an analysis of translation in not of the *Recherche* that will avoid some of the traditional conundrums of Proustian criticism *and open up different avenues, or angles of viewing the novel as itself both an original and a translation.* In order to do so, we must trace the development of *Proust's notion of translation from (dutiful) reading to (iconoclastic) rewriting, from necrophilia (in the form of idolatrous worship over the body or grave of the Master) to necrology (which takes the form of a thousand —page obituary), from translation, finally, as the transfer of relics (translation) or the stasis of metaphor (metaphorein) to the transpiercing movement of metonymic desire (*as in Peter Brook's formulation*). The test case of*

> *Ruskin will serve as the incipit of our analysis* (italics added).

Daniel Simon "Translating Ruskin: Marcel Proust's Orient of Devotion", *Comparative Literature Studies,* 38:2, (2001):142-169.

Introduction

The first paragraph of Daniel Simon's "A. Owen Aldridge Essay Contest Winner essay" has been quoted to show how comparatists have been adopting, to use Edward Said's term, "contrapuntal" approaches to translation in the new millennium. At the outset it is necessary to compliment the organizers for selecting this relevant interdisciplinary topic for the Seminar. Teaching Creative Writing and Comparative Literature (hereafter CW, CL, CS Culture Studies, CLC Comparative Literaturé and Culture, and CCS-Comparative Cultural Studies) in Goa University was an innovative experience for me. I was asked to write a book on Creative Writing in Marathi for the University curriculum. It not only brought me the Government of Maharashtra Award but also became a textbook in a number of universities. I (2005) argued in it how it can be taught and writers and translators are not born but made like doctors and engineers. Similar demystification of theories of fidelity, equivalence, purity, literaliness, liberalness etc., in translation has been made by structuralists and postcolonialists, culturalists and comparatists. There are separate departments for conferring distinct degrees in Creative Writing, Comparative Literature and Culture Studies in many countries. Our single paper in this area does more harm than any good.

My area of research is comparative literature and culture; and the topic of the Seminar reminded me of K.K. Ruthven's *Faking Literature* (2001) first and then of a feature film that is not only an adaptation but also about adaptation, and that is also actually entitled *Adaptation.* It adapts Susan Orlean's *The Orchid Thief,* a nonfiction account of a flower poacher. It focuses less on the poacher than on the book's adapter struggling to write a screenplay about adapter struggling to write an adaptation. Robert Stam (2005) has explained how in real life, the flesh-and-blood screen writer Charles Kaufman did indeed have a contract to adapt the Orlean book, but he developed a severe case of writer's block, broken only when he conceived the idea of thematizing the screenwriting struggle itself. According to Stam, "Thus *Adaptation is* simultaneously an adaptation and an original screenplay, one which turns a nonfiction book into a fictional adventure" (Introduction, 1).

The seminar on translation may lead to adaptation and help to link film studies with literature and culture studies. My thesis on *Western Influence on Marathi Drama* (1818-1947) included the analysis of translations, adaptations, imitations, offshoots, plagiarisms, fakedom and so on. But Ruthven's book and Stams theorization has led me to believe that the creative writing is more or less adaptation, amalgamation of texts and quotes without inverted commas and further think that there should be a film on the creative process of "Translation" itself! Vishram Bedekar's tale of a journey from translation of American *Send Me No Flowers* by Malati Bedekar to a number of "remakes", "prefabrications", "after performance repairs" and "alterations" by several actors, friends and finally his printed text of "fathered" adaptation entitled *Waje Paul Aapule* (1967) provides a fine plot for a film/play/ novel on a creative process in the writers' colony (Sahitya Sahavas). Bedekar anticipated Ruthven's theory. He frankly suggested to compile the encyclopedia of new terminology for understanding the complexities in such creative processes and to train the experts, reviewers and referees who evaluate such works of arts and performances. Except the title no other details of the source text, which he adapted, are mentioned in its Marathi avatar.

Perhaps this was the colonial legacy to give the post-colonial "retailored" text an aura of "originality." But today we can easily trace its textual affiliations on internet: Norman Barasch, (play "Send Me No Flowers: A Comedy in Three Acts") and. Carroll Moore, (play "Send Me No Flowers: A Comedy in Three Acts"). This can be further scrutinized in terms of Bakhtin's "dialogism", Henry Louis Gate's notion of "signifying",

Harold Bloom's "anxiety of influence" and Julia Kristeva's "intertextuality." What we have to do is to concentrate on the analytical productivity of new concepts developed in the context of internationalization of literature and translate those concepts in our language to replace superficial descriptive mythical terms such as "kayakalp" "avatar" "influence", "stage version", "reborn" etc.

Stam's detailed analysis of *Adaptation, in Literature and Film: A Guide to the Theory and Practice of Film Adaptation* has provided a "ready-made" model for imitation. V.S. Naipaul has already described how Indians are "mimic men" and Salman Rushdie the "shadow literature". Such complex relationships between translation and version, adaptations and renderings, fiction and non-fiction, creative literature and literature of information, literary text and other arts, literature-film and TV serials, stereotypes and hybridities etc., need to be analysed comparatively as cultural products in the present international contexts. A dozen junior writers are asked to develop sections of one theme and one senior novelist/dramatist creates a collaged text finally in his single name as "original" creation". Twenty screenwriters are shown thirty foreign films and asked to create one film script. Under such circumstances can a translation remain totally individualistic "original" creation in the age of liberalization? We have to deconstruct it contrapuntally and comparatively by taking into consideration varieties of national and international remote controls.

In the new millennium Anglocalization has given great impetus to the "business" of translation, and the UGC to CL and CLCS. Even international relations shape the trends in writing. In my book: *Comparative Literature: Theory and Practice* (Marathi and Hindi) three theories of comparison namely perception, discursive, disciplinary are discussed (29). In fact, comparison and translation are the twins and the process of knowledge begins with them. It has been accepted that translation is also a kind of creative writing and a newly designed advertisement on the electric pole can be more effective than a classic epic which is hardly read but much talked about. Unfortunately, translation and comparativism are much neglected areas in our education. The comparative perspectives on the entire history of criticism in Indian languages till date reveal too much resistance to analytical "comparatism" and fear of interference of translated, in Michael Escheuro's terms "exo-cultural" elements in the steel frame of hierarchical Vedic traditions. It was Frantz Fanon who said: "Black man is comparison."

It can be studied comparatively how our modern critical theories are dependent on international relations and indigenous hierarchical acculturation. Steven C. Roach has concluded his "Introduction: From Critical Theory to Critical IR Theory" to his edited *Critical Theory and International Relation: A Reader* (2008) as follows:

> As such, each of these periods reveals the impact of the changing social conditions on the evolution of critical IR theory: from purely abstract universalism to a hermeneutical understanding of global society. Together, they allow us to see critical IR theory as constituting an open ended dialectical project of critical theory, in which the opposing meanings of society and state have given way to a deeper understanding of the oppressive and liberating forces of world society (xxii-xxiii).

Moreover, the nature and scope of international relations and cultural contacts show how translations bring about the renaissance in literature and culture. Such renaissance in the 19th century was started after the British /Portuguese contact with a number of "masks of conquest." Exceptionally S.G. Malshe sincerely studied that by gone colonial century in *Gat Shatak Shodhitana.* But the neocolonialists cum modernists have been spreading the myths of genius, originiality, authenticity, creativity etc. "childishly" till today. Such myths of modernism were the part of agenda of Anglo-American grand Project of aesthetics to retain neocolonialism and imperialism after political decolonization of the whole world on the map. For instance, the comparatist will search the remotely controlling cultural contacts, not only between Anglo-American scholarships, PL480 etc., and modernism in Indian writing but also between the Report on the University of Iowa International

Writing Programme (see *Span* January, February 2011,1823) and also on how WikiLeaks' 'cash for votes' bombshell rock UPA Govt-Parliament as Opp cries "pro-US tilt" *(Times of India,* 18th March, 1), and later BJP's double dealing with America's nuclear policy. This "US friendly" politics has pushed the country in the mainstream of Americanization by elbowing Russian pulls which were equally strong in the Nehru era and Cold War. What WikiLeaks have exposed in politics can be traced in the American cultural and literary policies since the inception of their Modernist Project of emancipation. R. B. Patankar also wrote *Apuri Kranti* to demonstrate, with less awareness of aesthetics of resistance or comparison, how that Western Project of Enlightment remained incomplete in India.

Indian diaspora literature translation projects and "Petro-Arab dollar fests" are its outcomes today. Translations are gateways to foreign influences which revolutionize indigenous literary culture. Translation of an ordinary author's insignificant text in one culture may be a trend setter in the other and Joshua Reynold's fiction is its fine example. The travelling theories and travels in foreign lands make the writer wiser because he has to stay in "other" culture by translating everything with the help of second language. Mediator and medium determine the message. The Report in *Span* (18) explains how the Mumbai based internationalized (Americanized) young writer Chandrahas Choudhury found "a new voice" after he participated at Iowa International Programme. Similarly our Mardhekarian rats were born in Anglo-American barrel, Dalit writing in the American Black cradle, rural-regional writing in William Empson's horse carriage of "aesthetics of regionalism", and further back modern Indian language drama in the colonial British theatre. In the Report (*Span*, 20) the NRI Monica Bhide's, "a cookbook author, cooking teacher and food writer", claims that she is "writing about the relationship between food and family and culture ....It's all about relationships and how food brings people together" (20). Food festival of translation should be a separate paper in the syllabus; and the impact of vegetarian and non-vegetarian translations on our literature and culture industry will be the major component in it. Cookbooks and translations of Western (detective) bestsellers are sold more than any kind of indigenous literary works in India today. It was the Nobel laureate Gunter Grass who defined the craft of writing literature as "an art of cooking" and wrote a novel *The Fish* to give its demonstration. So I call translation an extraordinary art of cooking the Goan "khatkhatan" (a number of vegetables and fish mixed and cooked with coconut and spices). But as a post colonial creative writer, culturalist-comparatist and translator, I limit this discussion to the major terms used in the title of my paper.

Wider Frame of References: From Literature to Culture

The chapter on "Translation and Adaptation" in S.S. Prawer's *Comparative Literary Studies* begins with the following famous statement made by Wilhelm von Humboldt (1920):

> One of the labours most essential to any literature; partly because it introduces those ignorant of foreign languages to forms of art and humanity which otherwise they would never come to know- and this is an important gain for any nation; but partly also, and especially, because it widens the capacity for meaning and expression possessed by one's own language.

Prawer argues that translation "provides the most important channel through which international influences can flow; its investigation is therefore of greatest importance to the comparatist" (74). When I selected the influence study for my doctoral degree, it was the "wine and bread" of comparatists (Erwin Koppen). In the new millennium much water has flown under the bridge. The whole terminology of traditional influence study has been revolutionized in the Electronic Age. New concepts of "intercultural performance", interliterariness, internationalism, intertextualities, hybridities, remix and gimmicks etc., have demystified the romantic myths of originality, and authenticity. A new journey from literature to cultural study began in the second half of the previous century after the theory revolution (see Easthope, During). My various kinds of comparative and cultural studies opened new vistas; especially in Goa when I studied comparatively "literature in British Bombay and Portuguese Goa", supported by S.G. Malshe Fellowship and now invited by the German publisher for publication in English. So, the first part of the title of present essay is taken from the title of my recently released book *Literary into Comparative Culture Criticism* (2011). In the beginning of his "Foreword" to it, Steven Tötösy de Zeptnek, commented on my use of the term "criticism" in place of "studies" as follows:

> [H]e uses in the title of his book the British term "culture criticism" instead of the US-American "cultural studies," i.e., "cultural criticism" — is a welcome addition to the emerging field of "comparative cultural studies," a field that, as he points out, is, in the West, a field "in between." This is because comparative literature scholars in the U.S., Canada, and Europe in general often object to cultural studies owing to the perception of a lack of theoretical framework(s) and its ideological nature, while cultural studies scholars object — in my opinion rightly so — to comparative literature's (still and ongoing) adherence to the national approach and its Eurocentrism.

In the new millennium the spectrum of traditional concepts and theories has been changing with great momentum. The interdisciplinarity is a watchword and "technical writing" and its translation is privileged while traditional "literature is dead". This is called a new turn "from literature to culture" (see Easthope). A new cultural literacy is needed for rendering as well as interpreting hybridity, interculturalism (Bhide), internationalism (Choudhury) and intertextualities in the translated texts.

New Comparative Perspectives on Translation

The colonial background of our literary thought had put me, to use Spivak's words, in the "machine" of British "Otherness" while translating a new Western concept of "comparative culture studies" in Indian contextures. Madhav Apte has harshly commented on the difference between Indian traditional concept of culture and the same inflammatory term in Western theories. Such dependence, contradictions and oversimplifications of alien concepts and Western theories is our "intimate enemy" (Ashish Nandi). Relatively more neglected discussion of politics of translation involved in the colonial sociological twin process of Anglicization-Westernization/ modernization and Sanskritization /Brahmanization/ Orentialization in the nineteenth century speaks volumes for the production of poetics of ignorance in both inter and intra-colonialism. That "white man's burden" has been shifted to the same uppermost bourgeois class (castes) patronized by the Western colonisers, as Lord Macaulay declared, to develop it in their "own image" and of their "taste".

In the tsunami of globalization the same comprador intelligentsia has started the second Renaissance through trash translations, which might cause the "death" of indigenous languages, literatures and cultures due to, as Frantz Fanon had predicted, the attacks of "cheap entertainment" from Euro-America. Hence it is necessary to rethink the presence of Indian avataras of Rene Wellek and Austen Warren's *Theory of Literature,* which Wellek himself discarded after he became the first Professor of Comparative Literature, in Indian language curriculum today.

Immanuel Kant had stated that the theory of aesthetics needs to be supported by production of "ignorance" Such ignorance has become the bliss for the subalterns who hardly "translate" or "speak". It seems that the Anglo-American Project of Modernism and aesthetics after the First World War and PL480 after the Second one and later in the Cold War achieved its goals in case of politics of translation. Perhaps Gayatri Spivak's *Death of a Discipline* also inherits some of these features. What is "dead" for Euramerica-centric Susan Bassnett and Spivak is much needed for decolonizing our cultural identity. Spivak's argument for "planetary studies" needs to be supplemented by Indian theorization of "castealization" (I have coined and defined this term in a separate comparative essay, 2011) of translation and comparison as it has been done in case of "racialization" in the West. Shu-Meh Shih (2008) has discussed various aspects of "Comparative Racialization" and explained why such theories have not yet taken centrestage in Asia. It was Fanon who made another famous statement: "some streets are more comparative". So there is a greater need of comparative cultural studies of translations in India.

Such need for re-imagining not only literature but also the very process of translation was discussed in the International Conference at Bangkok (at which I participated). Its proceedings are edited by Suthira Duangsamosorn-*Re-imagigining Language and Literature for the 21st Century* (2005). Much more relevant to the present topic of the Seminar is Emily Apter's *The Translation Zone: A New Comparative Literature* (2006).

She has demonstrated how translation is the field and practice for innovating comparative literature. She observes:

> A new comparative literature, with the revalued labour of the translator and theories of translation placed centre stage, expands centripetally toward a genuinely planetary criticism extending emphasis on the transference of texts from one language to another, to criticism of the processes of linguistic creolization, the multilingual practices of poets and novelists over a vast range of major and "minor" literatures, and the development of new languages by marginal groups all over the world (10).

The first part of this discussion is intended to highlight Stephen Tötösy de Zeptnek's "criticism of "stars" such as Bassnett, Spivak et al., and his proposal for developing "The New Humanities: The Intercultural, the Comparative, and the Interdisciplinary" (2007). He has cited nearly hundred titles of recently published books in this area and proposed the merger of CL and CLCS which paves a path for interdisciplinary study of translations from comparative perspectives. Consequently, our fossilized monoliterary studies and theories of autonomy, originality, authenticity, 'national literature' and so on can be well deconstructed. For example, "style is the man", "style is the dress of though" and other such dictums in the study of translation can be challenged as half truths by use of the newly developed concept of "stylometer". Now it is accepted that "literature is the product of textual intercourse" and it is "littered by letters" and writer's imagination is, as Michael Escheuro has comparatively demonstrated in his *Culture Conditioned Imagination from Shakespeare to Conrad,* conditioned by semiotics of his culture. Similarly, the translator's imagination is double conditioned by both poetics and politics of many cultures. Both the text and its translator are cultural products, and a text is a Homeric/Valmikian cultural battlefield determined by Tuecer/Karna paradigm. The semiotic comparative study of translations is a greater "challenge" (Roland Barthes). Since pluralistic approaches and new interdisciplinarity have rejuvenated CLCS, a new terminology has come in vogue. The process of globalization has given greater momentum to internationalization of literature.

Internationalization of Faking Translation

The second half of the title contains two important concepts. First, "internationalization" means globalization, (in Indian context "Anglocalization" cum Americanization) which in its literal sense is "the process of transformation of local or regional phenomena into global ones." For example, P.L. Deshpande adapted *Three Penny Opera* in *Teen Paishacha Tamasha* and 90 per cent Apsaras from our elitist subculture group hybridized the indigenous dalit "lavani" in Tamasha into American rock-pop and ballet with the help of Surekha Punekar. It should be noted that comparatists have labelled P.L. Deshpande and Girish Karnad as "anti-national" writers for "misusing" Western texts. We will discuss how we have to coin appropriate terms to describe such processes of crosspollinations in translation at microscopic level. It does not mean that this is a very new process. Its roots can be traced to the Vedic times when different cultural contacts began. There has been trade, travel, communication, imitation, cross-pollination; and a number of comparative works, including P.S. Deshmukh's thesis cited below, which exhibit the international contacts that existed between Asia and Africa before the time of European imperialism. But today's globalization is a Janus-faced process, which has two sides: constructive and destructive. Our individualistic-impressionistic critics, sans comparative cultural capital, have not yet studied Janus-faced two tones/ two layers of Indian literary texts, like the Afrikaner and Caribbean. Translation is a means that strengthens this process in one way or the other. It develops "interculturalism," "intertextualities", "hybridities", remixes and gimmicks. As a result the traditional terms such as adaptation, imitation, emulation, transliteration, transformation, plagiarism, influence, and metamorphosis etc., used in the translation studies fall short in the analysis of complex literary relations. What Bruce King writes of "New National and Postcolonial Literature" and new centres of consciousness is applicable to comparative studies of translations; because translation is a means of continuing dialogue to build bridges between cultures. It develops comparative dialogic imagination. He finally argues:

> The dialogue, however, is important as mastery of international standards must be accompanied by the creation of a personal voice and other resources only available through consciousness of local society and culture. Many artists creatively use tensions between both positions. For Walcott all art and life begins in imitations; all culture starts in mimicry. The artist has a double consciousness; in watching himself imitate he imitates a new vision. Because of its many influences and the character of local life there is a distinctive Caribbean culture; the artist's job is to give it form ad make the people aware of it. . . (26).

Here lies the crux of the matter. How does the translator show this "double consciousness"? The question can be answered adequately only by comparisons which are more odious in our culture. At the risk of self aggrandizement, I (2002) have compared my Marathi translation of P.S. Deshmukh's *The Origin and Development of Religion in Vedic Literature* (OUP, 1933) with S. M. Ayachit's totally "faithless" Marathi rendering of the same text published in the same decade. It is interesting to note that the pioneering source text went into oblivion for sixty five years, because it was an "odious" scientific' philological and comparative study of Vedic religion. It was overshadowed by the Orientalist debates during the colonial renaissance and reformation in India. Thus the context and contexture of this research is historically significant. Its two translators belonged to two distinct upper castes and subculture groups. Their relationships with the source text differed on various grounds. Ayachit deleted all quotations in Greek, Latin, French, German and Avesta and freely transferred the content presented in English source text. He was a librarian and Sanskrit scholar. It was examined and recommended for publication by the Professor of English in the University. Both of them were Brahmans. The cultural, literary as well as linguistic competence of a translator matters most in granting cultural centrality. The cultural interferences in such works can be theorized well in new comparative cultural studies of translations. Here the caste factor matters most.

All Indian literature is a caste based product. However, the burning issues crop up when source texts are smuggled/ plagiarized, subverted or misused with few alterations. I (*Teekavastraharan* 2008) examined comparatively one hundred postcolonial plays performed and published in Marathi. Nearly 90% are dependent on Euro-American texts. Only five per cent Marathi adapters have mentioned the title of the source text but not the author. Very few have recorded both the details. The bibliographical annotated entries in their introductions are unheard of. A faithful translation can be hardly found in this corpus; 99 per cent adapters belong to a single subculture-caste section of the elitist middle class. For analysing such varied processes, I have used K.K.Ruthven's title *Faking Literature* (2001). This has been the major sector of our cultural industry run by the anglicized class since India's contact with the West.

Comparative culture study is a very effective tool to deconstruct forgeries of Western texts in Indian languages. Some of them can be regarded as spurious versions of genuine alien literature. That alien text might be full of foreign intertextualities. For instance, in *Othello* a number of non-native sources are traced by monoliterary researchers. But a comparatist has to distinguish between its very faithful literal translation in Mahadevshastri Gopalshastri Kolhatkar's *Othello Natak* (1867), cutting and pesting of parts in Krishanji Prabhakar Khadilkar's *Sawai Madhavravacha Mratu* (1896-*Hamlet+Othello)* V.V. Shirwadkar's adaptation in *Othello* (1949), *a* metamorphosis of a fragment of plot in Vasant Kanetkar's *Gaganbhedi* (1982-four in one) and spurious mutations in Dilip Paradeshi's *Nispap* (1993). It is beyond the reach of a mono-literary impressionist critic or a specialist to account for the total absence of its Indian subversions inspired by "colour" (caste) and "colonial consciousness", as they are in African or Caribbean languages. I have compared the use of *Antony and Cleopatra* by Derek Walcott and collage of Shakespeare's four Great Tragedies by Vasant Kanetkar (see *The Whirligig*). The resistance to *Antony and Cleopatra* in India can be studied comparatively in terms of reception theory. Translations and imitations pave the paths for masterpieces. In the global as well as "lobal" context a "postcolonial" culturalist comparatist can carry out this research more effectively than a psychoanalyst in the age of pluralism and multiculturalism.

Lack of adequate terminology for this venture is a main hurdle; and Ruthven has asked the scholars to compile a separate encyclopedia of literary terms to analyse such complexities involved in creative processes: literature and forgery, translation and adaptation, "dark twins" and hybrid crops, so-called originality, authenticity, imposture and identity, prose Shakespeare and dramatized Milton in Marathi (see Date's bibliography) and so forth. What Ruthven writes in the final paragraph of her "Preface" is more applicable to the subject of this Seminar. After commenting on the "fakedom" in the Western literary tradition she argues:

> In short, I argue that we should start thinking more positively about literary forgery, and not least because of its opposition to the establishment of no-go areas by cultural police of both the right and the left, who suspend their residual hostilities to one another by jointly condemning it as an unethical practice. Literary forgeries

> are worth studying because they display even more clearly than those other counterfactual assemblages we call literary works ...By doing so they provoke in our cultural gatekeepers anxieties displaced as anger and articulated as opprobrium ...They are also a serious embracement to people who see it as their duty to protect the institution of literature from critiques of it by literary theorists who question received ideas about authorship, originality and authenticity. This is one reason for integrating literary forgeries into studies of cultural values instead of ignoring them as anomalies ...Now that English studies is once again reappraising its activities, I think it timely to recall some of its repressed texts, and to consider how the discipline might refashion its agenda in the wake of such a reclamation (4).

If re-examined in the light of these remarks, P.L. Deshpande's sophisticated "remake" of G.B. Shaw's *Pygmalion* in *Tee Phularani* would be classified as "spurious" and the controversy about its "authenticity and originality" in Marathi is metaphorically "childish" in post-colonial critical terms. In contrast to it, Mahadev Babaji Rane's suppressed play *Sant Tukaram* (1914) will be rated as a batter cultural collage or offshoot. Thus, there is a greater need to rethink of translations in the following terms discussed by Ruthven:

Fake, generic hybridity, imitation, forgery, fraud, hoax, imposture, counterfeit, supercherie, spurious, bogus other, ghosting of already spectral, re-counterfeiting of the already counterfeiting re-tailor, collage, re-fabricate, remake, reinvent, offshoot, simulacrum, literary fakedom, pseudo-named products, affiliation, shenanigan, pseudepigraphia, apocryphal, fake masters, parody, subversion, version, duplicate, bastard version, corrupt, para-text, imposter, collaborative, ghost writing, anonymous, pseudo-anonymous, mononymity, allonymity, ananym, aristonym, cryptonym, demonym, geneonym, phracenym, phrenonym, polynym, pseudoj in, scenonym, tiltonym, translationym, alphabetism, asterism, initalism, pseudandry, telonism.

Some of these terms do not have equivalents in our languages. However, in my *Western Influence on Marathi*

Drama (1818-1947) I have discussed a number of sample cases to illustrate some of these terms. An account of the value of translation studies for students of comparative literature may begin with a glance at transposed Shakespeare texts in any Indian or foreign language. Prawer has compared translations of Hamlet's "To be or not to be" by Voltaire and A.W. Schlegel and cited Voltaire's comment (which has its counterparts in India):

> Do not believe that I have here rendered the English word for word; woe to the literal translators who, translating every word, enervate the sense. Here it may indeed be said that letter killeth, but the spirit giveth life (as quoted on 77).

Elsewhere, I (1999) have discussed at length how Europeans butchered the bard of Avon and "bardicide" has been the profit making cultural industry in India. Much neglected area is a comparative study of translations in Indian languages. Familiarity breeds contempt. Foreign things are always attractive. Yet experience of translating Basavraj Naikar's *Light in the House* into Marathi led me to think of comparative culture studies from Indian perspectives. Here our bilingualness and cultural "illiteracy" are put to test. Moreover, the knowledge of not only "bi-culturalness" of both the writer and translator but also of their subculture, class, caste, sect, region, religion, first language education, profession matter most for the culturalist-comparatist. Naikar, the Lingayat of a specific sect, has constructed the biographical English novel on the life and work of a Sufi Muslim saint of the early twentieth century in Karnataka. Govind Bhat, a Brahmin teaches him and appoints him as his successor of the Math (Shrine). This cultural complexity can hardly be rendered by any foreigner or Indian accurately in a foreign language. The issue of racialization of literature is being theorized by Western theorists; but Indian scholars have evaded more complex problematics of castealization of literature and cultural products in the name of secularism. In case of translation and adaptation it is, to use Prawer's words, "all-but-impossible ideal comparatists set themselves to accomplish; and it suggests a reason why the scrutiny of translation has come to loom large in comparative literature courses" (82). What he claimed thirty years before has become more relevant to us today in the age of globalization. Further he pointed out:

> Studies in the theory and history of translation are increasingly being supplemented by practice in the craft of literary translation as well as analysis of selected renderings by different translators at different times. This is a welcome development; for comparatists are uniquely qualified to perform the important task and that of gauging the degree of distortion introduced into literary criticism and literary theory by the use of translations (82).

Such comparative approach brings new realization as to how domination of modernist aesthetics in single text/author study nourishes ignorance in Kantian terms. Single approach study tells the half truth. "Literature is a mirror held to the society" is a good lie because it reflects the front side of the reality show. Similarly, translation is not a carbon copy of the source text. It is also "built of many books" echoes, and intertexts. My reading of Prawer's *Karl Marx and World Literature* led me to the writing of "Y.B. Chavan and World Literature". In course of its writing the reading of Thomas Wright's *Built of Books: How Reading Defined the Life of Oscar Wilde* (2009) demonstrated how translations also enrich and shape the "literary biography". Since translation involves two semiotically distinct texts relaying the same narrative, it brings up some issues not mentioned in intertextuality theory. Such issues are related to comparative narratology. For example, what words, images, segments etc., are eliminated, added, or changed in the translation, and why? A comparative narratology of translation also examines the ways in which translations add, eliminate or condense sentences, alter names, and other signifiers. What principles orient the changes? Who represents what, how, and why?

IMPACT, GENRE, MOVEMENT, STYLE AND OTHER CLCS

Traditional CL concerned itself with the impact of translations and also with the activity of translating, on the work of given writers or on literary movements. There was a mushroom growth of influence study of Shakespeare in India which has become a separate prosperous sector of a cultural industry. But there is the absence of the comparative cultural study of the literary hybridity caused by translations and adaptations of Moliere's plays which rivaled Shakespeare texts in our culture. It is necessary to study how translations of alien texts made by Indian writers moulded their own careers. Culture conditioned use or abuse of a foreign source text in translation/ adaptation is also an important subject for a comparative culture study. It can be comparatively analysed how a politically motivated adaptation of a Rumanian play, *The Lost Letter* by relatively less known playwright. Rangnath Kulkarni (1956) has added a new dimension to internationalization of faking the foreign texts. Without bothering to mention the name of the original writer, language, etc., he confesses in his "introduction":

> Shri Vidhyadhar Karmarkar, my friend from the days in Daund, gave me for reading the Rumanian play titled *The Lost Ticket* in the August of last year. I liked it so much that I sat down to adapt it immediately. I have stitched this Marathi shirt within ten to eleven months. While stitching it, Vijay Tendulkar was of great help to me (Preface).

Kulkarni's use of the indigenous term "tailoring" reminds us not only of Ruthven's theory of faking literature but also of the comparatist's motto "not to believe any author's/ translator's confessions.' R.S. Walimbe had attacked this colonial tendency of ignoring bibliographical details of the source text as "Marathi writers' intentional negligence of such details." Literature is a finely structured, good and convincing lie. Kulkarn's specifically "kesari" coloured "Marathi shirt" is not only culture conditioned but also politically determined. For one reader it may be a good use of the foreign text for exposing the indigenous corrupt politics. But for the other belonging to a rival party, it may be the misuse for political mileage in the name of freedom of expression. The translated text is stuffed with our communal conflicts and cultural prejudices. Often prejudice also gives rise to great works of art. But it is a poor rendering.

The history of translation of genres and subgenres is important for understanding cultural transformations in different periods of history. There are different versions of the same text which betray the original. Poetry of Shakespeare's plays is lost in their *avatar* not only because of Indian translators but also because of European altered prompt copies made available to them. The Konkani versions of the *Ramayana* and the *Mahabharata* owe their obvious departure from their Hindu literal faithfulness to shift in taste, sensibility and Christian cultural politics in Portuguese Goa (see *British Bombay ani Portuguese Govyateel Wangmay).*

Vilas Sarang (1988) has discussed the stylistic aspects of English and Marathi translations. Although it is not a comparative stylistic study, it shows how translation studies merge readily into 'stylistics'. Individualism overrated the specific qualities of an author's style without taking into account how both the author and his style are structured by the semiotics of different cultures and sociopolitical forces. The literary tradition in which the family romance of the writers plays an important role in shaping his works needs to be examined comparatively. Comparative scrutiny of the translated author's style may also reveal what is left out and what is added. A comparatist culturalist goes a step further in tracing the reason behind such changes. Elsewhere, 1 (2011) have demonstrated how comparative stylistics opens new vistas for CLCS and concluded that essay as follows:

> I believe that the fictional discourse is also a "social discourse" determined by our culture in a peculiar way. The umbrella term "discourse stylistics" may be used to analyse a dialectical interrelationship between first ad second languages and social structures. The foregoing discussion has made it clear that comparative stylistics

> takes us beyond the traditional concerns of stylistics with aesthetic values. It leads us towards its concern with social and political ideologies encoded in texts. So labelling an author as "a maker of style" is a half truth. There is no easy one to one correspondence between words and what they refer to "objectively" in the world. Edward Said's concept of "worldliness of text" throws light on the stylistic affiliations of the text. The use of word is historically determined. In Michael Foucault's words, our knowledge and beliefs, theories and practice are discursively produced. Hence not only poetics but also politics of culture is equally important in cultural products with certain trademarks and specific styles. Style also adopts political stance. Human knowledge, beliefs, theories etc., are not universal as humanitarians believe. Their origins are traced into socio-semiotics. If we scrutinize comparatively a few more sample texts from Indian regional languages, the significance of comparative stylistics will be more validated.
>
> It will reveal how 'meanings' are always discursively produced as well as it is a part of image building cultural industry. Bringing socio-historical and sociocultural comparative stylistics with scientific stylometer to the centre of interdisciplinary cultural comparativism is our main preoccupation here *(Literary into Comparative Culture Criticism).*

The conventional terms of discussion, unfortunately, do not account for complexities involved in styles of narration. The concepts based in language and grammar such as "third person narration", "I", "we" fall short in dissecting the mixed style and constantly changing relation between the narrator and the fiction. The stylistic study of use of "we" in politician's speech and writing or law and love poetry in translation will make a rewarding comparative culture study. The term's context also evokes issues of censorship, internal-external, indigenous-foreign, conscious-unconscious. The theories of fidelity and equivalence, purity and essence are being undermined by convergence between poststructuralist theory and new media. To be brief, the constellation of currents—multiculturalism, postcolonialism, race theory etc.—revolve around issues of identity and oppression. They also influence translation theories. The new technologies are associated with them.

The complexity of such intertextual and generic negotiations becomes manifest in the translations and adaptations. As a kind of methodological demonstration or taxonomic delirium, we can locate the major intertextual elements in *Godan,* its two translations in English and in many languages. From fidelity to intertextuality we should theorize transtextuality, intertextuality, paratextuality, metatextuality, architextuality and unmarked adaptations in translations. Similarly the other theoretical movements today have demoted the literary text from its position of authority after the declaration of Author-God's death. Such developments point to a possible reconceptualization of translation.

The interdisciplinary cultural studies explore "horizontal" relations between translation and its neighbouring media. That is why Vishram Bedekar, as we discussed realier, a film scriptwriter director was invited to retailor the version of an American *Send Me No Flowers* in order to make it run on the middle class Marathi stage. Long ago G.B. Deval had "mended" his *Falgurao athawa Tasabiricha Ghotala* - adaptation of Arthur Murphy's *All in the Wrong* (English version of Moliere's *Sganarellel)* — fifteen years after its failure in Pune, at the suggestion of Nanasaheb Phatak, the renowned actor, to Brahmanize it as *Sanshaykallol* (1912). Even the first musical play *Sangeet Saubhadra* (1883), which is supposed to be the "original" play, was the literal adaptation of the Music–Hall Mixture or Savoy Opera- *Thespis or Gods Turned Down* by Gilbert and Sullivan.

From cultural perspectives, translations and adaptations form a newly egalitarian spectrum of cultural productions. Within this textualized world of images and simulations, they become just other texts, forming the part of a broad discursive continuum. In this way "posts" in postconlonial, poststructural, postmodern, posttheory etc., have an impact on our discussion of translations. As stated above intertextuality theory certainly reshaped translation studies, other aspects of postcolonialism and poststructuralism have not yet been given prominence in the rethinking of the status and practice of translation. According to Roland Barthes, "The text is a tissue of innumerable quotations drawn from innumerable centres of culture." These centres of culture in India are many and the unity is traced in this diversity. Under such peculiar circumstance a translator himself is placed at the centre of a cultural battlefield called the work of art. How does he transcribe "a tissue of innumerable quotations" from the foreign culture? How does he face the tug of war between indigenous and alien cultural pulls?

Thus, the local and global contexts of translation lead us to the discussion of a wider concept of translation used by Patrice Pavis in the title of his edited book: *The Intercultural Performance: Reader* (1991). The translator's "cultural capital" plays a significant role in this intercultural performance. The literary fortune of the author, like Rabindranath Tagore in Spain and V.S. Khandekar in Tamil Nuda, does not depend only on his translator, but also on the need of the receptor culture. Translated ext is a gateway to another culture; and also a cultural laboratory. It is a network of very complex relationships and affiliations. Pavis writes:

> Every relationship with a foreign culture is determined by the purpose of the artists and cultural mediators who undertake its adaptations and its transmission. This purpose is as much aesthetic as ideological and, in both cases, often remains implicit or unconscious. Most often, the adaptor is not someone specifically charged with transposing the contents and forms from one cultural shore to another. It is rather a group of enunciators intervening at all levels and at every stage of production. An this sense, every intercultural project obeys the constraints and the needs tied specifically to the target culture that produces it .... It's so called universality, which subsumes all individual cultures is in fact only a construction of the dominant West (16, 17).

Apart from the limitations of comparison which falls short in analysis of cultural hierarchies. The comparatists have been pleading for development of comparative dialogic imagination in the Age of Terror. To the other extreme, it is considered "equally responsible for producing irreducible difference and manufacturing consent. Nor only does the field have a legendary history as a source for colonial and neocolonial epistemes, its traditional intransigence regarding challenge to the type of work we are advocating here." The debate is unending, but the field of comparision and translation is rapidly expanding in the digital space. Sophia A. McClennen and Joseph R. Slaughter argue:

> As comparative literature considers its role in the twenty-first century, it is clear that it is a discipline especially suited to the intellectual space form which to think about the work that we propose here.

As Kadir points out:

> Comparison is inevitably ethical: any course must be accompanied by the realization and forthright admission that Comparative Literature is and of this world and, as such, it is an eminently political endeavour, and, as with all political tasks, this too must be guided by a supple but steady sense of ethics.

The type of critical thinking needed to engage seriously with the complexities of human rights analysis demands an optic that exceeds the confines of traditional disciplinary formation. Such interdisciplinarity and cross-cultural attention also require comparative thinking, but this only when comparison is resolutely conscious of its own tendency to create hierarchies and reify difference. Reflecting on the possibilities of comparison necessarily leads to consideration of subjectivity and to the ethical motives behind comparison. If human rights are problems of representation, then they are a problem of comparison. Perhaps more importantly, it is only by means of comparison that there can be any sense of rights and their violations.

Thus translation as an "intercultural performance" is not an exception to these observations. This interculturalism has given rise to a more complex subject: comparative poetics conceived interculturally. What we have not yet done in India is being marketed by Euro-American comparatists with the help of NRI scholars. To cite only two examples: The following books have reached almost all libraries in our universities and colleges. They include essays on translations and adaptations also.

1. Patric Hogan and Lalita Pandit. (eds) *Literary India: Comparative Studies in Aesthetics, Colonialism and Culture,* State University of New York, rpt. New Delhi: Rawat Publication, 1997.
2. Stuart Blackburn and Vasudha Dalmia (eds.) *India's Literary History: Essays on the Nineteenth Century,* London: Orient Longman, Indian edition, Paramount Black, 2004.

As we began this discussion with the opening of Daniel Simon's essay, let us conclude it with the ending of Earl Miner's first chapter of his book: *Comparative Poetics:*

> Not all roads lead to comparative poetics. That point also needs making. But others do besides that followed here. Rene Etiemble clearly envisioned another double route that others have tried to set asunder. "By combining the two methods that consider themselves enemies...." The attitude is visionary in part, lofty, and set in a possible present. Others in the same enterprise may wish to follow different routes: ideology, interpretation, translation, the individual, society – the routes involve the manifold and familiar ones of literary study. It is, as Etiemble envisions, the purpose and the goal that determine whether a given route leads to comparative poetics (33).

This is the royal road, which is not taken by many, that leads to a global village.

13

Contesting "Newness" in Commonwealth Literatures

> *Difference*, spelled with an 'a', is notoriously unpindownable concept, but in fact it means something very close to 'unpindownability'. If so far we have had difference as the opposite of sameness, as the opposite of identity, the opposite of singularity and the opposite of reference, now, with the word 'difference', which Derrida claims is neither a word nor a concept at all, we are dealing with something like the opposite of presence, or even the opposite of concepthood. *This chapter explains the connection between presence and concepthood, and why Derrida saw, diffarance, as their opposite, but it also explores some other poststructuralist approaches to and modifications of ideas about difference.* (emphasis added)
>
> —Mark Currie, *Difference*, London: Routledge, 2004, 48.

It is a happy coincident that I had evaluated the PhD thesis on the folk tales in Angami submitted to the University of Pune by the Naga researcher; and today I am addressing the scholars from the same land. This shawl gifted by her has travelled back to her homeland, as Edward Said said "theories travel" with the travellers. India is a mini "commonwealth": itself. So the topic of this national Seminar on the Commonwealth Literatures demands a comparative cultural approach in the wake of globalization. It is a significant sign of change that there are five comparative presentations in this Seminar. At the outset, I congratulate the organizers for accepting this big challenge. It provides a good opportunity to think comparatively of the "newness" in all these cultural products produced in former British colonies. Are these literatures simply "new" in the historical sense for the Europeans or really "new" in the structuralist sense? Of course, they added new experiences to the mainstream literatures in Europe; but what about the forms and master narrative which determined it? The Blacks describe their literatures in Africa by using the image of Greek God Janus with two faces; but paradoxically Indians employ the culture-caste specific metaphor of "twice born" to describe fiction in English. We do not analyse Indian writing in English by using the image of Dattatraya with three faces or of ten headed Ravana. However, the twin process namely Anglicization-Westernization-Modernization plus Sanskritization-Brahmanization defined by sociologists was debated by the Anglicists and Orientalists in the early nineteenth century. Today the comparitists and culturalists claim that Indians suffer from extreme "Occidentosis". Now the international contexts and "affiliations' of the concept of "Commonwealth" (labelled as the "Commonwealth of crimes' by Jean Paul Sartre) Literatures have changed in the Age of Globalization and Terrorism. Since the old concept of literature littered by letters is dead in the digital space, it is necessary to resocialize literature to make the discipline of Humanities relevant in the Electronic Age. In order to resist the homogenizing impact of globalization, I have quoted some lines on the concept of "difference" in the beginning of this discussion. How far are these Commonwealth literatures different from each other as well as their counterparts in Europe? What are the salient features of their "newness"? Can we pinpoint Indian characters of Indian literature(s)?

I take up the last question first, because it was the theme of the International Seminar organized by Leiden University in the Netherlands where we were placed on the horns of a dilemma in 2001. In order to answer other questions, I would like to place Indian Writing in English at the centre and discuss "newness" comparatively with special references to other Commonwealth literatures. It is better to quote the leading comparatist, Steven Totosy de Zepetnek, at the outset to create a new frame of reference. He wrote a "Foreword" to my recent book titled *Literary into Comparative Culture Criticism*. He consciously pointed out how the use of the British concept of "culture criticism" instead of American "culture studies" displays the Eurocentricism in our literary thinking and further advised me to develop the "home grown theory" to resist such appropriations. I found his frame of ten principles of comparative literature and culture studies and systemic and empirical method more useful in rethinking of contesting "newness" in new literatures. I prefer to speak from the perspectives of a post-colonial creative writer, comparatist culturalist and translator. Earlier the Canadian historian of literature H.W. New had used the metaphor of "centre and periphery" to describe the complex relationships between European literatures and the "emerging new" literatures in its colonies. Steven Totosy applies three concepts, viz., "inbetweenness", "centerperipherality" and "center-marginality" to the literatures in East Central European countries. His observations about "cultures and peripherality" in this regard are relevant to varieties of literatures in the Indian sub-continent also. He argues:

> The problematics of peripherality are global event of our times. Not that peripherality has not always been evident in political, geographical, economical, cultural etc., situations; it has always been the case between the powerful and less powerful, between the coloniser and the colonized. What is now is the theoretical and political importance, the politics of postcolonialism and its attention to marginality attained in literary and cultural study. Here, my objective is to suggest a theoretical framework designated as "in between peripherality" for the current debate about postcoloniality, national identity, and post-Cold War narrative. Again the context is comparative; the method developed from the Systemic and Emperical approach and the application is with reference to the "Other", the peripheral, or the marginal. To start with, the problematic nature of postcoloniality, culture, and literature suggests that it may be advantageous to problematize the question further than use the usual British, French, American etc., mainstream focus and its historical or contemporary spheres of influence and colonialization...(129-30)

My influence studies (1993, 1999a) revealed how Indian/ indigenous literary systems and theories were slowly elbowed by "modern and advanced" Western theories and we are dependent on those ready made foreign textualities till today. Asia has never been the centre of theories after the contact with the West. It is a myth that modern literatures in Indian dialects and languages are more "Indian or nativistic" than Indian Writing in English. So Steven Tötösy's framework is applicable to a number of postcolonial and cultural situations and literatures including Indian mainstream literature as well as ethnic, diaspora, dalit or other instances of marginalized literatures. The application of this method to Aravind Adiga's *The White Tiger* might lead us to a culturally paradoxical conclusion that it is a neo-dalit fiction written by the savarna-high-caste elite.

There are a number of, to use the American concept, "border writings" such as aadiwasi (tribal), OBC (Other Backward Communities), Muslim, Jain, Christian and other minorities' writings. All of them exhibit, in Homi Bhabha's term, "ambivalent affiliations" to Western literary traditions to such extent that tolerant Hinduism and especially Gandhism seems to be unfavourable to the African /Fanonian violent aesthetic trend of "de-daffodilization" of indigenous literature. Ironically, the most westernized Indian literature produced by the traditional elite priestly class, having rich traditional cultural capital, has always remained at the local centre as an Indian representative English literature. All other emergent "vernacular literatures" were always at its 'margins' or 'borders'. The national and international politics in Frantz Fanon's term, "battle for recognition" also remotely controls indigenous "newness". There are innumerable margins of margins based on not only caste divisions but also on sub-casteist/religious fractions which have no parallels in the "colour/"aboriginal" divisions in the Commonwealth as well as Western countries. American critics have traced six faces of modernity but we have hundreds.

On this background, the traditional concepts such as "new/ modern/ "post" this and "after" that literatures, "Indian literature", "dalit literature" "Indianness," etc., need to be reconsidered in the light of new postcolonial theories and global contexts. We, especially the teachers of English, are the cultural products mostly determined by Anglo-American literatures and dominant cultures. Hence we have to place these concepts and texts in the contexts of social, cultural and literary discourses in the specific time and space from which they emanate. With such international references it can be argued that the regions' literatures in pre and postcolonial era manifest a specific 'narrative change"; but with some cultural difference. From these comparative and cultural perspectives, it would appear that the Indian writing in English, may be colonial or postcolonial, cannot be studied adequately without references to international, to use Edward Said's concepts, "affiliations" and "worldliness" of texts. Homi K. Bhabha finds it difficult to ascertain their cultural affiliations and lays more emphasis on their hybridity. European "culture and imperialism" have over determined Indian literary forms in such a way that the cultural amnesia has misled us to believe in the "authenticity" and "originality" of the modern Indian literatures.

The present caste-based Census reveals that 30 per cent Indian population lives in cities and the rest in villages. The dichotomy of India and Bharat is persistent in all debates. But the Indianness of English literary text is measured in urban terminology borrowed from the West. It represents the image of 30 per cent anglicized urban elites; because the foreign English falls short in transmitting rural reality. Indianization of English in *Kanthapura* and other 'twice born' priestly fiction amounts to cultural fakedom which was imitative of Joycean modernist experimentation with linguistic and individualistic stream of constiousness techniques. Of course, the implied Western reader governs the cultural intertextualities in the Commonwealth literary texts. Rarely an audacious Achebe or a resistant Rushdie rushes to "chuttanify" and pickle the European tradition. Caribbean civilisation is also more resistant.

It should be noted here that there is a need to reconsider Commonwealth literatures in terms of national self-referentiality and relative sovereignty of indigenous cultures and conflicting impacts of the other Western centres. Elsewhere, I (1999a) have demonstrated how the position of "margin" is in constant shift, depending on the locus of the speaker in any part of the subcontinent. For example, there is a great difference between colonial literary products in British Bombay and Portuguese Goa (see Patil 1999a). The relation of Indian mediators to the European literary texts, received to cater to the needs of the receptor's culture, stands in contrast to their counterparts in Africa and Caribbean in terms of resistance aesthetics. The first adapt them to recolonize their brethren, while the latter plagiarize them to subvert and resist the European dominant "culture and imperialism". A comparative study of Shakespeare's influence in these countries will illustrate this point. Both the European intellectuals and their counterparts in India, excepting very few, have not resisted to both inter- and intra- colonialisms. The cultural influences of Western centres such as London and New York are accepted with an eye on intracultural hegemony. If there is any opposition at all, it is based on ideological, economic, social etc.means. The term 'nationalism' and its self referentiality are considered less tenuous because of rich cultural diversity. Therefore, Saidian secular criticism is a better option for comparative analysis of European "culture and imperialism" which brings "newness" in Commonwealth literatures. Edward W. Said observes:

> You read... in order to keep with the best that was thought and known, and also to see yourself, *your people, society, and tradition in their best lights*. In time, culture comes to be associated, often aggressively, with the nation or the state; *this differentiates "us" from "them", almost always with some degree of xenophobia*. Culture in this sense is a source of identity (xiii emphasis added).

In India there are caste based differentiations and more complex cultural layers which can be hardly found in any "colour/class" based distinctions in other Commonwealth countries. Hence the language and literature curriculums in India include castealized semiotics in nomenclature of different papers such as dalit, rural, tribal etc. This constructivist approach shows how the imagination of Indian writer is culture conditioned not only by indigenous systems but also by Western culture and imperialism in a peculiar way. Here we should not loose sight of Said's analysis of national identity construction in and with culture in reference to the larger context of the West. It raises the problems of applicability of such new terms as "in between peripherality", "centre and marginality", "oppositional aesthetics", "Indianness", "border writing", "newness" etc. For instance, William Walsh and other Western critics did a good service to Commonwealth writings. But it is a time to comment comparatively on their "exo-cultural," patronizing attitude and inadequate understanding of cultural complexities.

After the colonial contact the comprador bourgeois class of intellectuals has been mediating Western culture. It is mediated through the political, social, economic and other leverages and powers. Therefore literary "newness" needs to be examined comparatively in terms of intertexuality, internationality, hybridity and politics of aesthetics. Although Britain and Portugal ruled India, French Moliere's influence countered Shakespeare worship which amounts to "bardicide". Thus, limitations of mechanical catalogues of influences, borrowings, adaptations etc., are brought to light by new culture studies. A new terminology, for example, devised by K.K.Ruthven, is necessary for tracing different modes and methods of "faking" literature in the Commonwealth. This process of internationalization of European kinds of literature demands more attention than its monolingual discussion in terms of "authenticity", "originality", novelty, experimentation and what not.

At least for this modest purpose, despite declaration of death of comparative literature by Susan Bassnett and Gayatri Spivak, we badly need comparative poetics and interdisciplinarity. Bruce King (1996) had pointed out "new centres of consciousness" and discussed "new postcolonial and international literature" in English as if it is a single entity. But his homogenizing effort falls short in dissecting innumerable aspects of these "new centers of consciousness". For example, the effects of sibling relationships of the writers writing in English and in the local languages, or mastery of a "foreign" language and lack of it should be studied comparatively. The term "new", according to King, is used to point out a phase in the historical development of literatures in the Age of Postcolonialism after the Second World War. This is the extension of Anglo-American Project of Modernity that makes him write about the "emergence of new literatures" from Eurocentric perspectives. But comparatists outside Europe and America have different stories to tell about the hidden agenda and politics of aesthetics behind that big project. King refers to the modernization of local cultures and crumbling of old traditions in the Commonwealth countries; but ignores mimicry, memorization, stereotyping, faking etc. in their reconstructions. He states:

> That English literature has changed radically since about 1960 is obvious; less clear is the nature of this new literature especially as the various descriptive terms have their own historical and political contexts. Many nationalists, Americans and cultural radicals regard *'Commonwealth' as a passing phase of British colonialism*. Others regard post-colonial as an American and *new Left ignorance of national differences* that also disregards the continuing links between many English-speaking nations. *International, Global, or World English homogenizes and suppresses differences* (4 emphases added).

The term "Indian English Literature" also homogenizes varieties of Englishes in the subcontinent. They are historically graded in hierarchy according to dates of Europe's cultural conquest of different regions in India. Gauri Viswanathnan's concept of the "mask of conquest" suits well for the indigenous agents of alien imperialism. The current scams and corruption cases related to Commonwealth Games conducted in Delhi may be used as a metaphor to describe the literary fakedom, barring very few exceptions, in our "shadow literature". The politics of not only use and misuse of Western texts but also of production of "ignorance" to maintain dominance of aesthetics of Anglo-

American modernism has been having the upper hand in our cultural industry. So we have to accept King's statements with some reservations. According to him, "post-colonialism is a further development of the decolonization and the changed cultural perspectives." If it is so, why did Ngugi wa Thiong'o, Namwar Singh and others write essays on "decolonizing mind"? Thiwang'o was right to demand that we should include as many Anglo-American texts as African and other non-Euramerican texts are prescribed by "them" in their syllabi. There is a battle cry against the marginalization of Commonwealth literatures in Europe and America. Apart from their classical traditions, the literatures produced after the colonial contacts are labelled as "shadow literatures". In order to put this wrong image straight one has to sort out "new" elements in Commonwealth literatures. Of course, Kumau Braithwaite and few others did try to develop the aesthetics of resistance based on surviving indigenous elements while Indians did a lip service to Sanskrit aesthetics without practising it.

It will be more interesting to juxtapose poetry of Jayant Mahapatra and Derek Walcott in order to trace different degrees of acculturation and enculturation. The first would appear, to a committed culturalist, more English and the latter more Indian! Similarly a comparative cultural study of critical writings of Frantz Fanon, Edward Said, Arunprabha Mukherjee, and M.K.Naik might reveal great disparity in their resistance to the dominant West. Fanon dissected the nature and scope of European colonization by theorizing it vehemently and revolutionized the postcolonial literary thought. Said is more known for his comparative scholarship and for striking a secular balance between Right and Left. Arunprabha Mukherjee's "oppositional aesthetics" is determined both by Indian "loss of inheritance" and "inbetween marginality" of a Brahman migrant in Canada. To the other extreme, M.K.Naik and Meenakshi Mukherjee represent the comprador class of Indian intellectuals. Especially Mukherjee's recent title "Perishable Empire" is a misnomer. The Indian diaspora continues the same tradition of "white man's burden" to "civilize others" in India.

Relatively fewer attempts are made to "de-scribe empire" theoretically in India than in other Commonwealth countries. So there is the absence of such canonical texts as *The Wretched of the Earth, Empire Writes Back, Culture and Imperialism. My life: Postcolonialism, Race, Writing and Difference, The Coloniser and the Colonized* etc., in our literati. Perhaps the comprador class's self interests and its Western cultural capital are invested in Indian local neo-colonialism. It is a paradox that Salman Rushdie's popular phrase "Empire Writes Back" appears in the title of the book edited by non-Indian scholars. Rushdie stands in contrast to V.S. Naipaul who was knighted by the Empire. Under such circumstances Ania Loomba and others, based in the centre of India, have edited *Postcolonial Studies and Beyond* (2006) in collaboration with the University of Illinois in the United States. The place of production of knowledge also matters in comparative culture studies. This collection of research papers exhibits the double bind of "globalization and neo-imperialism." The editors hope to draw on the tradition of anti-colonial thought and sociocultural analysis to suggest socioeconomically informed models of marginalization and innovative critical language. Their attempt to minimize Eurocentricism deserves compliments. They argue:

> Thus, the *beyond* in the title of this volume is not meant to indicate a facile hope for a transformative shift in the practical loosely clustered round the affiliation postcolonial studies, nor does it mean to point to a wholly new mode of understanding the links between the critical study and the neo-imperial structures of global inequality (although the volume does indicate significant new distinctions for future works). Rather it charts a path between Eurocentricism and "hip-defeatism", as much by renewing engagements with analytical models developed by older anti-colonial thinkers as by positing new forms of critique that will address the ideological and material dimensions of contemporary neo-imperialism (4).

The present Seminar offers a golden opportunity to evolve "new forms of critique" by amalgamation of indigenous elements and traditional terms drawn from crafts and grafts, travels and trades. By recapturing the morphology of transoceanic and transcontinental folk-tales and classical storehouse of concepts, a new generation can "address the ideological and material dimensions of contemporary neo-imperialism." For this change an equal importance should be given to the poetics as well as politics of literature. Going beyond the West and rest binary and the legacy of Eurocentricism is a real challenge today. The belated acquaintance with the death of literary theories and traditional terminology facilitates continuation of the colonized curriculums and talking in terms of impressionism and New Criticism, albeit they were dead long ago in their countries of birth. Thus, Euramerica-centricism continues through Western cultural attacks, as Fanon had predicted, of "cheap entertainments", songs, rock-pop-hip-hop, remixes, gimmicks and best-sellers which might cause the death of our languages, literatures and cultures. Loomba and others have rightly pointed out that Eurocentricism "continues to bedevil even its most ardent critics" and we are not exceptions. If the gold rusts, what can the iron do?

This dilemma has been haunting Indian literati since Lord Babington Macaulay introduced his famous "Minutes" in 1835. The changes in our literature are closely connected with his theory of filtration of English education through the mud pots in the hierarchical ladder of castes. It is necessary to trace the effects of this educational system, which is often called "miseducation of the natives", on unexpected and uneven developments during and after colonial modernity of different faces. Sometimes there are isolated comparisons of contemporary texts without taking into consideration the historical contexts and contextures. For example, Toral Jatin Gajarwala opens his article "Miseducation: Dalit and Beur Writers on Antiromance of Pedagogy" (2010) with the following "introduction":

> Farida Balghaul's novel *Georgette*! (1986) spans a single traumatic day in the life of a Beur schoolgirl. Sushila Takbhore's story *Silvya* (1997) traverses the entire educational life of the protagonist from grade school to college and beyond. This essay considers why the site of

> the school figures this prominently, this deliberately, in writing by Beurs (descendants of North African immigrants) and dalits "untouchable' caste), writing invested in the category of the marginal. As essential subsets of literatures characterized as "ethnic", "marginal", "minor" and so forth, these bodies of texts invariably negotiate mainstream bureaucratic institutions, indeed, their narrative drive, conflict, humour, and resolution drive from these entanglements (346-47).

The dalit literary texts display strong resistance to local orthodoxy, but the Blacks to the Euramerican domination. Such comparisons mostly focus on themes. In this way our criticism has been privileging European textuality and the colonial period over the continuity of the pre-colonial cultural heritage and the post-colonial cultural diversity. Perhaps the Vedic resistance to comparision hardly leaves any space for caste-based theorization of self and other as represented in literature. Such caste/colour conditioned discourses get stuck in the mire of content for preaching the cult of the under dog. They trim the wide ranging inter-textuality embedded in the texts. A comparative study of the movements and protest literatures of the oppressed, namely, apartheids in Africa, Black Panthers in America and dalits in India reveal more or less similar one sided dimensions of texts. For instance, why does the image of the "sun" repeatedly shine more brightly in them? Perhaps, the Fulbright and other fellowships in the First World make it shine in poetry first and then brighter in the Cold War!

Apart from the patronizing attitude of traditional critics towards the literatures of the oppressed, a well informed comparist might point a finger to the protagonists' schooldays depicted satirically in British *The Hard Times, The Portrait of an Artist as a Young Man,* Russian *Crime and Punishment* or Indian *Sorrowing Lies My Land* or similar texts in other cultures. Here lies the crux of the matter in relating literature of the formerly colonized countries to the West, and present globalization has further complicated this issue. Therefore, a shift in strategy of reading the text in the contexts of intertextualities, cultural hybridties and affiliations of interliterariness is necessary. It means turning Western norms upside down to deconstruct the text comparatively in order to get rid of the curse of "lie of the land," and find true "newness" categorically. Robert Young's (2003) postcolonial theory is of great help in developing such strategies. He argues:

> In a comparable way, 'postcolonial theory' involves a conceptual reorientation towards the perspectives of knowledge, as well as needs developed outside west. It is concerned with developing the driving ideas of a political practice morally committed to transforming the condition of exploitation and poverty in which large sections of the world's population live their daily lives (6).

Owing to such theorizations and globalization of media, the attention is now shifting to literary texts and cultures in Asian countries. For example, it is reported that a better postmodern novel, than Shashi Tharoor's *The Great Indian Epic,* has been published in Bangkok. It makes more effective use of more liberal intertextuality of the *Mahabharata* than its culture conditioned misuse in India. However, the capitalist politics of marketing such books does make a great difference in their reception. The pirated editions of Euramerican substandard best sellers are easily available on the footpaths of our cities, but not the classics of Nobel Laureates from Africa, Asia or from China and Japan. In fact, such new samples will provide new norms for tracing "newness' in our literatures.

Edward Said had pointed out the major weakness of Indians that they are "obsessed with West and suffer from Occidentosis". Such "daffodilization" enables them to know everything about Euro-American periodicals, but less about *Enact, Ariel* or *Kunapipi.* Perhaps that is why there is a rich intertextuality of Western literary texts in *The God of Small Things,* and *The Loss of Inheritance* rather than that of Indian language literatures, both oral and written. Since Commonwealth countries provide less financial support to study these literatures and cultures we cannot compare Premchand, Achebe and Atwood or movements in these countries. A university in the Unites States does not encourage a proposal to study nativism in American and Indian literatures. This leads us to the problem of in Homi K. Bhabha's words "nation and narration". Whose master's voice is heard in the dalit literature and which forms are used for representation of Indian reality? Which are the Western lark mirrors that entrap budding Commonwealth writers? A comparative study of travels by Naipaul, George Lamming, and I myself might reflect different images of cultures in Europe and Commonwealth countries. Elsewhere, I (2005) have demonstrated how adaptation of Shakespeare plays by Derek Walcott in *The Branch of Blue Nile* is more acculturated and internationalized than Vasant Kanetkar's superficial collage of four tragedies in one, in his Marathi *Gaganbhedi* (sky piercing cry).

The Walcott's innovative hybrid product could not be generically identified by critics. Walcott labelled it as "serio-comedy". His Nobel speech ironically opened with the reference to a performance of Ram Leela, which he called "the fragments of Indian epic culture", in a village called Felicity in the West Indies. He adapted the comic device of Vidushaka from Indian classical tradition of drama. On the contrary, Kanetkar's Shakespeare offshoot is more British than Shakespeare's plays. Plagiarism and misuse of European texts in India for vested interests is described by comparatists as an "anti-national" tendency. This is how Macaulay's policy of creating people not of the white man's colour but of their "culture and taste" continues till today. That is why we neither have Wole Soyinka, nor Boas, nor Kwame Anthony Appiah, nor Helen Tiffin, nor Gareth Griffiths, but more elitist comprador writers and no critic who has studied literatures in 24 languages constitutionally recognized by the Government of India. Sisirkumar Das was the first comparatist to conduct the comparative survey of Indian medieval critical terms which can be the source of constructing the home grown literary theory.

As a creative writer I have been pleading for a dialogic comparative imagination, a new international cultural literacy and neo-nativism to survive in the global literary market. Resistance to total appropriation can be acquired by comparative awareness of indigenous cultural inheritance and alert reception of foreign elements for the healthy growth of remixed genres. In fact, the adjective "Indian" marks the geographical boundaries but cultural. There are varieties of "Indiannesses" which change per kilometre. Blind nativism and nationalism lead to fascism. The whole pre-British Vedic and Muslim traditions cannot be discarded. It would be a simplistic nativistic view to think of pre-colonial past as "primal", innocent and pure. However, as A. Ahmad had pointed out, we have to pay attention to "the continuing pre-colonial and internal preoccupations of societies." The truth of this statement dawned upon me when I translated P.S. Deshmukh's *The Origin and Development of Religion in Vedic Literature* (OUP, 1933) into Marathi and wrote short stories also in the local dialect. Deshmukh's comparative, philological and scientific study remained totally neglected for nearly seventy years. This speaks volumes not only about intra-caste politics of cultural hegemony, but also about our postcolonial cultural "amnesia." These classical as well as folk cultural sources, which are the fountainheads of creativity, need to be explored in the electronic age. Here the comparative study can be blended with cultural study for a new interdisciplinarity. "A comparative study of death and pharmacy in Indian, African, Australian, Caribbean and Canadian fiction: A Case study" will be more rewarding and revealing than the traditional "analytical" author study of Arthur Miller in the run of the mill pattern.

After teaching English literature for forty long years and writing more than dozen books in the area of comparative literature and culture, it is a very painful realization for me. Our studies are embedded in the transplanted English literary culture and in vastly differing cultures of the colonized. We are nourished not only by Western theories of aesthetics, but also by the colonial "production of ignorance." Immanuel Kant had stated that the dominance of any aesthetic theory is always supported by equal "production of ignorance". It seems that our Humanities have been trading both Western theories and ignorance through double colonized curriculum. The British Romanticism and American formalist criticism teaches us how to appreciate the romance of Shahjahan and Mumtaz and beauty of Taj Mahal but not to think of labour put in its construction and the food those wage earners ate. This is why we do not find in our criticism a parallel to the apt term "deffodilization of minds" used in the Black aesthetics. On the contrary, we have the "vernacular" language writer from the priestly class who described English as "a milk of the tigress." It was a self defeating identity politics. In acceptance of superiority of foreign ruler's language there was the politics to retain traditional cultural hegemony. Here no resistance is implied like the Blacks, who tamed their "english" like a sheep. Such minor observations provide good grounds for comparisons of Commonwealth literatures at different levels. For example, the myth of the lazy natives is present in them, but awaits exploration. The problem of racialization of literature is being debated in the West. So Rosalind O'Hanlon, who has published her dissertation on the literature and reformist movement of Jotirao Phule, from Oxford University travels with her new cultural theories to trace nature and scope of the caste system in pre-British India. Indian cultural industry might import, like weapons and machines, good Western researchers one day!

This process of exporting knowledge about Commonwealth literature produced in Europe and America with the help of their masters of Indian languages and informer NRIs is a next phase of the Anglo-American Project of Modernity mentioned above. To cite a single example, Stuart Blackburn and Vasudha Dalmia write in the beginning of an "Introduction" to their edited collection of Seminar papers titled *India's Literary History: Essays on the Nineteenth Century* (2004):

> Ever since Clifford Geertz transformed the drama of Balinese cockfight into a text, and new historicism made the complementary gesture of returning culture of literary studies, students of literature, history and culture have shared a common vocabulary, key concepts and points of reference. This conversance has led to a orientation in the study of literary history. The periodization, assignment and attribution that characterized earlier historiography have been replaced by an effort to understand the place of literature in history, largely through an analysis of the textual production of cultural meaning and the socio-political conditions of creating texts... The present book,

> we hope opens up this enraging field of critical literary history to nineteenth century India.

This is how knowledge is produced in Europe and America and marketed in the Commonwealth and a new kind of Euramerica-centricism is strengthened in the name of globalization. One can imagine how Dalmia's *Poetics, Plays and Performances* (OUP, 2006), a comprehensive book on Indian modern drama, must have been determined by America-centricism and alienated from Sisirkumar Das's concepts explored from Indian dramaturgy. This is the tug of war between two cultures, super-power and the emerging power.

Hence we need a Gareth Griffiths to design "The Postcolonial Project: Critical Approaches and Problems" (1996). Before he presented it, he (1978) had pleaded for "Celebrating the Past: Facing the Future" and discussed the double exilement of the writer. Then he (1998) argued:

> The future study of the new literatures appears assured as it is difficult to see how a canon can be restored in a form which excludes such literatures, their concerns, and the theoretical problems they raise. Nevertheless, the theory of the construction of the field, as it has developed in recent years, has had both a positive and a negative effect. It has been positive in recognizing that merely accrediting literatures and literary texts onto a unified model of English studies, even one which accepts a plurality of differences, does not ensure a genuine equality of cultures and of diverse reading and speaking positives. Such formulations overcome the limitations of the more simplistic kind of pluralism which underpinned the earlier models of the field (175).

Griffiths is not totally opposed to Western influences. He suggests adequate measures to resist appropriation by them. Studying the factors which shaped these "new" literatures is the prime task of the new comparatists. They are closely embedded in internationalism. The structuralists demonstrated how Romantic theories of genius and autonomy of literature are lies and literature itself is a big convincing lie. It is necessary to trace the similarities and differences between new nativist literatures in Africa, America, Australia, India etc. It may reveal that nativism in India is weaker than that in Africa. What makes all this difference? Ngugi wa Thiong'o pleaded for abolition of Departments of English in the 1970s when Indian scholars resisted the emergence of comparative literature. Apart from Ashish Nandis theorisation there is hardly any scholarly study of colonialism in Indian writing in English and the role of Department of English in spreading or resisting it. So the term "postcolonial", which has become synonymous with all forms of oppression or resistance to it, needs to be contested in Indian contexts. There is a great tradition of anti-colonialists from Fanon and Amie Caesaire, Albert Memmi and Jan Mohmad, Stephen Slemon and Bill Ashcroft, A. Ahmad to Spivak in this field. Any marginalization and anti-oppressive act can be discussed under this rubric. The religious and other cultural markers have demarked Indian communities in such a way that every sub-culture group's literature tends to be a "minority discourse" determined by the domestic as well as international politics of aesthetics. Since we live in a postcolonial/post-independence period the development of postcolonial literary studies should have a firm base and its theoretical coherence. Stephen Slemon's observations on this theme are more useful for deliberations in this Seminar. He writes:

> 'Post-colonialism' as it is now used in various fields, describes a remarkably heterogeneous set of subject positions, professional fields, and critical enterprises. It has been used as a way of ordering a critique of totalizing forms of Western historicism; as a part of manteau term for a retooled notion of 'Class'; as a subset of both postmodernism and poststructuralism (and conversely, as the condition from which those two structures of cultural logic and cultural critique themselves are seen to emerge); as the name for the condition of nativist longing in post-independence national groupings; as a cultural marker of non-residency for a Third World intellectual cadre; as the inevitable underside of a fractured and ambivalent discourse of colonialist power; as an oppositional 'reading

> practice'; and this was my first encounter which sprang from a new and welcome political energy going on within what used to be called "Commonwealth Literary Studies" (16).

This leads us to the new concept of comprehensive as well comparative histories of "new" literatures and tneir "affiliations" to the West. So far we are used to the mono-literary histories of specific countries from above modelled on the patterns evolved by scholars in Cambridge and Princeton. They exhibit cultural parade of the hierarchically arranged authors and their books. In the digital age they are not more significant than a telephone directory (outdated one?). Most of them are determined by nationalism, cultural hegemonies and elitists who own the cultural capital. Under such circumstances the glaring limitations of the literary histories compiled single handedly by K.R. Srinivas Iyengar, M. K. Naik and others will be revealed only if they are juxtaposed with histories of "New" literatures in other countries. Almost all histories are compiled by Brahmans except very few.

We have a fine example of the post-colonial alternative model of the subaltern history edited by Ranjit Guha. It is necessary to expand the "postcolonial project" and compile the comparative and compendious history of new literatures to gain deeper insights into the effects of colonialism and globalization. Of course, the traditional literary histories of Commonwealth countries show how they share the continuous international circulation of ideas and intellectual trends.

It is necessary to link the "emergence" of "regional literatures" in different dialects in the 1930s with the publication of William Empson's essay "Aesthetics of Regionalism" in the 1920s. Such comparativism exposes the loud claims of originality, experimentation and innovation in so called "new" literatures in the Commonwealth (without any wealth owned by the natives?).

Postcolonial scholars are placed on the horns of dilemma because they are sandwithched between the print culture of the Third World and the digital media culture of the First World. The recent developments in the information science have changed the original meanings of the concepts such as literature, Commonwealth literature, author, critic, theory, genre etc. to such an extent that the whole literati is ridden with a tremendous epidemic of death. Elsewhere I (2011) have discussed the impact of media and globalization on Indian literature(s). The concepts such as "Time", "Space", "worldview", "authorial voice" etc., are utterly changed by the electronic and information revolution. We need a stylometer to scrutinize the characteristics of an author's style. Compu-novels, remixed poems, soap serials, retailored plays, and hypertexts are taught by organizing the food Festivals of literary texts. Such a festival of Indian literary texts is likely to expose the myth that writings of the writers belonging to the priestly class are strictly vegetarian! I (2011) have discussed at length the impact of globalization on language and literature.

Before we conclude, a passing reference to the post-colonial literary Renaissance brought about by translations in Indian languages might show how there is a tough competition between the Euramerican mainstream and Commonwealth literatures. Along with attacks of "cheap entertainments" through electronic media, there is the aggression of translations of Euramerican best-sellers. There is nothing wrong in such ventures when we have signed the GAAT. Nature does not tolerate any vacuum. They are doing what our culture conditioned imagination never dreams of. For example, Emily Apter, the young scholar in America, underwent the traumatic experience during the terrible terrorist attack on 2001 in New York. Her thinking of traditional translation theories was revolutionized by that single shocking international event to such an extent that she wrote a very innovative book. It will soon become a *Bible* for new studies in this area and occupy a permanent position like Rene Wellek's *Theory of Literature*, which he himself dismantled after he became a comparatist, but it survives in Indian curriculum till today! In contrast to our submissive tradition, Apter writes in her "Introduction":

> It is this political situation that *The Translation Zone: A New Comparative Literature* took shape. The book aims to rethink translation studies a field traditionally defined by

> problems of linguistic and textual fidelity to the original in a broad theoretical framework that emphasizes the role played by mistranslation in war, the influence of language and literature wars on canon formation and literary fields, the aesthetic significance of experiments with non-standard language, and the status of the humanist tradition of *translation studii* in an era of technical literacy (3).

26/11, 13/7 and several other numerical signs have become parts of our "cultural conflict." Terrorist attracts on India have never inspired such theorizations. This "newness" is lacking in the Commonwealth literatures. Therefore, we should strike a serious note that neither language nor literature nor culture can survive without the strong armies of "home-grown" theories.

The electronic media has brought about a revolutionary change in the concept of 'newness' because of international interculturalness. Each nation has been renewing its cultural policy to guard against total appropriation. In this context globalisation is an opportunity as well as a greater challenge. It is a responsibly not only to resist appropriation but also to set out in search of new comparitivism and creativity. There lies a great inheritance of profit in a rich diversity and hybridity of Indian culture.

Bibliography

Abrams, Tevia. (1974). "Tamasha: Peoples's Theatre of Maharashatra State, India." Ph.D. Mischigan State University, U.S.A.

Achebe, Chinua. (1958). *Things Fall Apart,* London: Hienaman, 1972.

________ Hopes *and Impedements: Selected* Essays 1945-1987. London: Heinemann International, 1988.

Adiga, Aravind. (2008). Between *the Assassinations.* London: Picador.

Ahmad, A. *In Theory, Class, Nations, Literatures,* London: Verso, 1992.

Amannudin, Syed. (1989). "The Novels of Salman Rushdie: Mediated Reality as Fantasy" *World Literature Today,* 63-16: (Winter): 42-45. Hereafter cited as *WLT.*

Anzaldua, Gloria. (1987). *Borderlands / La Frontera,* The New Mestiza Spinsters/ Aunt Lute.

Appiah, Kwame Anthony. (1991). "Is the Post in Postmodernism the Post in Postcolonial?" *New Literary History,* 2-17: 136-237. Here after all periodicals are abridged as *NLH.*

Apte, Madhav. (1978). ed. *Mass Culture Language and Arts in India*: Bombay: Popular.

Apter, Emily. (2006). *The Translation Zone:* A *New Comparative Literature.* Princeton: Princeton UP.

Ashcroft, Bill et al. (1989) *Empire Writes Back: The Theory and Practice in Postcolonial Literature,* London: Routledge, 1991.

Axton, Richard. (1979). "Folk Plays in Tudor Interludes", in *English Drama: Form* and *Development,* eds. Marie Axton and Raymond Williams, Cambridge: Cambridge University Press.

Bachelli, R. R. (1991). "The Double Meaning of Humorous Writings and its Translatibility," *International Journal of Translation,* III 1-2: 91-98. Hereafter abridged as *IJT.*

Baker, Ernest A. (1936). *The History of English Novel,* London: Barnes and Noble, 1968.

Bakhtin, Mikhail. (1981). "Epic and Novel", in Michael Helquist and Caryl Emerson, eds. *The Dialogic Imagination*, Texas: University of Texas

Press; 12-38.

Balakian, Anna. (1995). "Theorising Comparison", *WLT* 62-2 (Spring): 263-267.

Baldo Jonathan (1975). "Exporting Oblivion in the Tempest," *Modern Language Quarterly* 56-2; 112-114.

Barry, Peter. (1995). *Beginning Theory: An Introduction to Literary and Cultural Theory*. Manchester: Manchester University Press.

Bedekar, Vishram. (1967). *Waje Paul Aapule*. Pune: Sadhana Prakashan.

Berg, Stephen ed. (1973). *In Praise of What Persists,* New York: Harper and Row Publication.

Bhabha, Homi K. ed. (1994) *The Location of Culture*, London: Routledge.

________ (1996). "The Other Question: Difference, Discrimination and Discourse of Colonialism," in Barker Francis and Hume Peter eds. *Literature, Politics and Theory,* London: Methuen.

________ (1995). ed. *Nation and Narration*. London: Routledge.

Bhende, Subhash. (1974). *Jogin*, Mumbai: Majestic Prakashan.

Bhosale S. S. ed. (1861). *Raja Shivaji by* M.M. Kunte. Aurangabad: Sahitya Seva Prakashan, 1992.

Blackburn, Stuart and Vasudha Dalmia. (2004). *India's Literary History: Essays on the Nineteenth Century*. Delhi: OUP.

Bourdieu, Pierre. (1979). trans. from French *Distinction: A Social Critique of Judgement of Taste*. London: Routledge and Kegan Paul.

Brathwaite, Edward Kamau. (1992). "The Search for a Caribbean Aesthetics", as quoted by Synthia James "The Unknown Text," *WLT* 68-4: 762.

Brennan, Timothy. (1993). "The National Longing for Form", in Bhabha, Homi K. (ed.) *Nation and Narration, op. cit.* 44-67.

Breslow, Stephen. (1989). "Trinidadian Heteroglossia : A Bakhtinian View of Derek Walcott's Play, *A Branch of the Blue Nile"*, *WLT* 63-1:36-39.

________ . (1993). "Derek Wlacott: 1992 Nobel Laureate in Literature", *WLT* 62-2: 267-271.

Brown B. H. ed. (1959). The Twain Must Meet: *Study in Cultural Understanding*, East Lancing: Michigan State University.

Cardoz, Tomzinho. (1992) *Tiatr: Mhowal Wikh, Samaj* Seva, Kandoli-Goa: Amer Prakashan.

Chandra, Sudhir. (1992). *The Oppressive Present: Literature and Social Consciousness in Colonial India,* Delhi: OUP.

Chitre, Dilip. ed. (1967). *An Anthology of Marathi Poetry,* Bombay: Nirmala.

________ . (1990). trans. *Abhang Gatha: Tuka Says—Tukaram,* Harmondsworth: Penguin Classics.

Cohn, Ruby. (1997). *Modern Shakespeare Offshoots,* New Jersey: Princeton University.

Cunha, T.B. (1961). *Goa's Freedom Struggle,* Bombay: T.B. Cunha Memorial Committee.

Currie, Mark. (2004). *Difference,* London: Routledge.

D'Souza, Eduard Bruno. (1899). *Ev ani Mari,* transcribed into Konkani and ed. by Olivinho Gomes, Chander Goa: Saraspat Prakashan, 1992.

Dalmia, Vasudha. (2006). *Poetics, Plays and Performances.* New Delhi: OUP.

Das, Sisir Kumar. (1984) "Terms for the Medieval Indian Long Poems" *Jadhavpur Journal of Comparative Literature* 22:74-84.

Desai, Ranjit. (1962). *Swami,* Pune: Deshmukh ani Co.

Deshmukh, Panjabrao Shamrao. (1933). *The Origin and Development of Religion in Vedic Religion.* Delhi: OUP,

Devi, Ganesh. (1992). *After* Amnesia: *Tradition and Change in Indian Literary Criticism.* New Delhi: Orient Longman.

________ . (1992b). "Bhartiya Sandharbhat Taulanik Sahityabhyas," in Chandrashekhar Jahagirdar ed. *Taulanik Sahityabhyas: Tatve ani Disha*, Kolhapur: Saurabh Prakashan, 21-52.

Dey, Susnigdha. (1998). *Contemporary Latin American Literature,* Delhi: B. R. Publishing Co.

Dharwadkar, Aparna. (1995a). "John Gay, Bertolt Brecht and Postcolonial anti-colonialism", *Modern Drama* 38: 101-127.

________ . (1995b). "Historical Fiction and Postcolonial Representations: Girish Karnad's *Tughlaq PMLA* 38-104:21.

Dhale, Raja. (1990). *Astitwachya Resha* ed. J. V. Pawar, Mumbai: Pranali.

Dhasal Namdev. (1997). "Interview", *Anusthubh (July)* 47-74.

Dirlik, Arif. (1994). "The Postcolonial Aura: Third World Criticism in the Age of the Global Capitalism", *Critical Inquiry* 20-2:324-56.

Donnely, Mary E. (1995). "Mother Country, Father Country: in *The Castle of My Skin* and Oedipal Structures of Colonialism," *Ariel* 26-4 (Oct.): 7-20.

Draudt, Manfred. (1993). "Committing Outrage against the Bard: Nineteenth Century Travesties of Shakespeare in England and Australia" *Modern Language Review,* 80-1:1-9.

During, Simon. (1993). ed. *The Cultural Studies: Reader,* London: Routledge.

Eagleton, Terry. (1993). *Literary Theory: An Introduction,* Oxford: Basil Blackwell.

Easthope, Anthony. (1996). *Literary into Cultural Studies,* London: Routledge.

Edmonson, Belinda. (1992). "Black Aesthetics, Feminist Aesthetics and the Problems of Oppositional Discourse", *Cultural Critic* (Fall): 75-96.

________ . (1994). "Race, Tradition, and Construction of the Caribbean Aesthetics," *New Literary History* 25:109-119.

Ekam, Keir. (d 980). *The Semiotics of Theatre and Drama,* London: Methuen.

Escheruo, Michael J. C. (1978). *The Culture Conditioned Imagination from Shakespeare to Conrad,* London: Macmillan.

Fanon, Frantz. (1961). bans. *The Wretched* of *the Earth,* Harmondsworth: Penguin, 1967.

________ . (1952). trans. The *Black Skin, White Masks,* New York: Grove Weidenfield, 1967; rpt. 1982.

Freire, Paulo. (1977). trans. *Pedagogy* of *the Oppressed,* Hannondsworth: Penguin.

Gaikwad, Baburao. (1994). *Dalitetar Lekhak ani Dalit Jeevan,* Pune: Adhik Prakashan.

Gajarawala, Toral Jatin. "Miseducation: Dalit and Beur Writers on Antiromance of Pedagogy ". *Comparative Literature Studies,* 47:3 (2010) 346-68.

Geetha, V. (1993). "Re-writing History in the Brahmin's Shadow: Caste and Modem Historical Imagination", *Journal of Arts and Ideas,* 25-26 (Dec.): 127-151:

Ghose, Sagarika. (1955). "Journalistic Writing as a Literary Genre" *Literature Alive* 2:53-57.

Godase, D. G. (1979) *Lokdhati,* Mumbai: Popular Prakashan.

Goldberg, S.I. (1974). *An Essay on King Lear,* London: Cambridge University Press.

Gomes Olivinho. (1987). *Village Goa,* New Delhi: S. Chand and Co.

Gomes, Francisco Louis. (1866). *Os Brahmanes,* Lisbon: Typographia da Gazette De; translated into English *The Brahmans,* Bombay: Siudhu Publication 1971: into Marathi: Laxmanrao Sardesai, *Brahman,*. Bombay:. Maharashtra Rajya Sahitya ani Sanskrit Mandal, 1973.

Gracyk Theodre A. (1994). "Rethinking Flume's Standard of Taste", *Journal* of *Aesthetics and Art Criticism*, 52-2, (Spring): 169-182.

Greenberger, Allen. (1969). *The British Image of India: A Study in the Literature of Imperialism 1880-1960,* London: Oxford University Press.

Griffith, Gareth. (1978). *A Double Exile: African and West Indian* Writing *Between Two Cultures*, London: Marion Bayers.

________ "The Postcolonial Project: Critical Approaches and Problems," in Bruse King, Op. Cit. 175.

Guha, Ranajit (1987). ed. *Subaltern Studies: V.*. Writing *on South Asian History and Society*, New Delhi: Oxford University Press.

________ . (ed.) " On some aspects of the Historiography of Colonial India". *Subaltern Studies I. Writings on South-Asian History and Society*. Delhi: OUP, 1982:1-8.

Gune V. T. (1979). ed. *Gazetter of India: Union Territory of Goa, Daman and Diu,* Part I, Goa, Panaji.

Habicht, Werner. (1989) "Shakespeare and Theatre Politics in the Third Reich," in Hanna Scolnicov and Peter Holland eds. *The Play Out of Context: Transferring Plays from Culture to Culture,* Cambridge: Cambridge University Press.

Handoo, Jawaharlal. (1994) "Oral Tradition: Words, Signs and Gestures," *Indian Literature 163* (Oct.): 69-87.

Hirsh, Edward. (1981). "The Imaginary Irish Peasant", *PMLA* 105-106: 1116-1133.

Hogan, Patrick C. (1992). "Mimeticism, Reactionary Nativism and Possibility of Postcolonial Identity in Derek Walcott's *Dream on Monkey Mountain," Research In African Literature* 25-21:103-117.

Holmes S. (1991). "The Name and Nature of Translation Studies," *International Journal of Translation III* 1-2:31-47.

Holub, Robert C. (1984). *Reception* Theory: A *Critical Introduction.* London: Methuen.

Hutcheon, Linda. (1998) A Poetics *of Postmodernism: History, Theory, Fiction,* New York: Routledge.

________ . (1986) "Literary Borrowing... and Stealing: Plagiarism, Sources, Influences and Intertexts", *English Studies in Canada* 12:229-239.

________ . (1989) "Circling the Downspout of Empire: Post-colonialism and Postmodernism," *Ariel* 20-4 (Autumn): 149-174.

________ . (1995) "Introduction: Colonialism and the Postcolonial Condition Complexities Abounding", *PMLA* 1 10-(January) 7-13.

Ivir, Vladimir. (1981). "Procedures and Strategies for Translation...", *International Journal of Translation III 1-2:* 48-60.

Jadhav, Narendra. (1993). *Amacha Bap ani Amhi,* Bombay: Granthali.

Jaidev. (1998). "Intertextuality and Influence: Connections and Boundaries," in Amiya Dev and Sisir Kumar Das eds. *Comparative Literature: Theory and Practice:* New Delhi: IAS, Shimla and Allied Publisher.

James, Synthia. (1994). "The' Unknown Text", *WLT* 64-4 (Autumn): 758-764.

Jarvis, Kelvin. (1995). "V. S. Naipaul: A Select Bibliographical Update (1987-1994)" *Ariel* 26-4 (Oct.): 71-85.

Joan, Dayan (1994). "Who's Got History? Kamau Brathwaite's Gods Middle Passage." Ibid., 71-85.

Jog, R S. (1959). *Marath: Wangmay Abhiruchiche Whangamavdlokan,* Pune: Pune Vidyapeeth.

Johnson, Alex C. (1984). "Creative Tension in West African Drama in English: The Linguistic Dimension," *World Literature Written in English* 24-1: 65.

Johnson, Lesley. (1979). *The Cultural Critics from Mathew Arnold to Raymond Williams,* London: Routledge.

Kale, Pandharinath. (1984). "Marathi Tamasha: Ek Kalaprakar," Ph.D. Diss. University of Pune.

Kanetkar Vasant. (1982). *Gaganbhedi,* Mumbai: Parachute Prakashan.

________ S.K. (1965). *Swapnabuhmi: Madhav Julian yanche charitra* Pune: Venus.

________ N.B. (1882). *Shashikala ani Ratnapal,* Pune: Aryabhushan.

Karandikar, Vinda. (1974). *Raja Lear,* trans. Bombay: Mouj Prakashan.

Kermode, Frank. (1990). *Poetry, Narrative, History,* London: Basil Blackwell.

King, Bruce. (1996). (ed.) *New National and Postcolonial Literatures: Introduction. Oxford.'* Clarendon.

Kirtane, V.J. and Dev B. N. (1927). *Thorale Madhavrao Peshave va Jaypal anı B. N. Dev yani lihilele raobahaddur V. J. Kirtane yanche charitra,* Pune: Balodhyan Press.

Kolhatkar, M.G. (1867). *Othello Natak,* Mumbai: Modern Book Depot; 1962.

Kolwakar, Deepa. (1991). "Francisco Louis Gomes: His Contribution to the Growth of Political Consciousness in Goa", M.A. Diss. Goa University.

Komarpant, Somnath. (1993). "Gomantakatil Lokwangmay", in Ramesh Warkhede (ed). *Lokrahitya va Lokparampara.*

Kott, Jan. (1975). *Shakespeare Our Contemporary,* London: Methuen.

Kulkami, D.B. (1975). *Mahakavy Swaroop va Samiksha,* Nagpur Vijay Prakashan.

Kulkarni, Rangnath. *The Ticket,* Mumbai: Shubha Prakashan, 1956, performed.

Kunha, T.B. (1961). *Goa's Freedom Struggle,* Mumbai: T. B. Kunha Smarak Samiti.

Kunte, M.M. (1961). *Raja Shivaji,* Pune: Sarasvat Prakashan Mandali.

Kurundkar, Narhar. (1972). *Dhar ani Kath,* Pune: Deshmukh ani Co

Lefever, Andre. (1987). "Systems Thinking and Cultural Relations," *Jadhavpur Journal of Comparative Literature* 26-27: 60.

Levin, Richard. (1990). "The Poetics and Politics of Bardicide" *PMLA* 105-3: 491-504.

Limaye, Pushpa Moreswar. (1976) "Mahadev Moreswar Kunte: Kal va Kartratva", Ph. D. Diss. University of Pune.

Lowe, Lisa. (1993). "Literary Nomadics in Francophone Allergories of Postmodemism: Pham van Ky and Thar Ben Jelloun", *Yale French Review* 82:43-61.

Mack, Maynerd. (1996). *King Lear in Our Time*. London: Methuen.

MaCracken, Ellen. (1991). "Metaplagiarism and the. Critic's Role as Detective: Ricardo Piglia's Reinvention of Roberto Arlt," *PM1.A* 106-5 (Oct.) 1071-1082.

Mande, Prabhakar. (1975). *Loksahityache Antparva,* Pune: Continental.

Marquez, Gabriel Garcia. (1970). *One Hundred Years of Solitude,* trans. London: Picador Pan Books.

Mardhekar B. S. (1955) *Saundarya ani Sahitya;* Bombay: Mouj.

_______ . (1960). *Arts and Man Lectures and Essays,* Bombay: Popular.

Mascarenhas, Lambert. (1955). *Sorrowing Lies My Land,* Panjim: Goa Publications, 1970.

McLennan, Sophia, A. and Joseph R. Slaughter, (eds) Special Issue of *Comparative Literature Studies* 46:1, 2009, 1-19 on "Introducing Human Rights and Literary Forms; or, The Vehicles and Vocabularies of Human Rights."

Mehta, Kumudini. (1960). "English Drama on the Bombay Stage in the Late Eighteenth and Nineteenth Centuries,: Ph.D. Dim.; University of Bombay.

Memmi, Albert. (1974). *The Coloniser and The Colonised.* 1957, trans. Howard Greenfield. New York: The Orion Press, 1965.

Miller, Jane. (1983). *Many Voices: Bilingualism, Culture and Education,* London: Routledge and Kegan Paul.

Miner, Earl. *Comparative Poetics: An Intercultural Essay on Theories of Art.* New Jersey: PUP, 1990.

Mitchell, W.J.T. (1995). "Postcolonial Culture, Postcolonial Criticism" in Bill Ashcroft et al., eds. *The Postcolonial Studies: Reader,* London: Routledge, 475-477.

Moraje, Gangadhar. (1995). *Loksahitya,* Pune: Moghe Prakashan.

Muir, Kenneth. (1972). *Shakespeare's Tragic Sequence,* Liverpool: University of Liverpool.

Mukherjee, Arun. (1994). *Oppositional Aesthetics: Readings from a Hyphenated Space,* Toronto: Tsar Publications.

________ , Meenakshi. (1985). *Realism and Reality: Novel and Society in India,* New Delhi: Oxford University Press.

________ , *Perishable Empire*. (2005). Delhi: OUP.

Namade, Bhalchandra. (1990 a). *The Influence of English on Marathi,* Panaji-Goa: Rajhauns Vitaran.

________ . (1990 b). *Teekasvyamvar,* Aurangabad: Saket Prakashan.

________ . (1991). *Indo-Anglian Writings,* Dharwad: Kamatak University.

________ . (1994). "Semantics of Orality," *Indian Literature* 163 (Oct.): 78-88.

Naipaul, V S. (1961). *A House for Mr Biswas. London:* Russell Edition.

Nandi, Ashish. (1983). *The Intimate Enemy: Loss and Recovery of Self under Colonialism,* New Delhi: Oxford University Press.

Narayan, R.K. *The English Teacher*. Great Britain: Eyre and Sportiswoode, 1945, reissued by William Heinemann, 1978.

Nayak, Pundalik. (1977). *Acehev,* Preyol: Jag Prakashan.

Nazareth, Peter. (1978). *The Third World Writer: His Social Responsibility,* Nairobi: Kenya Literature Bureau..

New, H. W. (1 989). *A History of Canadian Literature,* London: Macmillan.

Nida, E. A. (1976). "A Framework for the Analysis and Evaluation of Theories of Translation", in W. R. Brislin ed. *Translation: Application and Research,* New York: Gardner Press.

Niranjan, Tejaswini. (1993). "Whose Culture? Contesting the Modern, "*Journal of Arts and* Ideas 25-26: 139-150.

O'Connor, Marion. (1979). "The Adaptation of Shakespearian Tragedy in the Twentieth Century. English Drama," Diss. University of London.

Padmanji, Baba. (1857). *Yamuna Paryalan*, Mumbai: E. V. Padmanji, 1935.

Pantawane, Gangadhar. (! 993). ed. *Dalit Sahitya: Charchya ani Chintan,* Aurangabad: Saket Prakashan.

Patankar, R. B. (1974). *Saundarya Mimansa,* Mumbai: Mouj Prakashan.

Patil Anand. The Bells in 'Post'-Colonial Indian Novels: A Semiotic Comparative Study", *Perspectives and Progression: Essays in Comparative Literature*. New Delhi: Creative Books Publication, 2005:15-30.

Patil, Anand. (1993). "The Whirligig of Literary Taste: Impact or alienation?" *Indian Literature* 156 (Aug.): 156-161.

________ . (1995). "Colonial and Post-neocolonial Discourse in Two Goan Novels: A Fanonian Study", *Ariel* 26-4 (Oct.). 87-112.

________ . (1997). "Bardicide in the Third World Theatre: A Comparative Case Study", *Critical Practice* 32 (June): 34-50.

________ . (1988). "Image of Lear in Marathi", *Indian .Scholar* 8-12: 11-31.

________ . (1992). "The Whirligig of Taste: Decolonization of Teaching Literature and Research in English", *New Quest* 96 (Nov.): 345-5.

________ . (1993, b). *Marathi Natakavaril Ingraji Prabhav,* Murnbai: Lokwangmay Griha.

________ . (1997). "A Comparative Study of the Nativistic Intertextuality in Indian Fiction," in Makarand Paranjape, *op. cit.*, 177-21.

________ . (1998). *Taulanik Sahitya: Nave Siddhant ani Upayojan*, Aurangabad: Saket Prakashan.

________ ed. (1993 a). *Western Influence on Marathi Drama*, Panaji-Goa: Rajhauns Vitaran.

________ . *The Whirligig of Taste: Essays in Comparative Literature*. New Delhi: Creative Books. 1999.

________ . "Bardicide in *the Postcolonial Theatre:*" in *The Whirligig of Taste: Essays in Comparative Literature*. New Delhi: Creative Books, 1999 pp.147-60..

________ . "Yashwantrao Chavan ani Vishwasahitya" rpt in *Samiksha "up' haran*. Aurangabad: Rajat Prakashan, 2010.

________ . *Dharmacha Vaidik Wangmayateel Uday ani Vikas*. Amaravati: Amaravati University, 2004. Marathi Translation of P.S. Deshmukh's *The Origin and Development of Religion in Vedic Literature*, Delhi: OUP. 1933.

________ . *Literary into Comparative Culture Criticism*. Ambala: Associate, Publishers, 2011.

________ . *Taulanik Sahitya: Nave Siddhanta ani Upayojan*. Aurangabad: Saket, 1997; translated in to Hindi by Chandralekha, Tulanatmak Sahitya: Naye Siddhant our Upayojan, New Delhi: New Bharatiya Book Corporation, 2006.

________ . *Urus*. Pune: Dnyandatta Prakashan, 2009, Marathi translation of Basavraj Naikar's, *Light in the House* (2006).

________ . *Teekavastraharan*. Nagpur: Akanksha Prakashan, 2008.

Patil, Sharad. (1988). *Abrahmani Sahityanche Saundaryashtra,* Pune: Sugava.

Patrice, Pavis. (1989). "Problems of Translation for Stage: Interculturalism and Postomodern Theatre," in Hanna Scolnicov et al., *op. cit.,* 111-119.

Pavis, Patrice. (ed). *The Intercultural Performance: Reader*. London: Routledge, 1991.

Pendase, S.N. (1952). *Garambicha Bapu,* Bombay: Mouj Prakashan.

Perry, John Oliver. (1992). *Absent Authority: Issues in Contemporary Indian Criticism,* Delhi: Sterling.

Pinge, S. M. (1980). "Europeanancha Marathi Bhasha va Wangmayacha Abhyas va Seva," Ph.D. Diss. University of Bombay.

Pondrom, Cyrena. (1974). *The Roads From Paris: French Influences on English Poetry,* London: Cambridge University Press.

Porter, Lawrence M. (1995). "Amie Cesaire's Reworking of Shakespeare: Anti-colonialist Discourse in *Une Tempeste, "Comparative Literature Studies* 22-3: 360-380.

Prabhubhembre, Laxmikant Vyankatesh. (1979). ed. *Portugali Rajwatipurviche Govyateel Dharmik Wangmaya,* Panaji Goa: Gomantak Marathi Bhasha Parishad.

Pradhan N. S. (1978). *Modern American Drama: A Study in Myth and Tradition,* Delhi: Arnold Heinemann.

Paranjape, Makarand. (1991). "The Ideology of Form: Notes on the Third World Novel, *Journal of Commonwealth Literature* 27:19-32.

________ . (1997). *Nativism: Essays in Criticism,* New Delhi: Sahitya Akademi.

Prasad, Madhav. (1992). "The 'Other' Worldliness of Postcolonial Discourse: A Discourse," *Critical Quarterly* 34-3 (Autumn): 87-88.

Prawer, S.S. *Comparative Literary Studies.* London: Duckworth, 1973.

Priyolkar, Anant Kakaba. (1959). ed. *Christache Yatanageet by* Manuel Jacques de Noronha, Mumbai: Mumbai Marathi Grantha Sangrahalay.

Ranade, M.G. (1867) *The Miscellaneous Writings.* Bombay: Ramabai-Manoranjan Press.

________ . Moro Shankar. (1981) *Atipeedcharit Natak,* Bombay: Induprasad Press.

Randall, Marilyn. (1991). "Approriate(d) Discourse: Plagiarism and Decolonization," *NLH,* 22:325-339.

Rannen, Autis. (1991) "On the Treatment of Elements that have to be left Untranslated," *IJT* II 1-2: 1-12.

Rao, Raja. (1938). *Kanthapura,* New Delhi: Orient Paperback, 1995.

Raza, Rahi Masoom. (1966). *Adha Gaon,* New Delhi: Rajkamal, 1993.

Roach, Steven C. (ed). *Critical Theory and International Relation: A Reader.* New York: Routledge, 2008.

Rushdie, Salman. (1981). *Midnight's Children,* pirated edition.

Ruthven, K.K. *Faking Literature.* Cambridge: CUP.2001.

Said Edward W. "Representing the Colonized: Anthropology's Interiocutors" *Critical Inquiry, winter* 15:2 (1989): 205-226.

________ *Culture and Imperialism.* London: Vintage, 1993.

________ E. (1979) *Orientalism.* London: Routledge and Kegan Paul.

________ . (1996). "Orientalism Reconsidered", in Barker et al, *op, cit.* 221.

Sankar, S. (1994) "The Thumb of Ekalavya: Postcolonial Studies and the 'Third World' Scholar in a Neocolonial World, *WLT* 683: 479-488.

Sarang, Vilas Govind. *English and Marathi: Stylistic Aspects of Literary Translation.* Mumbai: Mumbai University, 1988.

________ (1994) "On Confessions of a Marathi Writer," *WLT* 68-2: 309-312.

Savory, T. H. (1957) *The Art of Translation,* London: Jonathan Cape, 1968.

Schucking Levin L. (1931). *The Sociology of Literary Taste,* trans. London: Kegan Paul, 1944.

Sen, Nabneeta Dev (1995) *Counter Points: Essays in Comparative Literature,* Calcutta: Papyrus Publication.

Shahane, Ashok. (1963). "Marathi Sahityavaril X-Kiran," *Manohar* Nov. Dec.

Sharma Knippling, Alpana. "Fiction of the Indian subcontinent". *Modern Fiction Studies,* 39:1, (Spring 1993) 169-186.

Shih, Shu-Meh. "Comparative Racialization: An Introduction." *PMLA,* 123:5, 2008, 1348-1362.

Shinde, Vishwanaih. (1994). *Paramparik Marathi Tamasha ani Adhunik Yagnatya,* Pune: Pratima Prakashan.

Shirawadkar V. V. (1971). *Natsamrat,* Mumbai: Popular Prakashan.

Singh, Namwar. (1992). "Decolonizing The Indian Mind," *Indian Literature 152* (Sept.): 151-155.

Sisson, C. J. (1926). *Shakespeare In India,* London: Oxford University Press.

Snead, James. (1989). "European Pedigree/African Cotagions: Nationality, Narrative and Community in Tutuota, Achebe and Read," in H. K. Bhabha, ed. *Nation and Narration,* Op. Cit., 231-249.

Spivak, Gayatri. (1996). *The Spivak Reader* ed. Donna Landry and Gerald Maclean, London: Routledge.

Spuffort, Margaret. (1981). *Small Books and Pleasant Histories, Popular Fiction and its Readership ın Seventeenth Century England,* London: Methuen.

Stam, Robert and Alessandra Raengo. (eds) *Literature and Film: A Guide to the Theory and Practice of Film Adaptation.* Oxford: Blackwell Publishing, 2005.

Tendulkar, Vijay, (1971). *Ratrarani,* Mumbai: Chaufer Prakashan.

Thali, Prakash (1993) *Tiatrcho Itihas,* Panaji-Goa: Konkani Akademi.

Theroux, Paul. *VS. Naipaul:* An *Introduction to His Works.* London: Hienemann, 1972.

Tötösy de Zeptnek, Steven. (1998). *Comparative Literature: Theory, Method, Application.* Amstradam: Atlanta.

________ (2011). "Foreword" in Anand Patil, *Literary into Comparative Culture Criticism,* Ambala: Associated Publishers.

________ "The New Humanities: The Intercultural, the Comparative, and the Interdisciplinary" *The Global South, 1;* 2 (2007), 50.

Thiong'o, wa Ngugi. (1972.) *Homecoming. Essays on African and Caribbean Literature, Culture and Politics.* London: Heinemann Educational Books.

________ . *Narayan: A Critical Appreciation.* New Delhi: Allied Publishers 1982.

Verghese, C. Paul. (1975). *Essays on Indian Writing in English,* New Delhi: N. C. Publication.

Viswanathan, Gauri. (1990). Masks *of Conquest: Literary Study and British Rule in India,* London: Faber and Faber.

Vogley, Nancy. (1987). "Defining the 'Colonial Reader': El-periquillo Sorniento", *PMLA* 102-5:784-799.

Volpe, Galvano Della. (1966). *Critique of Taste,* translated from Italian, Western Printing Sources.

Walcott, Derek. (1974). "The Caribbean: Culture and Mimicry: "as quoted from *The Journal of InterAmerican and World Affairs* 16-1 (Feb.): 3-13, in *The Journal of Commonwealth Literature* 15-2 (1982): 313.

________ . (1986). *A Branch of Blue Nile,* in *Three Plays,* London: Farrar, Straus and Giroux.

________ . (1993). "The Antilles Fragments of Epic Memory: the *1992* Nobel Laureate,." *WLT* 62-2:262-267.

Walsh, William. (1973). *V.S. Naipaul.* Edinburgh: Oliver and Boyed.

Wankhade, M. N. (1981). *Dalit Vidhrohi Wangmaya,* Nagpur. Probodh Prakashan.

Wasadikar, Lata. (1969). "Paschyatyancha Marathi Natakavaril Prabhav 1850-1950: Shakespeare", Ph. D. Diss. Aurangabad: Marathwada University.

Wells, H. W. (1963). *The Classical Drama of India,* Bombay: Asia Publishing.

Williams, Raymond. (1961). *Culture and Society,* Harmondsworth: Penguin.

________ . (1984). *English Novel From Dickens to Lawrence,* London: Chatto and Windus.

Wilson, H. H. (1971) *Theatre of the Hindus,* Third reprint, Delhi: Indological Book House.

Wright, Thomas. (2009). *Built of Books: How Reading Defined the Life of Oscar Wilde,* New York: Henry Holt and Co.

Wyatt, Hyacinth Cynthia. (1997). "R. K. Narayan as a Brahman Novelist" Thesis Doctoral, Universitat Rovira, iVirgili.

Xavier, P. D. (1993). *Goa: A Social History,* Panaji-Goa: Rajhauns Vitaran.

Yadav, Anand. (1979). *Gramin Sahitya, Swaroop ani Samasya,* Pune: Mehta Publishing House.

Young, Robert J.C. (2003). *Postcolonial Theory: A Very Short Introduction.* London: OUP.

Index